Crime and Society

99

SOCIOLOGY FOR A CHANGING WORLD
Series Editors: Roger King and Janet Finch

Editorial Advisory Board:
Frank Bechhofer, Sheila Cunnison, Sara Delamont,
Geoff Payne and Liz Stanley

This new series, published in conjunction with the British Sociological Association, evaluates and reflects major developments in contemporary sociology. The books will focus on key changes in social and economic life in recent years and on the ways in which the discipline of sociology has analysed those changes. The books will reflect the state of the art in contemporary British sociology, while at the same time drawing upon comparative material to set debates in an international perspective.

Published
Rosamund Billington, Annette Fitzsimons, Leonore Greensides
  and Sheelagh Strawbridge, *Culture and Society*
Lois Bryson, *Welfare and the State: Who Benefits?*
Frances Heidensohn, *Crime and Society*
Glenn Morgan, *Organisations in Society*
Andrew Webster, *Science and Society*

Forthcoming
Angela Glasner, *Life and Labour in Contemporary Society*
Marilyn Porter, *Gender Relations*
Mike Savage and Alan Warde, *The New Urban Sociology*
Claire Wallace, *Youth and Society*

Series Standing Order
If you would like to receive future titles in this series as they are published, you can make use of our standing order facility. To place astanding order please contact your bookseller or, in case of difficulty,write to us at the address below with your name and address and the name of the series. Please state with which title you wish to begin yourstanding order. (If you live outside the United Kingdom we may not have the rights for your area, in which case we will forward your order to the publisher concerned.)

Customer Services Department, Macmillan Distribution Ltd
Houndmills, Basingstoke, Hampshire RG21 2XS, England

CRIME AND SOCIETY

Frances Heidensohn

MACMILLAN

First published 1989 by
THE MACMILLAN PRESS LTD
Houndmills, Basingstoke, Hampshire RG21 2XS
and London
Companies and representatives
throughout the world

ISBN 0–333–43527–3 (hardcover)
ISBN 0–333–43528–1 (paperback)

A catalogue record for this book is available
from the British Library

Printed in Hong Kong

Reprinted 1990, 1991, 1992 (twice)

To my parents

Contents

Preface

This book is intended to provide two things: first a guide to the major sociological contributions to the study of crime; and second suggestions as to how this work may be used in the rapidly changing world of today and tomorrow. I am, I suppose, a hardened criminologist, having taught the subject on many courses and to varied audiences over the years. From this experience, I have, I hope, learnt the kinds of approaches which can be most helpful to the study of criminology and I have tried to use them here.

The structure of the book is as follows: in Chapter 1 the questions of defining and measuring criminality are raised and accounts of crime today which suggest the key issues to be followed up in later chapters. Among these issues are the urban focus of much crime, the participation rates of young males from less privileged backgrounds and the growing public concern with law and order problems. Chapter 2 then deals with cities and crime, Chapter 3 with juvenile delinquency and social structure and Chapter 4 with new approaches to the study of crime with an emphasis on societal reactions. Sex and gender and crime are the topics covered in Chapter 5 and Chapter 6 deals with the contentious area of policing, while in Chapter 7 the newest issues in criminology, those of victims and of crime control, are considered. While there are major thematic links between them, each section stands reasonably discretely as an account of theories and substantive issues in that area. In Chapter 8, I propose ways in which this text can be used as an aid to future understanding and application in the study of crime by students, by professionals in the criminal justice system and by those growing numbers of the general public who are concerned about crime. *Crime and Society* is thus meant to be a guide and companion to the terrain of crime and its sociological study; there are no guaranteed prescriptions for altering the territory or redrawing the maps, though they may be discerned here, too, by the adventurous traveller who is not averse to taking some risks. What social scientists can most confidently do in this and other fields is to pose and clarify questions and inform discussions. I hope this book will aid in those tasks.

Steven Kennedy and Roger King encouraged me to write this book, and I acknowledge their characteristic contributions to its editing and production. Many friends and colleagues in criminology have helped me with advice and suggestions and the loan of papers and texts still in draft; Paul Rock in particular was characteristically generous in this way and I am most grateful to him. David Downes, Mary Eaton and Betsy Stanko have all given me ideas and advice as well as a sense of criminological fellowship which has been most supportive. Martin Farrell, Director of the Institute for the Study and Treatment of Delinquency, answered questions patiently and guided me to sources, as did the staff of the Intermediate Treatment Fund and the Community Architecture Office of the Royal Institute of British Architects. Robert Harris and David Webb kindly allowed me to have a draft of their *Welfare, Power and Juvenile Justice* before it was published. In the Department of Social Science and Administration at Goldsmiths' College several people have contributed both moral and practical support to the completion of this book, especially Sue Balloch, Mike Levin, John Stone and Iris Swain. Lucy and Edmund Pereira once again prepared my manuscript for publication with great care and patience.

By a curious tradition whose origins I do not fully understand, families always come last in these lists of credits. Mine know, I hope, that they are certainly not least but most deserving in acknowledgement. They ensured that I had companionship and refreshment while I was writing and never allowed me to lose my sense of proportion or of humour by becoming too absorbed in the project. Their affectionate encouragement has been all-important to me. Everyone mentioned has been very helpful, as have many others, and I am most appreciative of their kindness. As it is, however, only proper to admit in a book about crime, I am solely responsible for the deeds committed here, all the others are innocent.

FRANCES HEIDENSOHN

1 The Social Construction of Crime

Crime is a major source of social concern today. Look at any daily newspaper, certainly those published in Western countries, and you will find a significant proportion of their column inches devoted to reports of murder and theft and accounts of sensational trials. For films and television, stories of crimes and their detection are the sources of many plots and series. Increases in crime rates will often be treated as headline news, and many people see the 'law and order issue' as one of the most pressing in modern society.

While there are, as we shall see later, certain distinctive features about our reactions to crime in the modern world, concern about crimes appears to be age old. Abel's murder by his brother Cain is one of the first episodes recounted in the Bible. In Greek mythology, the actions of the gods from Olympus included a considerable number of acts of rape, incest and impersonation. Later, similar and grosser crimes were to be the central themes of classical Greek drama. Folk tales in many cultures have law-breaking figures as their heroes, and their exploits are often recounted with admiration: Robin Hood in England, or Annansi in Afro-Caribbean tales.

There is not only a widespread popular concern about crime; 'experts' on the subject have also long flourished. Plato put forward theories of punishment and was one of the earliest of a long line of philosophers to propose an innovative prison system. In an infamous and influential text published in Nuremberg in 1494, two German monks outlined the types and characteristics of witches. They also included devices for obtaining 'confessions' from suspects and procedures for torture and extermination. Modern scientific and systematic study of crime and criminals is usually held to have begun with the work of Cesare Beccaria, whose *Essays on Crime*

1

and Punishment were first published in Italy in 1764 and had immense influence.

In the late nineteenth century, constitutional or dispositional theories were first put forward within a positivist framework, with the emphasis on the scientific study and comparison of offenders. Criminals, who were equated largely with prison inmates, were said to be physiologically distinctive (Lombroso, 1913; Sheldon, 1949). Later in the twentieth century they were seen as disordered in a psychopathological sense (Bowlby, 1946) or because of faulty conditioning (Eysenck, 1977). Physicians, psychiatrists, psychologists, and more recently even economists have sought to explain criminal behaviour using the concepts of their own disciplines. They have shared the stage with armies of lay and shadow criminologists, ranging from experienced former police officers to investigative journalists, who also confidently proclaim their versions of theories of crime.

Yet of all the interpretations of the strange phenomenon called crime which have been offered, none has been more successful and more convincing than those of sociologists. They have succeeded in portraying crime as a socially situated and defined problem both to an academic and a lay audience. The editors of a major American series on research on *Crime and Justice* point out that 'the criminological journals present largely the work of sociologists', and their purpose in producing their volumes is to introduce 'contributions from disciplines and on topics less fashionable in the criminological literature' (Morris and Tonry, 1980, p. vii).

In examining the state of criminology in Britain in the 1980s, Paul Rock (1988a) focuses almost exclusively on sociologists. Such influence and status can be at once powerful and precarious: 'Crime [is] now . . . a sympton of social distress. For the first time since sociology came to dominate our view of how society worked, it is sending off alarm signals' (Benton, 1986).

Sociological understanding of crime consists of a series of paradoxes. It is broadly comprehensive, yet exists in discrete developments which have not been integrated with one another. While concepts and empirical work have been well developed, the subject has not grown cumulatively: lessons from one generation may be cast aside by the next. Furthermore, there is not a set of theories organised round key issues, as is perhaps the case with social class or modernisation, but a range of varied theories and concepts.

These paradoxes occur because the study of crime is distinguished by two sets of factors, one to do with its academic development, the second and more significant due to special features of the issue itself. The study of crime has been a multidisciplinary enterprise, or, put another way, almost everyone has approached it at some time or other. This has made it a contested area, with contests between proponents of particular perspectives, rather than within a discipline. In addition, crime has sometimes featured as a social science tourist attraction, a Taj Mahal or Tower of Pisa which everyone visits – once. Hence major theorists such as Durkheim, Parsons or Merton have made key but brief appearances on the crime scene.

The social construction of crime

The main problems in studying crime for the interested student, concerned professional or anyone else lie in its distinctiveness as an issue and the consequent difficulties of studying it. Crime is a socially constructed concept; so too, of course, is religion. Religion, however, is not *artificially* constructed in the way that crime is, and there are therefore not the same doubts and uncertainties about definition with religion as there are in defining crime.

Defining crime

It might at first glance seem simple enough to define crime as the sum of all those actions deemed as 'violation of the criminal law' to equate crime with law-breaking. Paul Tappan (1947) did advocate just such a definition, arguing that criminal law embodied 'conduct norms' marking out acceptable and deviant behaviour in any society. Using this approach gives rise to a number of problems. Criminal laws are not fixed or permanent in any society. In the twentieth century almost all Western societies have introduced legislation, or strengthened existing sanctions, against the use of certain drugs. In the same period most (the Republic of Ireland excepted) have removed sanctions against abortion under certain conditions. Such changes are not random; a growing body of research has shown that, at various times in history, class and power have influenced the scope of the criminal law – in eighteenth-century English laws on poaching game, for example (Hay, 1975). In the nineteenth century in Britain, an alliance of middle-class feminists and male trade unionists campaigned successfully *against* the Contagious Diseases Acts, which criminalised certain prostitute women, but also *in favour of* raising the age of consent of sexual intercourse, thus criminalising the child prostitution common at the time (Petrie, 1971; Walkowitz, 1980). In twentieth-century America another alliance of middle-class women and other anti-alcohol groups combined to introduce prohibition. The formal limits of criminal law, in short, can be shifted by many different social pressures.

If criminal laws do in any sense constitute 'conduct norms' in a society, they must by definition change to reflect social changes. Sometimes the source of change is technological – the introduction and growth of car ownership has provided enormous scope for criminal behaviour, from taking and driving away to causing death by dangerous driving. This has been accompanied by a host of laws and regulations about the speed, use and parking of vehicles. Motoring offences do not arouse the same public concern as, say, murder or sexual offences. This raises a further problem about defining crime: infractions of criminal law do not make a meaningful or homogeneous category of action. Arson, burglary, living on immoral earnings or possessing heroin are all behaviours whose only common feature is that they are criminal acts. Even within the categories imposed by the legal system, there may be little coherence, no shared meanings in the everyday world of discourse. Stealing a loaf of bread if you are hungry does not seem to have much in common with taking mink coats from Harrods intending not to pay for them.

Sociologists have tried to overcome some of these difficulties. Sutherland (1945), for example, proposed that an action that causes an injury and incurs a penalty should be added to the legal definitions of crime. In this way, he argued, acts violating administrative codes or regulating business practices would be included, and some of the bias of criminal law against the poor and in favour of the well-to-do would be redressed. However, Sutherland still retained the notion of legal infraction at the core of his concept. In an important later shift, sociologists focused on deviant rather than criminal behaviour, taking social reaction as the key to the concept. Deviance was thus whatever a society at any time labelled as deviant (Becker, 1963).

This approach (see Chapter 3) led to numerous key studies of behaviour on the margins of disrepute – of drug taking, prostitution and other deviant lifestyles. One must then ask such key questions as 'who defines such behaviour as deviant and why'? Studies of the sociology of law and law-making have explored these questions.

Such studies reveal the many institutions and processes involved in the social construction of crime. Positivist 'scientific' criminology itself, Garland (1985) argues, played a crucial role in the 1890s in redefining who and what was regarded as criminal. Smart (1981) and Edwards (1981) have examined laws relating to sexual behaviour and point to the ways in which these embody 'patriarchal' concepts of male and female sexuality. Despite the permanently impermanent and inherently unstable nature of legally defined criminality, many social scientists in the later twentieth century have returned to the study of 'officially' defined crime. I explore some of the reasons for this in Chapter 7. The key one is the public concern over crime. Crime is not merely socially constructed, it is in part socially concernedly constructed, and this has always had a bearing on its study. There has also been a considerable volume of research available which suggests that is is possible to define what Toby (1974) calls 'consensual' crimes – such as homicide and rape – which are regarded as serious crimes by most members of society (Rossi *et al.*, 1974). National and local surveys (for example, Mayhew, 1983 and 1985; Jones *et al.*, 1986) indicate much public concern about such crimes and widespread support for measures to control them.

Even when there is congruence between types of definition – the criminal law, 'social harm' and 'social reaction' – there are still many difficulties to be faced in the study of crime. The central issue can be summed up by the observation that the *processing and recording* of crime is as much a socially constructed event as the definition of crime. You can hardly ever convict yourself of crime and almost certainly never record your own offence. A host of agencies, including the public, are involved. Nowadays the caution in handling the data which such complexities of origin deserve is much more widespread. Nevertheless, anyone embarking on the study of crime needs to be reminded of some of the key issues.

The social construction of crime records

> Any official crime rate is more or less artificially constructed on the basis of a variety of administrative and legal considerations which inevitably vary from time to time and between countries and regions. (Bottomley and Pease, 1986, p. 3)

This quotation, from a detailed study of crime records and their limitations, encapsulates the main points: conventional crime records were devised and continue to be kept for purposes other than the study of crime – such as accountability. They are, moreover, the product of a most elaborate if incoherent series of social processes. Crime rates, as publicised in the mass media, are seen as 'hard' data, evidence of real events which can meaningfully said to be 'rising' or 'out of control', and therefore events about which someone should act or intervene. Yet they are in fact fragile and soft data, susceptible to changes and manipulations by many factors. Among the many aspects affecting the construction processes the following can be highlighted.

1. Stages in the recording process
Many studies have pointed to the long series of stages in the recording process which occur if an event is to be recorded as a crime: there must be an observer; a report must be made to the police; the police must record it and then act upon it, perhaps going on to apprehend and charge an offender who then might be cautioned or appear in court and then be convicted (or not) and sentenced. Attrition can occur at every stage, and there can also be intervention from many sources. Thus Farrington and Dowds (1985) found that three adjoining police forces had differing methods of logging telephone calls on to crime complaint forms, and this affected their respective overall crime figures. Chambers and Millar (1987, p. 59) found 'considerable case attrition' in their study of 196 incidents of serious sexual assault in Glasgow and Edinburgh. Only forty of these incidents resulted in a trial. Chambers and Millar raise another point about reporting crime which also qualifies the official data: the existence of the so-called 'iceberg'. Known, reported and recorded crime is only the tip of the iceberg. Beneath lies an unknown and uncertain mass of hidden material.

Several techniques have been developed in modern times to measure the hidden dimensions of the iceberg. In self-report studies respondents are asked which of a list of offences they have committed. Most admit to some and a few to many (Nye and Short, 1957; Polsky, 1969). Crime surveys, which are discussed further in Chapter 7, additionally record incidence of crime by asking for reports of victimisation and sometimes also self-report (Hough and Mayhew, 1983 and 1985). All such devices reveal that the base of the iceberg (a) is larger than its tip, and (b) varies considerably by offence category in such relations. Most car thefts are reported to the police, for example, while this is much less likely with burglaries. Sometimes the relationship between the hidden mass and the reported crimes changes, i.e. more crime from a stable pool of crimes is reported. Home Office research suggests this happened in the case of burglary in the 1970s.

2. Negotiable procedures

Studies of police discretion suggest that the defining and recording of offences is a matter of negotiation and relates to a constellation of factors. Sudnow (1965) found that what constituted 'burglary' or 'robbery' could be very flexibly negotiated. Chambers and Millar (1987, p. 61) found that it was police officers who suggested to women that they should withdraw their complaints about rape or sexual assault. Plea bargaining in or around criminal courts is a procedure recognised only tacitly in Britain but acknowledged in the USA. This can lead to a guilty plea by the accused after negotiations over sentence.

Complexity and interaction

Crime is not an invariant and universal phenomenon, consistently the same in all places and at all times. (Gibbons, 1968, p. 6)

What is conventionally called crime, the 'social facts' taken as crime rates, are the outcome of a remarkable number of complex interactions and negotiations between different groups of actors, all of which can be subject to change. In Chapter 6 we shall see how the strong occupational culture of police officers produces a culture and values which can have a marked effect on the priorities they give to their work and hence to their responses to calls and reports from the public.

So far I have discussed the problems of defining crime and

reporting offences as acts and events. These have proved sufficiently uncertain and problematic. Once we move further along the recording process from offence to offender, these factors are compounded. Criminologists use the term 'dark figure' to describe the crimes which are not 'cleared up' in police records and about whose perpetrators little can be known. Clear-up rates vary: between types of offence – most homicide is 'solved', very little burglary is – and over time – clear-up rates fell in Britain in the 1980s (Kinsey *et al.*, 1986). This makes for problems in studying known offenders: they cannot be regarded as a 'sample' since the population from which they are drawn is not known. Groups such as imprisoned offenders are even less typical, since they represent only a tiny proportion of all convicted criminals.

At times in the history of the study of crime, a kind of terminal pessimism has been achieved. Since the concept is so flexible and the records so unreliable, and so far outside the control of researchers, there has been a tendency to avoid confrontation, to argue against any engagement with the concept or especially with official records (Douglas, 1967; Atkinson, 1971). While sociologists have been able to carry out crucial and fascinating work by focusing on concepts such as deviance and conducting small-scale qualitative studies (see Chapter 4), there are several reasons for persevering with the study of crime despite the conceptual hurdles with which one is confronted.

First, 'deviance' is no less problematic a notion than crime. There are many well-rehearsed reasons why people do not feport crime to the police: shame, fear, lack of confidence, ignorance, the triviality of the episode, close dependence on the perpetrator. Many of these factors prevent people being frank about bizarre or unconventional behaviour. It is as difficult to label such behaviour securely as constantly 'deviant' as it is to find stability and consistency in the notion of crime. Academic sociologists who pursued the deviance perspective in the 1960s and 1970s have been criticised by feminists for their sexist construction of deviance (see Chapter 5). In fact it has proved very fruitful, as examples in this chapter have shown, to bring 'sceptical' sociological insights (Cohen, 1971) to bear on the study of crime and the generation of crime 'data'. The most fertile approach now is to link quantitative and qualitative material, to treat official records with proper wariness, while acknowledging that they record something worth exploring: 'any reference to official statistics at the front end of the criminal justice system needs information from elsewhere to make any sort of sense' (Bottomley and Pease, 1986, p. 31).

Concepts of crime will no doubt always be both arbitrary and contested. Yet social scientists confront one certainty: that there is a large public and political concern about crime and its consequences (Dahrendorf, 1985; Benton, 1986; and see Chapter 7). Even if sociologists decide that such concern is spurious and based on 'moral panics' manufactured by the mass media (Cohen, 1980) or that the focus is inappropriate and should instead be on the crimes of the powerful and not those of the poor and weak (Box, 1983), such episodes are in themselves significant and worthy of study. What causes fear of crime? Is it purely media hype? Careful research suggests that fear of crime itself is a product of the relations between social vulnerability, perceived and actual, and the risks of victimisation, and not just 'false' or manipulated consciousness (Maxfield, 1984; Smith, 1986; Jones, 1987).

Despite the hazards involved, crime has undoubtedly proved to be a fruitful area for sociologists to study. They have in turn contributed greatly to a more sophisticated understanding of crime and its social construction. Crime is a social phenomenon and needs to be studied in its social settings.

What public and politicians have looked for in the past century – before that there were other demands (Garland, 1985) – have been explanations and solutions. Why do some people commit crimes? how can they be controlled or prevented? Early criminologists, who were often psychologists and psychiatrists or physical anthropologists, accepted such demands confidently, and a scientific criminology was born. It was never lived up to early expectations (Clarke, 1983), although its influence has been immense. Sociologists came somewhat later and less confidently on to the scene. They have rarely claimed to be able to 'solve' crime problems and have often recognised the central problem of values and 'correctionalism' (Matza, 1969; Pearson, 1974) and have asked the question 'whose side are we on'?

The thrust of most sociological work on crime has not been to explain and solve the problem but rather to picture and to understand. Since the earliest contributions of the founding fathers (sic) sociologists have recognised the complexity of crime in its social setting. Durkheim (1973) put forward the bold suggestion that a certain level of crime was healthy sign in a normal society. We can look to sociology, then, for a picture of crime, a depiction of the social landscape and portraits of the figures which interact upon it. This may seem a lesser and less useful task than that of solving the problem of finding solvents to wipe the canvas clean. Yet it has not proved so. We can learn a great deal from images. These images too have often been animated as sociologists have tried to script encounters and record dialogue.

Sociological perspectives on crime have been as socially located as the phenomena they seek to illuminate. We shall find as we explore the contributions of sociologists that they reflect very much the intellectual preoccupations of their times and places and that their focus is on particular social constructions of crime. Often such constructions are derived from readings of official records described above. From these readings crime and delinquency appear to be the activities of young males in urban settings for whom various kinds of property crime – theft, burglary, forms of criminal damage – are the predominant and characteristic crimes. Yet an advantage of sociological perspectives on crime is that they have proved almost as variable and flexible as the phenomena they are used for studying. It is also true that, as so often in the study of society, we are dealing with behaviour which has meaning for actors, and part of that meaning may itself be constructed from or adapted to sociological findings. A plausible case can be made: for example, that the idea of the 'new female criminal' derived from the work of Adler and Simon produced a 'self-fulfilling prophecy' response from some of the control agencies dealing with criminal women (Chesney-Lind, 1980; Heidensohn, 1985). Sociological cast lists of crime did not for a long time include the victims of crime, but victim movements and the challenge they posed to conventional, especially radical, criminology, were ultimately acknowledged and accommodated (see Chapter 7).

Crime can be examined as a social phenomenon on at least three levels. It can be studied systematically, using concepts, theories and available data to test ideas. Most of this book is concerned with looking at crime in that way, as it has been and is being analysed. Public reaction plays an important part in shaping responses to crime – and even crime itself. Therefore another level on which we shall touch is the public reaction to crime and the media response. There is also the phenomenon of crime itself.

Social scientists have contributed hugely to the logging and mapping of many events and patterns, not least crime. The Victimisation surveys (see Chapter 7) have formed a major development in recording crime in the USA, Britain and elsewhere in modern times and owe their origins to concerns about accuracy and validity on the part of empirical social scientists. Much of the sociological endeavour described later in these pages has involved depicting crime and especially offenders. Indeed that has been, in my view, one of its principal themes. The focus has, however, been partial, subjective, sometimes even idiosyncratic. We can build up a portrait of criminality from these accounts and we can learn some important models of analysis and explanation, and how to apply them.

Sociologists have not generally been employed (although some have been and still are) in permanent Presidential or Royal Commissions, looking for answers to policy-makers' questions such as: How much crime is there? Of what kind? Are rates rising or falling? What can we do about this? It is possible to give answers of a tentative kind to some of these questions, though they are bound to be subject to the limitations I have pointed out above.

When considering the accounts outlined in this book, it may be helpful to compare these with the broader picture gained from the wide variety of sources now available. These include official data, such as the Federal Bureau of Investigation's *Uniform Crime Reports* and the Home Office's *Criminal Statistics*; victim surveys like US Bureau of the Census's *National Crime Surveys* and the *British Crime Surveys* (for details see Chapter 7); and a range of useful studies such as Meier (1984), Bottomley and Pease (1986), and Walker (1987).

From all these, certain compass points can be set on the map of the known world of crime. Crime is widespread and pervasive; there is a great deal more of it committed than is generally supposed. However, many offences are trivial in the costs they incur and the harm they cause. In all modern technological societies offences related to motor vehicles are the most prevalent – about one million in England and Wales each year. Next in prevalence come thefts and frauds: some 18 million US households were subjected to larceny in 1982 (Hepburn, 1984). Serious crimes such as homicide or robbery are much less common; death on the road is far more frequent in Britain than at the hands of an assailant. Once we start to make comparisons between societies, or within groups or regions in any one country, distinctions do occur.

Some societies or cultures appear to be more criminal or criminogenic than others. Rates of homicide and of violent crime are substantially higher in the USA than in comparable Western societies such as Canada and England and Wales (Luckenbill, 1984; Hagan, 1977) although they are lower than those found in several Latin American countries.

Whether crime rates are rising, nationally and internationally, and how far and how fast, are tricky questions to which the proper, if unsatisfactory, answer should begin 'it all depends . . .!' More particularly, it depends on how you interpret the data. There do seem to have been large and long-term increases in the numbers of offences recorded in many countries (Box, 1987; Bottomley and Pease, 1986). Some historical studies, however, have suggested a *decline* in violent crime in the nineteenth century in Britain and Europe and possibly the USA, with episodes of upsurge (Gurr, 1979). Evidence suggests that some increases in crime rates reflect an increased willingness to report crimes as well as 'true' increases (Box, 1987). Rape is a very clear example of a serious crime whose reported incidence is much affected by victims' willingness to come forward and tell police and also by the police's reaction (Blair, 1984). Recent dramatic increases in rates in some jurisdictions probably reflect an interaction between a dark figure of hidden rape and victim, and police and public attitudes, as well as possible 'real' increases.

Media spotlights focus on a rather different pattern of crime than the one reflected above. The mass media in many Western, though not in Eastern bloc, countries are often filled with accounts of criminal behaviour. News stories are often about crime, and fictions on film and television are often what the French aptly call '*policiers*'. Yet the image of criminality therein reflected is often a distorted one. Most space is given to crimes of violence and sexual crimes, although these are comparatively infrequent. Street crime, rather than the more common domestic assaults, are depicted (Young, 1986). Most underrepresented in both official and media depictions have been, until recently, the mass of violations by companies and their employees, the corporate crimes, which incur huge costs if modest penalties (Braithwaite, 1984; Clinard and Yeager, 1986).

However, that situation is probably changing. In the USA and

Britain, frauds associated with financial markets and dealing have been more widely discussed and pursued in the 1980s. From the 1960s on, organised crime, whose existence was scarcely acknowledged, has been both recognised and pursued more vigorously (Morash, 1984). This may also reflect wider international concern as organised crime has been linked to some of the 'newer' forms of crime.

It can be argued that there are no new crimes: the ten commandments record all the main transgressions one can commit. Yet criminality does take novel forms from time to time, reflecting technological development: no one could hijack an aeroplane until powered flight was possible, or the relevant social and political pressures arose. Modern terrorism, which has involved arson, bombing and kidnapping, had its roots in political discontent, especially in some minority groups, and in the possibilities offered by instant mass media attention (Becker, 1977).

A more widespread and probably more feared wave has been caused by the use of new substances. Abusing drugs or alcohol and behaving offensively as a result is one of the most ancient forms of human behaviour. The USA prohibited the production and sale of alcohol in the 1920s, as do many Muslim countries today. In the 1960s people in Western countries began to experiment more widely with illegal 'soft' drugs such as marijuana, and some harder ones like LSD. More recently, hard drugs such as heroin and cocaine have become much more widely available and used, and there have been moral panics in Britain and other European countries (Pearson, 1987).

Sometimes crimes are not so much new in themselves, rather they involve conceptual shifts as police or other agencies change their policies and practices, and this affects public perceptions in turn. For reasons discussed more fully in Chapter 5, the whole question of sexual abuse, and especially of the sexual abuse of children by relatives and others close to them, has been rethought. As a result there have been several major cases and considerable public reaction. Yet child sex abuse is most unlikely to be 'new'; indeed, in the new climate there is plenty of evidence of victims whose sufferings occurred long ago (Stanko, 1984).

As we shall see later, sociologists have had a good deal to say about this particular development, and an understanding grounded in their work can help both to explain the 'child sex abuse' crime wave and perhaps anticipate future kindred developments. This is a bold claim, and I have in general tried to be fairly modest about the subject of this book. There are no quick answers, nor easy solutions, to the questions I listed earlier. In any case, sociologists have not always addressed these kinds of questions. They have heard a different drum and sought to respond to it. Nevertheless it is possible to use the heritage of social science to illuminate many of the core policy problems associated with crime. It is also important, and arguably a prior task anyway, to find out what the structural relationships, the causal links or interactive patterns are before starting in any way to change and improve or eradicate the criminogenic ones.

A note on international comparisons

'Research on crime and its causes has been lamentably insular' declare the authors of one of the few texts dedicated to remedying this situation (Archer and Gartner, 1984, p. 3). It is because, as they point out, 'the field has suffered from a spectacular lack of international information . . . what has been missing in short, is information from many nations over many years' (p. 4). Some countries keep no records at all, in others the records are confidential. All the problems already noted about defining and recording crime are of course compounded when one is using data from more than one country. Legal systems differ as do cultures. Over time, political boundaries change and populations shift.

Nevertheless, comparative data are important in the understanding of crime, and some attempts have been made in modern times to develop comparisons. Historical studies provide intra-country and international cross-nation studies. Gurr (1976) suggests that there was actually an overall decline in violent crime in several Western societies during the eighteenth and nineteenth centuries, including the USA. Archer and Gartner have sought to remedy the lack of comparative material by assembling their own 'comparative crime data file', which files material on some 110 different nations. This material gives them the opportunity to make some interesting comparative analyses. They found, for example, that a majority of combatant nations in both the Second World War and the Vietnam War experienced increased levels of homicide after each war, increases with did not occur in the noncombatant countries (1984, Chapter 4). They attribute this to what they call the

> legitimation of violence model . . . which suggests that the presence of authorised or sanctioned killing during war has a residual effect on the level of homicide in peacetime society. (1984, p. 96).

These findings (and there are, of course, limitations to such exercises) and their results contradict those of Mannheim (1940) who did not find such effects in wartime England.

Such comparisons as are available to us suggest some curious paradoxes. Some features of and factors in crime appear to be broadly constant. In advanced countries and in cities everywhere, it is a phenomenon associated with urban, male youth from the less advantaged social groups. In many nations, over a long period, violence has relatively declined (but with minor upsurges), and property and fraud offences have increased. However, when one examines the tables in the CCDF files (1984, pp. 171 *et seq.*), what is striking is the vast variation in the recorded rates of crime between countries. Thus Japan appears as an orderly country with low rates of violence. England and Wales too have, internationally, relatively modest rates of robbery and violence, compared for example with the USA, where both kinds of offending are far more frequently recorded. The period covered in this collection, however, includes the onset of the 'troubles' in Northern Ireland, when the numbers of robberies recorded kept dramatically much nearer US levels for a short period.

Where possible I have used such worldwide comparative data in this book, but it has to be acknowledged that it is sparse and that its use must be cautious. In fact much of the research in this field has been done in the USA and Britain, and thus references to those countries will predominate. What these observations suggest is that although there are probably some *criminologically* constant relationships, there are such differences between observed levels of crime in different cultures that it is to *sociological* variables and to societal levels of explanation that we have to look.

2 Cities, Crime and Social Disorganisation

There are thousands of neglected children loitering about the low neighbourhoods of the metropolis and prowling about the streets, begging and stealing for their daily bread. They are to be found in Westminster, Whitechapel, Shoreditch, St Giles's, New Cut, Lambeth, the Borough. (Mayhew, 1862, p. 133)

The characteristic habitat of Chicago's numerous gangs is that broad twilight zone of railroads and factories, of deteriorating neighbourhoods and shifting populations, which borders the city's central business district on the north, on the west and on the south. The gangs dwell among the shadows of the slum. (Thrasher, 1963, p. 3)

The inner city is now, and is likely to remain Britain's most dramatic and intractable social problem. For here are concentrated the worst housing, the highest unemployment, the greatest density of poor people, the highest crime rates and, more recently, the most serious threat posed to established law and order since the Second World War. (Harrison, 1983, p. 21)

As the above quotations make clear, the links between cities and crimes have long been a focus of concern. Nor has this concern been unique to sociologists: writers such as Mayhew and Binney mapped out crime in London in the nineteenth century in vivid detail. The sociological contribution to understanding the link has been profound and lasting. Its main and most important embodiment is in the work of the Chicago School (Bulmer, 1984). Sociologists in Chicago *conceptualised* the interactions of life in inner cities in distinctive ways; they used *innovative methods* of sociological research such as life histories and participant observation; they were

16

involved in and committed to *social policy* developments in relation to crime and delinquency; and they used their studies skilfully to *communicate* their views of city life. The Chicago School's volumes on crime and deviance are probably still the richest source for sociologists in this field. In addition to achieving this they set out an agenda, and some of the tools for completing it, for the future study of crime as an urban problem and for urban studies in general.

In the late twentieth century inner-city crime is again a matter of major concern in many societies. However, the links between rising crime rates and growing urbanisation appear not to be entirely straightforward. In one comparison of homicide rates in some forty-four cities across the world, the cities generally had higher homicide rates than the nations to which they belonged, but the rates varied very widely from country to country. Thus Paris had a higher rate than France, while New York City (which also exceeded the USA rate) had a rate some twenty times higher than Paris, although both cities are of comparable size (Archer and Gartner, 1984, p. 106). The point is that urban crimes are seen as serious problems in both cities, but they are *relative* problems.

In this chapter I shall examine the key aspects of the Chicago approach, and also later developments influenced by this approach and their relevance for today. The history of the University of Chicago, and especially of its remarkable school of sociology, have been well documented and rehearsed (Faris, 1970; Bulmer, 1984). Time, place and people all seem to have converged and combined to produce a remarkable flowering of intellectual activity. During the nineteenth and early twentieth centuries, Chicago grew very rapidly: from a little town with 10,000 citizens in 1860 to a huge city of two million in 1910. The source of its growth was migration from many different European countries. The city teemed with life and with social problems. High rates of crime and delinquency, prostitution, alcoholism and illegitimacy were recorded. The University of Chicago School of Sociology was located in, and addressed itself to, this busy setting. Many sociologists worked there in the 1920s and 1930s, when it arguably was *the* home of American sociology. The key figures in its early development were Robert Park and W. E. Burgess, and some of its most characteristic writings are found in life histories such as C. Shaw's *The Jack Roller: A Delinquent Boy's Own Story* (1930) and appreciative studies such as Frederic Thrasher's *The Gang* (1927). Park was the key figure in focusing on the city itself and in developing what Plummer (1983, p. 50) calls 'the Chicago vision'.

Park had studied sociology in Germany and had long journalistic experience; He saw 'the city [as] an advantageous place to study social life [with] the character of a social laboratory' (Park, 1967, pp. 17–18). Building on an eclectic, empirical tradition already established in Chicago, Park encouraged his students and colleagues to go out, observe and record in the social laboratory around them. The results were very rewarding. Chicago, its mores and problems, inhabitants and culture, crime and delinquents were all carefully logged and mapped. Howard Becker has tellingly described the scope and effects of that endeavour:

> when I first went to San Francisco . . . and began to think about doing research there, I automatically began looking for the Local Community Fact Book, the demographic studies, the analyses of neighbourhoods and institutions and all the other kinds of background material I had come to take for granted when I worked in Chicago. But they were not there; no one had done them. Perhaps it is because no one group of researchers had ever existed there as well organized as the group that got its start under Park during the twenties. That group *saw connections between all the various problems they were working on.* (Becker, 1966, p. vii–viii)

Crime was not the only concern of Chicago sociology. 'But', suggest Downes and Rock (1981, p. 61), 'there were discernible strains which encouraged the development of criminology'. These included sponsorship from bodies seeking solutions to social problems, a reforming tradition in the department and what Downes and Rock describe as 'the sheer availability of deviance' and its accessibility to students. Thus, although the social researches of Chicago sociologists were of a general kind, they were particularly focused on crime and deviance in urban settings.

The Chicago vision was thus very much concerned with the highly visible and visibly high levels of social upheaval in the city. There is no single definitive view in their work; indeed, as was inevitable in such a productive group, ideas diverged both between different writers and even within the work of one man (Turner, 1967). Asserting that one discerns firm and coherent ideas and clear patterns in any body of past work is the sociological equivalent of claiming that the emperor has a fine suit of new clothes. It is an enterprise fraught with the likelihood of error and ridicule. In the case of the Chicago sociologists it is particularly challenging, since their work was not systematised and did not generate a 'finished system of sociology' but rather

> a series of general ideas and sensitizing concepts that could appropriately guide the empirical work of . . . students . . . and . . . that still inspire a great number of contemporary investigations. (Coser, 1978, p. 317)

In attempting to present these ideas they have to be set down and simplified in ways which cannot reflect their full diversity.

Concepts

As I suggested at the beginning of this chapter, others had observed that city streets were often the scenes of crimes. The distinctive nature of the Chicago vision was in arguing for an *area-based* theory of crime, in presenting models of urban crime and deviance in terms of *social disorganisation* and *cultural transmission* and in recognising the *spatial conflict* in cities.

Areas, crime and ecology

The ecological theories developed by Park, Burgess and Mckenzie from plant biology have been much criticised. Observing high concentrations of crime and deviance in certain inner-city districts, they sought to explain these by analogies with plants. The city was patterned in concentric formation with 'zones of ascending conformity'. Of the five zones, the second ring, the 'transitional' or interstitial area, had the highest crime rates. Within the zones were segmental subdivisions into 'natural areas' where the inhabitants were likely to be similar, rather like plants grown in the same natural habitat (Park, 1929). This notion has been heavily criticised by several generations of sociologists. Heathcote (1981, p. 354) sums up the key points:

The positivist overtones of social determinism, of inert human beings being acted upon and constrained by their physical and social environment, are clear to see.

Taylor *et al.* (1973, p. 281) insist on the need to break entirely with such approaches to form 'a fully social theory of deviance'. Downes and Rock, however, suggest that ecology was only used as a useful metaphor: 'Biological ecology was rarely taken to be more than a convenient working description of an otherwise excessively complex process' (1981, p. 59).

It is not necessary to accept the invasion–dominance–succession sequence of city population movements as literally true, nor that by some symbiotic process different groups successively inhabiting the same city district will always have similar crime levels. Empirical observation, even in Chicago, demonstrated that this was not so (Heathcote, 1981, p. 360). The importance of the approach for subsequent research lies in the way in which social conditions and relationships were perceived as interrelated in a spatial sense. As Morris (1957, p. 17) put it, in what is still the fullest account of area studies, 'it is the natural area which stands out as a concept of obvious value'. Morris pointed to the importance of socio-economic and class factors in determining patterns of residence: 'the natural area as a cultural isolate is to a considerable degree the coincidental product of the economic differentiation between different physical areas'.

The Criminal Area (1957), Morris's own study of the spatial distribution of offending in the London suburb of Croydon in the 1950s is testimony to the value of the ecological approach, if only as an heuristic device. For Morris did not find a causative link between area and delinquency; instead he suggests that there were concentrations of 'delinquency potential' on certain council housing estates, largely due to the segregation policies for 'problem families' adopted by the local authority (1957, chapter xi). Several decades later, this conclusion sounds remarkably like much more modern concerns: Lord Scarman listed poor location, environment and housing as the key social conditions leading to the 1981 Brixton disorders in London (Scarman, 1981).

Some contemporary criminologists insist that 'the notion of the criminal area must be rejected' because, they argue, it is not permissible [sic] to refer to criminal areas . . . as if crime were a central and typical cultural activity. For this would signify that crime was an activity of a majority of people most of the time, and of central importance to the economy of the area. In reality crime, even in such high-crime areas, is almost always the activity of a minority of individuals at any one time. (Lea and Young, 1984, p. 39)

Some of this argument seems questionable to me. After all, not everyone in a criminal area need be criminal, nor need criminals be constantly involved in crime. Few social roles and occupations are totally absorbing all the time: not everyone in a 'Catholic country' is devout, nor are even the devout always at mass or confession. Lea and Young seem on slighly surer ground with their emphasis on the *over-prediction* of ecological theory: if areas are criminogenic, why are 'the old, the female and the respectable working class' (p. 39) not affected? They are also anxious about a dangerous urban myth: 'the fake stereotype of the criminal area – of the wild beasts that live at the margins of the social order – has a whole series of real effects for the community concerned' (p. 41).

Moral panics, especially those caused by fake stereotypes, are of course deplorable, especially if they lead to heavy-handed policing or other over-reactions. That, however, is a very different point from the value or otherwise of focusing on areas with high crime rates. It is possible to retain the concept of an area approach while jettisoning the ecological theory.

Area studies have, in fact, been robust offspring of the Chicago approach. Heathcote notes:

as a result of Morris's work, the focus of subsequent British area studies widened to include the study of differential access to housing space, of policies concerning the utilisation and allocation of publicly-owned housing and of the effects on people compelled to live in low-grade housing in 'rough' areas with regard to criminal and delinquent behaviour. (Heathcote, 1981, p. 364)

The area concept has survived and been to some extent redirected, in a series of later studies which, even where they challenge the ecological fallacy in principle, begin in practice with a spatial approach.

We find a core concept of Chicago ecology retained, revived and reconstructed. The competitive struggle for space . . . returns as the basis of the organisation of urban life and of many contemporary urban area studies. It has however now become transformed into the struggle for housing space. (Heathcote, 1981, p. 364)

Rex and Moore's (1967) study of housing in Sparkbrook in Birmingham, while not primarily focused on crime, showed how housing policies led to the forming of 'housing classes' and the concentration of disadvantaged ethnic groups into private rented accommodation in the inner city. Baldwin and Bottoms (1976) found similar links in Sheffield. In Cardiff's docklands, Evans (1980, p. 17) found that 'there does appear to be established a delinquent tradition. . . . These areas also include high rates of offenders committing the more serious crimes'. Davidson (1981) found like concentrations in Hull, and reviewing the literature declared: 'in most British cities one would expect to find a residential concentration of adult male offenders in the older inner areas' (p. 55). Susan Smith (1986) comes to the same view: 'There is sufficient evidence to suggest that the high crime rate of Britain's inner cities is matched by high rates of offender residence.' She then goes on to present her findings from a study in Birmingham. She pays explicit tribute throughout her study to Chicago sociology, while making clear its limitations. In Birmingham she too found higher inner-city crime rates, but argues:

I favour an explanation of the concentration of offenders in the inner city that is couched first in terms of those disadvantages which derive from the unequal distribution of material wealth and life chances within cities. (p. 73)

Later Smith adds what she calls a 'neighbourhood effect' in victimisation 'which arises not only from an insecure *built* environment but also from a social environment where [there are] sudden and severe erosions of primary group bonds' (p. 107).

Smith uses the concept of 'territoriality' in a very interesting discussion of the dimensions of race, power and danger in the inner city (ch. 7). Her work is testimony to the continuing, if much adapted, urban area approach to crime, which has continued in the UK and been revived in the USA (see Baldwin, 1979, for a review).

The debate in the USA has been especially focused on the relationship between urbanisation, economic status and crime.

American cities are rather more clearly divided by social and ethnic groupings than European and British ones. While in one study (based on the US National Crime Survey) extent of urbanisation was an important factor in affecting crime rates, this was more significant for adult than for juvenile offending (Sampson and Castellano, 1982). Greater freedom of reporting in the USSR in the 1980s has suggested that urban crime rates are rising there too (Walker, Martin, 1987). If true (and reliable crime statistics are not available) this would be remarkable, since research has suggested that Soviet crime rates were *higher* by the early 1980s than USA ones (Zeldes, 1981).

What is curious is that the area concept and focus have also been adopted by some of the most vehement critics of ecological positivism. In a series of studies of crime in inner-city areas commissioned mainly by local authorities, Kinsey and Young and their colleagues have examined urban crime in Merseyside and the London suburbs of Islington and Tottenham (Kinsey, 1984); Kinsey *et al.*, 1986; Jones *et al.*, 1986). These studies merely use the area focus as a framework. They do not always report increased crime rates (e.g. on the Broadwater Farm Housing estate in Tottenham, crime rates were *falling*) and their emphasis is very much on remedies for crime. Their starting point is clearly the often expressed fear of crime found in inner-city populations, especially among women and the elderly (see Chapter 7 for a review). In short, what sociologists have to face here is that the public, especially vulnerable citizens of inner cities, perceive crime as an area problem, as *their* area problem:

> in the inner cities crime is a social problem, second only to unemployment. It is the problem of the poor, the weak and the vulnerable. For them, losing the fight against crime is the worst crime of all. (Kinsey *et al.*, 1986)

In seeking to explain and understand the patterns of crime and deviance in their city, the Chicagoans put forward the concept of 'social disorganisation'. This, as Downes and Rock (1981, p. 62) remark, 'is a most awkward conception which deserves some reflection'. They define it as part of experience, or possibly a property of social structure during periods of rapid change. But 'social disorganisation' has surely most value as a 'sensitising concept', an idea which draws our attention to others and to a wide range of evidence. It needs to be seen, too, in relation to its opposite, social organisation. Chicagoans were not often precise in defining such terms, but we can derive meanings from their usage in various studies. It is clear, for example, that there were at least two strands in the idea of 'disorganisation': one of 'fun', the other of almost romanticised celebration. Thrasher, for instance, argues that

> The gang . . . is one manifestation of the disorganization incident to cultural conflict among diverse nations and races gathered together in one place and themselves in contact with a civilization foreign and largely inimical to them. (Thrasher, 1963, p. 154)

At the same time, Thrasher also had a celebratory attitude to the gangs he studied. He did not wish to abolish or eradicate them, rather he sought to retain the gang's social activities and *to transform them*.

> The important point to be noted is that when the gang is broken up, the social world of the boy disintegrates and a new one must be substituted for it – not of the artificial type found in institution, but one which will provide for a redirection of his energies in the habitat in which he must live. (p. 353)

This assertion is printed as a caption under two photographs which illustrate just such a transformation, from street gang to Boy Scout troop. This ambivalence, both celebrating what Matza (1969) calls 'diversity' and insisting on the need for social order, distinctively characterise the Chicago School. Their approach to diversity and deviance were inherited by other bearers of their tradition. But however humane and reformist, there was also a correctional stance in much of their work, an at least implied notion of order, a longing for another world. Clifford Shaw's discussion of the career of Stanley, the Jack Roller (a thief from drunks) concludes:

> More than five years have elapsed since Stanley was released from the House of Correction. During this period there has not been any recurrence of any delinquent behaviour. Furthermore, he has developed interests and a philosophy of life which are in keeping with the standards of conventional society. (Shaw, 1966, p. 183)

In Zorbaugh's study, *The Goldcoast and the Slum*, which records the very diverse worlds of groups living close to each other, he makes a very telling comparison:

> The rooming-house which has replaced the boarding house is a very different sort of place to live. It has no dining room, no parlour, no common meeting place. Few acquaintances spring up . . . [it] is a place of anonymous relationships. (Zorbaugh, 1929, pp. 73–5)

Chicago sociologists thus were among the first to sensitise people to an awareness of the ordering effect of communities and groups. This of course is an awareness which has permeated many areas of social policy – often quite explicitly related to curbing crime. As Loney notes about the formulation of a British programme of Community Development Projects:

> Joan Cooper spelt out what she saw as the community dimension of the treatment of delinquency . . . the next stage is to work with communities producing the socially disadvantaged . . . highly skilled treatment with the individual is wasted if he is returned to a disordered community which can offer little support! (Loney, 1983, p. 45)

Conceptually the Chicago School represents a major shift in sociological thinking about crime. Crime was seen as socially, not individually, located, and although the approach is generally associated with disorganisation and unpleasant conditions, it was not one of a 'bad causes bad' kind. Crime was viewed, if not as normal, then at least as everyday and commonplace. Its location in and association with cities raises many problems, methodologically and theoretically, but it did help to set an agenda which is still being referred to and will have relevance for the future.

Methods

Sociology is not noted for its methodological innovations. But Chicago did introduce several of these which have been of lasting importance. I have already mentioned Park's idea of the city as social laboratory. Chicago certainly served in that role and was fully documented and observed. No one has since equalled that endeavour. But it does suggest at least partial models for recording and observing – for example the community study based on local residence and observation, as in Smith (1986). More readily replicated are the ethnographic studies, especially the life histories, which graphically record the careers of vagrants and delinquents in their own words (Shaw, 1930; Anderson, 1961). Bennett (1981) has raised some issues about how data were recorded and used in Chicago, while Plummer (1983, pp. 60–1) has a discussion of the life history method which emphasises the importance of Chicago. In Plummer's view, Chicago naturalism – 'lived life' – shows that 'concrete humans cannot be grasped in abstraction'. There are problems with such approaches, not least with criminals. Is the respondent telling the truth? How should his/her words be shaped and edited? Nevertheless, life histories and personal documents can provide enormously valuable accounts of criminal careers. Before and since the work of Shaw and Mackay and their colleagues, journalists and other writers as well as some offenders themselves have provided fascinating accounts. Tony Parker has published a series of such studies of sex offenders, fraudsters and mentally disturbed prisoners (Parker, 1962, 1963, 1965); Studying women criminals has, until recently, been much hampered by the lack of research on them (Heidensohn, 1985; Carlen, 1985), but the position has begun to improve (Heidensohn, 1987). Parker has produced one case study of the lives of five deviant women (Parker, 1965). Samuel's (1981) account of the life of Arthur Harding, an East End criminal, is a good modern example, set within the framework of oral social history. Life histories are an invaluable source and one which sociologists always need to encourage. The Chicago archive, for example, yields studies covering decades in the lives of individual delinquents.

Participant observation, in which the researcher records the everyday world around her/him was developed in Chicago and has much to offer sociologists of deviance. Perhaps the most complete and subtly reflective example is Whyte's *Street Corner Society* (1955), which was actually carried out in Boston in the 1930s, although it was clearly influenced by Chicago. Whyte, reflecting on his experience many years later, insists: 'I was seeking to build a sociology based upon observed interpersonal events' (p. 358). The main requirements he sets out for such a study are daunting and could hardly be met today. Such a study needs to take a long time, since it cannot be hurried, and to begin in a relatively unfocused way and be changed and modified as it progresses. Research constraints and resource limitations make such an approach fairly unrealistic today. But that does not mean that 'barefoot sociologists' cannot record their own experiences, charting the developments of areas and institutions. For some situations and problems, it is critical to do so. The voices of ethnic minorities are heard, but authentic voices, expressing the lived experience of being black in white society, of experience of racial prejudice and harassment, have remained silent.

Policy

Matza, in *Becoming Deviant* (1969, p. 15), distinguishes between what he calls appreciation and correction in relation to crime. Appreciation

> entails a commitment – to the phenomenon and to those exemplifying it – to render it with fidelity and without violating its integrity. . . . The decision to appreciate . . . delivers the analyst into the arms of the subject . . . and commits him . . . to the subject's definition of the situation. This does not mean the analyst always concurs with the subject's definition of the situation; rather that his aim is to comprehend and to illuminate the subject's view and to interpret the world *as it appears to him.* (Matza, 1969, pp. 24–5)

Taking an appreciative stance was, Matza argues, an important step developed in Chicago, with considerable consequences for sociological development (see below). He contrasts this position with that of 'correctionalism': 'the purpose of much research on deviation has been to assist established society ultimately to rid itself of such troublesome activities' (Matza, 1969, p. 15). I have observed above that in much of the Chicago work the two approaches were more closely linked than Matza's dichotomy suggests.

Much Chicago enterprise was certainly devoted to social welfare developments. The Chicago Area Project has been described as

> an almost legendary experiment in community based crime prevention which represented the first systematic applied chal-

lenge by sociologists to the psychiatric treatment of delinquency. (Smith, 1986, p. 15)

Shaw used the life history technique not just to empathise with and appreciate his subjects but also as a basis for *treatment*, and life histories are presented partly to demonstrate successful 'cures' (Burgess, 1966, p. 194). The kinds of social policy changes pursued by Chicagoans were of fairly specific and limited kinds. They focused either on what we would now perhaps call intervention projects or on community development types of programmes, with local and voluntary emphases. As Downes and Rock point out,

> The theory of 'social disorganization' seemed readily translatable into terms of social practice. If the causes of delinquency were to be found in the attenuation of social controls born of 'social disorganization' then the most effective responses should be the fostering of such potential for social organization as did exist in the areas most affected. (Downes and Rock, 1981, p. 229)

Downes and Rock trace the links between these projects and more modern ones run by the New York City Youth Board, as well as their influence on parts of the 'War on Poverty' programmes in the USA in the 1960s.

The Chicago approach did not originally involve either an appreciation of victims' or of non-deviants' perceptions. Nor, on the whole, did they build power or economy into their model. As a result, the *sources* of the inequalities and deprivations they recorded were neither analysed nor challenged. Political change was not on their policy agenda.

However, we have already seen that many writers since have used the Chicago framework as a structure on which to build a more dynamic and complex model. It is possible to move from comparing the Gold Coast and the slum to analysing housing classes and reconceptualising the inner city as an arena of conflict (Castells, 1978). While such a political economy of the inner city, and the place of crime within it, can be derived from area studies, albeit with major changes in theoretical constructs on the way (Loney, 1983, pp. 134–41), it nevertherless remains the case that policy changes within the reformist tradition are more naturally the heirs of Chicago.

Two modern area-related studies of crime and disorganisation incidence in Britain follow in many ways the Chicago path and exemplify both its possibilities and its limitations. I want to use them both to illustrate the continuing value and distinctiveness of the cities–crime–disorganisation theme both in sociology and in terms of current public and policy concerns.

Tim Hope's *Drinking and Disorder in the City Centre: A Policy Analysis* was published in 1985 as one of three studies in *Implementing Crime Prevention Measures*. While it is quite explicitly linked with initiatives within the Home Office on crime prevention (Tuck, 1985), it does not share the characteristics of many of those studies which are discussed below. Notably, Hope sets out to achieve an understanding and an explanation of the public disorder associated with drinking in central Newcastle upon Tyne (Hope, 1985, p. 45). Faithful to the customs of area studies, he uses occurrence logs to chart the patterns of incidents and disorder, locating as a result three key trouble spots: an area of (1) four streets with twelve public houses, (2) two large dance halls, and (3) the 'Metro' rail system (pp. 47–8). Hope then goes on to examine disorder (fights, assaults, criminal damage) 'to take account of a complex interaction between a wide range of possible contributory factors' (p. 48). These he sets out as *socio-cultural*, noting that there are strong associations between youth, drink, disorderly conduct and gender, as well as *situational factors* of space, public domain and physical structure. Finally, he lists *managerial and economic factors* where he suggests, albeit tentatively, that inner–city planning policies and macroeconomic trends, as well as conditions in the licensed trade, all contribute to the production of disorder (pp. 48–53). Having reviewed causative factors, Hope then suggests some preventive measures, which range widely from 'social reforms to affect the "root causes" of heavy drinking and violence' to situational ones: 'alter the character of pubs and clubs' (p. 57). Hope concludes by noting the value of research and planning 'for clarifying problems and objectives', but he also stresses the need 'for gaining consent' (p. 62).

In some ways Hope's study has an authentic tang of Chicago and later area studies, in the careful logging and mapping and the attempt to describe and explain disorder. It lacks, though, the authentic, participative voices of the city, the drinkers and the fights. Power, poverty and inequality are only hinted at in the brief analysis, and there is the merest nod in the direction of gender relations and patriarchal dominance. But Hope is able to adapt the

Chicago model for modern policy purposes arguing that his approach can be used at the local level (p. 58), although he appears to mean the *official* local level, rather than members of the local community. Nevertheless, this approach could well be adopted by any group wishing to monitor activities in their area (see below) and it is possible to see a variety of future uses for it.

Alice Coleman's *Utopia on Trial* (1985) is a full-length study of 'design disadvantage' in modern public housing. Coleman's thesis is that 'design can be a powerful influence for bad' and that reductions in social malaise and crime could be achieved through design modification, which will bring down the

> levels of litter, graffiti, vandalism, excrement and the number of children in care [and] in practice . . . achieve far more, including a spinoff in the reduction of stress and trauma, mental illness and crime. (Coleman, 1985, p. 5)

Coleman's work is very much in the ecological tradition and strongly positivist in approach. Housing designs actually produce social malaise in her view (p. 118). She bases her theory on Oscar Newman's *Defensible Space* (1982) in which, having studied all the housing projects in New York, he related design features to indices of crime and vandalism. Newman found three principles 'that explained how crime was made easy to commit and difficult to prevent: anonymity, lack of surveillance and the presence of alternative escape routes' (1985, p. 14). If, on the other hand, 'defensible spaces' were *designed into* public housing, then crime rates should fall. Coleman argues that natural selection leads to territoriality in species and the need to make one's mark. Contemporary designs, influenced by the Swiss architect and planner, Le Corbusier, reduce individuality and produce anonymous uniformity, 'confused spatial organisation' and massive scope for crime and breakdown.

Sociologists may understandably feel uneasy with the sociobiological basis of this thesis. They will recognise kinship more readily, with some reservations, with Coleman's empirical testing, carried out in association with her team at the Land Use Research Unit at King's College, London. The team surveyed over 4,000 blocks of flats and more than 4,000 houses in London and elsewhere and made precise measures of the incidence of 'malaise' by observing litter, graffiti, vandalism, amounts of urine and faeces deposited.

They also logged numbers of children in care. These factors were then linked to design features. They found that

The five most powerful designs are dwellings per entrance, dwellings per block, number of storeys, overhead walkways and spatial organisation. These, it is submitted, are the ringleaders of the anti-social design gang . . . various forms of social breakdown tend to occur in a set order as design features worsen to the successive degrees of depravity needed to undermine each social taboo in turn. (Coleman, 1985, p. 80)

Coleman goes on to make a series of recommendations about housing and design. These are summarised as follows:

— No more flats should be built.
— House designers should renounce the unstabilising layouts of the last decade.
— Existing flats should be modified to remove their worst design features.

There are also two extensive lists of design guides for preventing design disadvantage and to promote defensible space and improving the streetscape. Coleman insists that 'design–disadvantagement research has . . . led to a more general understanding of the way human behaviour tends to deteriorate under the stress of inappropriate habitats' (p. 177). She concludes with data and a chart which shows crime rates in certain blocks of flats in Southwark in London strongly related to design (p. 178).

This study has both great strengths and weaknesses. For sociologists, its environmental determinism is too simple and hard to swallow, for the reasons outlined in relation to the Chicago School. If habitats affect action so drastically, why are criminals mostly young and male? In part, Coleman answers this by including sociological notions of family, socialisation and even power in her causative model (p. 19), although she ignores gender. Methodologically, too, there is a naive empiricism in the careful measurements. Data on crime (pp. 178–9) are treated as unproblematic. The legend to Figure 40 on crime trends reads: 'No crimes were reported from the blocks with zero disadvantagement score' (p. 179). What, one wonders, were the categories recorded? Was domestic violence or child abuse measured in any way? Or only public crime? And what of known factors of underrecording even within the conventional model of real crime?

Despite these criticisms, Coleman's is a highly instructive book. She has reminded sociologists that ecological ideas are not dead and that they can be used to frame policy-related research that can have powerful impact, for this study has undoubtedly had considerable effect on housing and crime prevention policies. Several London boroughs and the Metropolitan Police have worked with Coleman on the redesigning of housing estates and blocks of flats, just as Oscar Newman has advised on design in other countries. A climate in which housing problems are rife and urban riots a recent memory was obviously one which would be responsive to such confidently expressed solutions. Sociology can learn that key ideas can be powerful when cogently expressed and addressed to recognisable problems. Sociologists should not be possessive about their models and their heritage, but should ensure, by contributing the crucial aspects missing from this analysis – for example, the dimensions of power, gender and race – that they are improved and made more successful. Coleman herself describes an analysis undertaken together with Anne Power, who has introduced the concept of housing management to a series of experimental projects on council estates in London. Housing improvement through better management, like design modification, focuses on the built environment – repairs, security, etc. – but it is based on a concept of devolving *power* from central authority to tenants (Power, 1981 & 1988). It therefore has distinct similarities with the concept of 'community architecture' advocated by Rod Hackney and the Community Architecture Office at the Royal Institute of British Architects. The scope for valuable and challenging work here is immense.

Communication

I have tried so far to set out the main themes of the Chicago heritage, why they seem worth cherishing, and the ways in which they have flourished despite having been, metaphorically at least, sometimes in store for years. There remains to explore perhaps the greatest gift of all to later sociologists. In a discipline not renowned for notable communicators, Chicagoans wrought a transformation and set exacting standards. We should remember, of course, that Park was a journalist for many years and that others had not followed conventional academic routes. In addition, there is perhaps the exotic excitement factor. Chicagoans were, on the whole, fascinated by the deviant, the bizarre and the down and out. They sometimes exaggerated these traits. Matza (1969, p. 71) points out that 'Taxi-dancers, studied by Paul Cressey . . . were very impressed with how different their lives were from those of conventional girls,' yet their lives as taxi-dancers (a kind of partner-for-hire in the large, male-dominated dance halls of 1920s Chicago) were very transient, and 'many girls left their deviant world, settled down and married'.

Notwithstanding these advantages of communications skills and human interest stories, the Chicago sociologists achieved a remarkable breakthrough. Their paradigm of the inner-city zone as linked to crime constitutes the first and vital step in a systematic empirical sociology of crime. (Durkheim, as I shall suggest later, also provided initial insights, but did not develop them himself. They were, as we shall see, critical at a much later period in American sociology.) Assumed links between urbanisation and crime are now taken for granted, so that it is vital to stress the importance of the conceptual shift that the Chicago school achieved and conveyed. For example, Mayhew as we saw, observed and recorded London street life and crime in great detail in the nineteenth century. But he believed that crime was caused by various 'wandering tribes' who were unfitted for modern life.

In America itself the Chicago tradition of bringing the bad news back from the mean city streets has survived in powerful sociological and journalistic accounts by Suttles (1968, 1972), and others. In Britain in the 1980s the hardest realities of inner-city life and crime have been most directly and tellingly conveyed by media reporting of riots, drug abuse and fears of crime. The urge to make sense of and explain the disturbing phenomena of crime and victimisation is, as I suggested earlier, very strong, especially since urban crime seems peculiarly threatening and disturbing. The two television soap operas developed in Britain in the 1980s – 'Brookside' on Channel 4 and 'EastEnders' (BBC 1) – both depict relatively disadvantaged groups in urban settings. Crimes such as drug abuse, rape, kidnapping, assault and murder all feature prominently and are tackled as issues to be explained within social and environmental contexts. Liverpool and London's East End are a long way from Chicago, but that is where this enterprise began.

That there is still scope for serious and popular studies of urban life and problems on the Chicago model is demonstrated by Paul Harrison's *Inside the Inner City* (1983), a comprehensive study of London's most deprived borough, Hackney. Harrison paints a careful picture of the district, physically, socially and economically, and devotes considerable space to the complex problem of crime in the area. He has no doubt that it is a major issue:

> The level of crime is one of the key features that distinguishes the inner city from other kinds of area. It casts a shadow over life and the poorer the family and the neighbourhood, the deeper is that shadow. (Harrison, 1983, p. 324)

Harrison sees crime as a product of poverty, bad housing, inequality, family breakdown and what he terms 'the collapse of social control' (p. 326) – a very full and broad indictment. He combines some economic analysis with some well-observed pictures of both Hackney criminals and victims, as well as giving a perceptive account of the supercharged problems of policing in the borough and the reactions of blacks and others to the police. Without major economic, political and social changes, Harrison argues, the polarisation of inner cities with the rest of the country will continue: 'Crimes of theft and of violence will continue to grow. Riots will recur and urban terrorism reappear' (p. 435).

Conclusions

Despite Harrison's rather gloomy scenario, we do not actually know what will happen in our cities in the future. Certain trends are established and will probably continue, but, as I suggested earlier, it is the uncertainties of change we need to prepare for. When the University of Chicago was founded the city around it was growing fast, as were most cities in the developing world. Many Western countries were in the classic take-off period of industrialisation and urbanisation (only Britain had passed effectively through that stage). The cities of industrial society attracted young migrant workers. Most of the problems perceived as urban issues had to do with youth, growth, lack of space, cultural clashes, etc. Today, in most Western countries at least, the picture is very different. Urban areas tend to be losing population to their outer suburbs, satellite towns and even the countryside. The population of London has declined since the 1920s. Areas which are growing, now that new technology removes the need for industrial concentrations, including previously 'green spaces' such as Southern California, East Anglia in Britain, and rural Bavaria (Hall, 1985). At the same time, in Second and Third World countries, cities are often growing exponentially. Mexico City is the world's biggest metropolis.

Cities, especially their inner areas, are therefore in relative decline, losing population and having tracts burnt out or boarded-up. Yet crime is perceived as much a problem in such areas as it was fifty or a hundred years ago (Pearson, 1983). Many people currently offer what they regard as panaceas for preventing crime (see Chapter 7). Some of these, such as neighbourhood watch and community policing, are likely not to be feasible in inner-city areas, or may confront and expose considerable conflicts within those areas. It seems unlikely that cities will cease to be stage sets for the ritual enactment of certain dramas of crime and control.

Yet we must always beware of uncertainty. Populations in many Western countries are 'ageing', and the youthful at-risk age groups are likely to decrease in numbers for much of the remainder of the century (*Social Trends*, 1987). Furthermore, signs of inner-city regeneration can be observed in parts of London's docklands and in the Marais district of Paris. Of course, the influx of some affluent, middle-class inhabitants into traditional working-class areas is not an unalloyed benefit. House prices rise steeply, local people are 'crowded out' and cannot live near their families. Where social groups with very different incomes and life styles do coexist, crime rates seem to rise as opportunity and conflict arise. This was a pattern described by Zorbaugh in Chicago and since also observed by Hunt.

Whatever future our cities face, it seems unlikely that it will be peaceful and unproblematic. Cities are not merely places, they are also symbols and metaphors, states of mind and styles of life. In so far as modern societies are pluralistic, diverse and prone to conflict, cities are likely to be where these are focused. (Although, during the miners' strike in Britain in 1985, it was in pit villages and in relatively rural settings that confrontations took place between groups of miners, and between miners, their supporters and the police.)

The well equipped sociologist or the concerned citizen who wishes to understand and be prepared for change can learn a great deal from the Chicago experience. For sociology, Chicago provided most of the main steps and ideas used and developed later in the study of crime. Crime as a social phenomenon and symbolic interactionism came from Chicago. Methodologically and empirically the subject was enriched. A legacy of studies has followed which show the power of the Chicago vision, even if, perhaps because, it is an impressive one. A sensible and grateful inheritor of this rich tradition will use it wisely and well. She/he will note its limits – whatever happened, in the family treasures, to power, race and gender? – and build them back in, since the loose nature of the model allows them to fit in. From large, city-wide surveys, to local ethnographic observation and life histories, there is scope for innovation and development.

For those who do not call themselves sociologists, the organising concepts of Chicago produced a mass of fascinating material, penetrating insights and useful tools for analysis. They have been borrowed by urban geographers, policemen, and by criminals themselves. Every authentic villain's autobiography I have ever read begins with a vivid description of the 'manor' (neighbourhood) in which he was reared. That, at least, is true of male criminals; women, when they confess, begin with their families. If you want authentic and fascinating versions, Chicago criminologists and their subjects are unsurpassed.

To demonstrate just how important it is to be adaptable, to expect the unexpected, I want to end this chapter with one last fascinating area study of crime and the messages it carries for the future. Jerry White's *The Worst Street in North London* (1986) is a vivid account of a vanished place and its problems. In the 1920s and 1930s – indeed, during the heyday of the Chicago School – Campbell Bunk was 'the worst street in North London', notorious for its high crime rate, poverty, high unemployment and high levels of interpersonal violence. White carefully reconstructs life in that part of Islington, through oral history and old records, recreating in the process a whole, vanished community and way of life. White is a Marxist historian, not a sociologist, but he found Marxist theory inadequate to explain change in Campbell Bunk. He builds in concepts of 'psychic compensation' for men who created a 'hierarchy of masculinity'. Building the social construction of gender into his model enabled him to see that it was the changing positions of young women in the street, in their social class and in the economy of London, which finally wrought change in the Bunk.

White's work is a fascinating piece of retrospective ethnography. Despite his resistance, his analysis is highly sociological. There is another message worth pondering, too. The Bunk has totally disappeared. Whatever the problems of the people and the area now, they seem very different from those of Campbell Bunk.

3 Youth, Delinquency and Subculture

Sociology has not developed in neat, well-defined stages which have, like all good stories, a beginning, a middle and an end. It is rather a never-ending tale, or series of tales, for a series of story-tellers have, so to speak, settled at the fireside and started their fables before others have finished. In other words, when a new voice presenting novel ideas or concepts has appeared, it has not generally been because others have stopped talking. Moreover, the process of succession has been random and haphazard; it has not obeyed systematic laws. It is often a convenience in text books to impose an apparent order on the theories being conveyed; this helps the author in selecting topics and the student to learn them, but such a system is only a learning device and an aid to mastering the subject.

All this is by way of a preamble to this chapter, in which I shall discuss two crucial and recurring themes in the sociology of crime: the links between social structures and crime and the related topic of youthful deliquency. The first is a major concern both of mainstream sociology (Becker, 1964) and of the sociology of crime and deviance, and thus has a dual importance in the discipline. The focus on youthful crime is due to similar twin origins: much of the work done in developing sociological theories of crime from the late 1930s onwards took male urban delinquent youth as its subject (although there were important exceptions, such as Sutherland's (1945) work on professional thieves and white-collar criminals. In addition, for much of this period 'juvenile delinquency' was the main form in which the problem of crime was conceptualised, and consequently it was the issue to which most remedies and policy programmes were addressed. To give just one example from

38

Britain, in 1964 a Labour Party Study Group under the chairmanship of Lord Longford produced an important report, *Crime – A Challenge to Us All*; most of the report's analysis and recommendations (which influenced later policies) were devoted to juveniles.

Society, social structure and crime

Sociology students sometimes find that in the study of crime they cannot use key concepts from their disciplinary tool kit such as 'family', 'class' and 'equality' as readily as in fields like education. Nor are they usually able to call in the ideas and the blessing of the theoretical Holy Trinity of the subject – Marx, Weber and Durkheim. As several sociologists have remarked, not always sorrowfully, this is not an altogether respectable topic (S. Cohen, 1981; Pearson, 1975). On this occasion, however, we start in excellent company with the contributions to the sociology of crime of Emile Durkheim.

I use the plural here advisedly, as Durkheim's importance extends to more than one of our areas of interest. As I have already suggested, sociology developed in a somewhat jerky fashion, and Durkheim, who did not himself write a great deal directly about crime, has come to have had considerable influence on several areas since his death. As Reiner summarises:

> The Durkheimian legacy is manifest primarily in three strands of contemporary work on crime and the law: (a) the influence of his conception of crime on 'labelling' theory; (b) theories of crime causation within the 'anomie' framework; (c) debates about legal and penal evolution. (Reiner, 1984, p. 185).

We shall look at the second of these now and the first in later chapters.

Durkheim's legacy is to be found both in the specific concept of anomie and his more general formulation of the nature of society and the ways in which 'social solidarity' are developed and maintained. In *Division of Labour in Society* (1949) he distinguished the 'mechanical' solidarity of simple preindustrial societies, 'which comes from a certain number of states of conscience which are common to all the members of the same society'. Such a society is characterised by 'repressive' law. In contrast, there is 'organic' solidarity which derives from the division of labour and is associated with restitutive laws. It is clear that understanding the processes by which order is maintained in societies was central to Durkheim's sociology. So, too, was a need to explain the phenomenon of crime and its persistence. Durkheim came to the conclusion that

> what is normal, simply is the existence of criminality, provided that it attains and does not exceed . . . a certain level . . . crime . . . is . . . an integral part of all healthy societies. (Durkheim, 1964, p. 66)

Crime is normal, according to Durkheim, 'In the first place . . . because a society exempt from it is utterly impossible' (p. 67). Further, it is in the nature of societies to generate rules and sanction their breaking, and it also serves a function (p. 69). Crime is thus an inescapable feature of society.

Such notions of the origins of crime in society itself, rather than in individuals or in abnormal conditions, were crucial in making *sociologies* of crime possible. Durkheim's direct heirs here are mainly American sociologists in the structural-functionalist line, but all who have since worked in this field are indebted to him.

The direct line runs through Robert Merton, who used Durkheim's concept of anomie, developed in his analysis of suicide. In *Suicide* (1952) Durkheim distinguished three types of self-destruction: egotistic, altruistic, and anomic. Anomic suicide is cased by a lack of social regulation and restraint (Durkheim did consider a possible fourth category, of 'fatalistic' suicide, the opposite of anomic suicide, which he describes as 'deriving from excessive regulation'. He decided, however, that it was too rare to be worth including) (Durkheim, 1951, p. 272).

Merton followed Durkheim in adapting a key concept, in his concern for 'sociological perspectives' as against biological, and in wishing to explore

> why it is that the frequency of deviant behaviour varies within different social structures and how it happens that the deviations have different shapes and patterns in different social structures. (Merton, 1949, p. 131)

Merton's central aim was

to discover how *some social structures exert a definite pressure upon certain persons in the society to engage in nonconforming rather than conforming conduct.* (Merton, 1949, p. 132, original emphasis)

Here Merton was in effect setting out the manifesto for a powerful regime that was to dominate sociological study of crime for several decades.

Merton's own first formulation was anomie theory. Among social and cultural structures he distinguished two elements: first, 'culturally defined goals, purposes and interests . . . they are the things worth striving for'; second were 'the acceptable modes of reaching out for these goals' (Merton, 1949, pp. 132–3). These 'cultural goals and institutionalized norms operate jointly to shape prevailing practices'.

Merton goes on to note that

contemporary American culture continues to be characterised by a heavy emphasis on wealth as a basic symbol of success, without a corresponding emphasis upon the legitimate avenues on which to march towards this goal. (1949, p. 139)

He then sets out his 'five types of adaptation' in a schema which has become one of the most famous typologies in all sociology; it is reproduced below as Table 3.1. Apart from conformity, all the

Table 3.1 Typology of modes of individual adaptation

	Modes of adaptation	Culture goals	Institutionalised means
I	Conformity	+	+
II	Innovation	+	−
III	Ritualism	−	+
IV	Retreatism	−	−
V	Rebellion	±	±

+ signifies acceptance
− signifies rejection
± signifies rejection of prevailing values and substitution of new values
Source: Merton, 1949, p. 140

forms of adaptation have some deviant potential, although it is the last category into which most of the American crime related to economic activity is classified. The result of the lack of fit between goals and means in Merton's view 'produces a strain toward anomie and deviant behaviour' (p. 157). Stress 'makes for the breakdown of the regulatory structure'.

Criticising anomie theory has become, Downes and Rock (1981, p. 94) suggest, a kind of alternative undergraduate sport: 'it has become a routine conceptual folly for students to demolish before moving on to more rewarding ground'. Critics have been numerous and vocal. Clinard (1968, p. 158) lists six types of criticism, which he calls 'only a few'. Anomie theory is based on what Matza (1969, p. 97) called 'the dubious reliability of official estimates regarding the distribution of deviation', since Merton assumes that most 'strain' is experienced in the lower class where poverty and distance from the realisation of the American dream are greatest. Yet Merton was already aware, as Matza points out, of research on the problematic nature of the construction of such records; a mass of work has since demonstrated this.

Universal cultural goals are hard to identify, and this is clearly one of the key flaws in functionalist theory as defined in the model (Cohen, 1968). As Merton suggests, societies clearly differ over the nature of these goals, and there are difficulties in interpreting the support for, and acceptance of, such goals. In modern Poland, for instance, where there is an official commitment to a socialist work ethic, and 'economic crimes' such as bribery and corruption attract severe penalities, a study of public attitudes to deviance showed that there was very mixed attachment to official values and marked indifference to state versions of 'social plagues' (Kwasniewski, 1984). According to Lemert (1964), social structure is too broad and simple a concept, while Clinard (1968, p. 160) argues that Merton 'neglects the important role of social control in defining who is a "deviant" that is how the label comes to be attached to a person.' Cohen (1965), in the most thorough of such analyses, points out that the theory is surprisingly simple, mechanistic and isolated in its treatment of the complex of roles and interactions of which the lives of delinquents and others consist.

To complete the ritual debunking of anomie it is now virtually compulsory to quote Taylor (1971, p. 148): 'It is as though individuals in society are playing on a gigantic fruit machine, but the machine is rigged and only some players are consistently rewarded'. (As a matter of fact, I think that the more appropriate analogy is with the skittle or bowling alley where some of the channels or roads are blocked or bent and participants cannot reach the target.) But the main point of Taylor's criticism is the lack of historical and critical perspective: 'nobody appeared to ask who put the machine there in the first place and who takes the profits'.

Reiner together with Downes and Rock all try to rebut some of the criticism and rescue anomie from, so to speak, the sociologists' builders' skip to which it has been consigned. Reiner (1984, p. 191) argues: 'It is reasonable to suppose (with Merton) that law-breaking (as defined by the state) is more prevalent among the less successful'. He also insists that it is perfectly possible to fill in the many gaps in the model without any great incompatibility (p. 192). Substantially similar points are made by Downes and Rock, who conclude that the theory could be strengthened by incorporating many of the missing aspects in it.

I have set out Merton's theory and the criticism it attracted for several reasons:

1. First, I think it is an important if undeveloped model: 'there is a great deal of unexpected mileage in anomie theory' (Downes and Rock, 1981, p. 114).
2. Second, it provided a sociological paradigm, however inadequate, for a range of studies of crime and deviance.
3. Those studies are in themselves important and also form part of developments in sociology which have provided one of the most interesting parts of our heritage.
4. The outline given above gives only some idea of the debate which anomie theory engendered. This debate and subsequent ones characterised American criminological research after the Second World War and played an important part in its development. This feature distinguishes this period from Chicago in its heyday when the school *was* American sociology, and interaction and dialogue was *within* that setting. By the 1950s, the scope of academic criticism had widened considerably. (It is worth pointing out that this was mainly intra- not interdisciplinary, although Wootton's (1957) book is an important exception.) Despite the persuasive claims for an interdisciplinary approach to the study of delinquency, especially in Britain, this usually meant leaving out sociology (S. Cohen, 1981).
5. Finally, as we shall see, much of both the conceptual and empirical urges had faded in these areas by the 1980s (Parker and Giller, 1981). If there is to be a renewal of this sociological lineage it may be useful to start with the source.

In the next section I want to explore some of these themes and show how American subcultural studies of delinquency developed, and to examine parallel but distinct studies of youth cultures in Britain. I conclude with Parker and Giller's observation: 'Criminology, dominated for twenty years by the sociological perspective, has clearly lost its preoccupation with delinquency' (1981, p. 233).

Society, sub-cultures and delinquency

One of the main confusions which seem to underpin much of the criticism of anomie theory is the assumption that it is meant to be a precise description of American society at a particular time – that it is a case study in the Chicago sense. Yet it is clear that what Merton sought to present was, as he says, a 'framework' 'schematically set out' (1949, pp. 139–140). In short, it was intended as an ideal type, in the sense used by Max Weber for analytic purposes. As Weber himself suggested, 'in order to untangle real casual relations, we construct unreal ones'. Now, in order to develop the model in a rigorous, Weberian manner, there should have been further, alternative versions put forward and tested and a vast range of empirical data used in the proving and firing processes. Lacking these steps, the schema is limited. Nevertheless it provided a framework for an important series of studies of delinquency, and a debate about those studies.

> Merton's strain theory . . . has served as the basis of so many other theoretical efforts and provided the framework within which many empiral inquiries have been interpreted. (Kornhauser, 1978, p. 150)

Albert Cohen was the first socioligist systematically to use the concepts of culture and subculture to explain delinquency. The delinquent subculture, insists Cohen in *Delinquent Boys* (1955, p. 24), is 'Non utilitarian and malicious and negativistic'. It is further characterised by its versatility, by short-run hedonism and by primary loyalty to the delinquent gang. Like Merton, Cohen assumes a functionalist model of society and a universal set of achievement-oriented standards. Working-class male youth (Cohen suggests a different theory for girls which he does not develop) have little chance of achieving standards set by the middle classes.

These boys then have three possibilities: (a) the brightest may try for upward mobility – the 'college boy solution', as vividly described by Whyte (1955); (b) less able boys may settle for becoming 'stable corner boys' who adjust to middle-class values without attaining them and rely on the street peer group for mutual support; (c) a third group choose the 'delinquent subculture' which is 'a way of dealing with the problems of adjustment'.

Delinquent boys experience failure and status frustration in schools, but are also aware of society's dominant values. The delinquent subculture provides an alternative source of status and a legitimation of the use of aggression. Cohen argues that by a psychological mechanism (derived from Sigmund Freud) the attachment to middle-class values of utilitarianism, respectability, deferred gratification, etc. is transformed into a powerful inversion and rejection of them, characterised by a powerful ambivalence. This process is called 'reaction formation'.

Delinquent Boys has been an immensely influential study (Kitsuse and Dietrick, 1959). Many sociologists have contributed to its critique and many more to empirically testing or extending it (see, for example, Giallombardo, 1972, for a selection). Although it was not itself strongly based empirically, the theory did appear to '"fit the facts" extremely well; to aid in both explaining and understanding . . . and to go beyond previous theories while retaining their more valuable insights' (Downes and Rock, 1981, p. 120). Yet, as other sociologists made increasingly clear, Cohen's concept of the delinquent subculture did *not* fit the facts.

Kitsuse and Dietrick (1959, p. 125) pointed out that middle-class gang delinquency was under-reported. Moreover, most delinquency does not involve group activities but individuals or pairs. Miller proposed a much more autonomous view of 'Lower Class Culture as a Generating Milieu of Gang Delinquency' (1958). Far from being produced by reaction to the dominant culture and an inversion of its 'protestant ethic' values, 'lower class culture' had its own established values, or 'focal concerns' of: (1) trouble, (2) toughness, (3) smartness, (4) excitement, (5) fate, (6) autonomy. Each of these 'is conceived as a "dimension" within which a fairly wide and varied range of alternative behaviour patterns may be followed' (Miller, 1958, pp. 138–9). Working-class boys studied by Miller often came from mother-dominated one-parent homes and sought to achieve masculine status through peer group activities, such as fighting in street gangs. In this perspective subcultures are perceived to be in conflict with dominant values rather than reacting to them.

Cohen responded to his critics and refined his typology to produce three kinds of subcultural response to dominant values:

1. the violent, conflict subculture;
2. the drug subculture;
3. the semi-professional thief subculture (Cohen and Short, 1958).

This typology is, as Downes (1966, p. 23) pointed out, similar to Cloward and Ohlin's. They too followed Merton in looking at achievement values and means of attaining them, but argued that 'discontented, lower class youths do not wish to adopt a middle-class way of life, or to disrupt their present associations' (1960, p. 62). Instead, Cloward and Ohlin assert that they seek status *within* their own community and, where these exist, by illegitimate means. They divide neighbourhoods into types, characterised by deviant 'parent' subcultures; like Cohen and Short, they suggest a threefold pattern of delinquent subculture. These are

1. the criminal subculture, located in a stable working-class areas, where juvenile delinquents 'graduate' into organised crime;
2. the conflict violent subculture;
3. the retreatist, drug subculture.

Both the latter develop in disorganised areas where legitimate and illegitimate opportunities are lacking.

Great effort and all the techniques of sophisticated modern sociological research have been used to try and test these theories. Martin Gold, for example, compared delinquents and non-delinquents in Flint, Michigan in respect of their occupational aspirations; he found no real difference, although subculture theory predicts otherwise (Gold, 1963). Downes also concluded that

> the English evidence lends no support for the existence of delinquent subcultures on the Cloward–Ohlin basis, and the material suggestive of Cohen's . . . subculture is not clarified to the point where a definitive conclusion could be offered. (1966, p. 134)

Short and Strodtbeck (1965) drew a similar blank in Chicago, where gangs specialising in certain forms of delinquency were not to be found.

Ironically, then, the strength of the response which subculture theory evoked proved its undoing. Since almost everyone interested in crime wanted to explore it and test it out, its limits and inadequacies and its lack of fit with experience were the more quickly exposed. In the final analysis, perhaps almost a post mortem, conducted by David Matza it is the central conceptual flaws which proved terminal.

Matza (1964) argues that subcultural theories massively *overpredict* delinquent behaviour. This is essentially because subculture theorists conceive of human nature in a passive, functionalist sense, in what Dennis Wrong has described as the 'oversocialized conception of modern man'. Although Matza does not bring this out fully, it is worth stressing here that subculture theory encapsulates a fundamental irony: in order to become deviant and *break* society's rules, delinquent boys have to learn to *conform* steadfastly to subcultural norms.

Matza first puts forward a different notion of human nature: he perceives human actors as having choice about their behaviour and being able to exercise 'free will' to some extent. This is certainly a break not only with strain theories but with functionalist notions of social order. In describing and typifying delinquency Matza is also at odds with the strain theorists, and much of what might be called the 'hard men on mean streets' genre of sociology. Delinquency, argues Matz, is not tough or thrilling, not a way of life but something much more mundane and episodic. Far from being romantic rebel heroes (Heindensohn, 1985) delinquents as depicted by Matza are almost boring. He avers (in a paper with Sykes) that

> the juvenile delinquent frequently accords admiration and respect to law-abiding persons . . . A fierce attachment to a humble pious mother or a forgiving upright priest . . . is often encountered in . . . juvenile delinquents. (Sykes and Matza, 1957, p. 130)

Some aspects of strain theory are retained by Matza, but he is concerned to develop alternative hypotheses, and proposes that young offenders 'drift' into delinquency, despite otherwise supporting the norms and values of society. Their drift into delinquency is aided by what he and Sykes call 'techniques of neutralisation' (p. 132).

Social controls that serve to check or inhibit deviant motivational patterns are rendered inoperative and the individual is freed to engage in delinquency without serious damage to his self-image. (p. 132)

The five techniques are:

1. denial of responsibility – deviant acts are an accident;
2. denial of injury – no one got hurt;
3. denial of the victim – he deserved it;
4. condemnation of the condemners – the police/judges etc., are just as bad;
5. appeal to higher loyalties – I did it for my mate.

Matza's work marked a radical step back from sociological determinism and was one of the reasons that this particular trend in explaining crime slowed down. The discipline had nevertheless developed enormously within the framework of strain theory and had outgrown that framework.

Youth culture and delinquency

Writing the history of sociological concepts, one is sometimes suddenly forced to bridge gaps, rather like a continuity announcer who can't find a record. I do not, however, want to say 'and now for something completely different', but rather to introduce another range of studies characterised (a) by their British origin and (b) by also being subcultural but also by increasingly using the notion of 'youth culture' in relation to delinquency. Brake (1985) distinguishes four categories of approach:

1. early social ecology;
2. studies of the sociology education and anti-school culture;
3. local youth studies;
4. the Birmingham School.

We looked at Morris's work in the first category in Chapter 2: I propose to take this category no further here. Otherwise I have used Brake's classification, but added and subtracted authors I found more or less interesting.

Anti-school culture

Downes (1966) explored delinquency in Stepney and Poplar in London's East End, and Hargreaves spent two years looking at social relations in a secondary school in a town in the North of England (1967). In the inner London study, Downes found that delinquency was not a product of reaction to broad concepts like society's dominant values, but stemmed instead from economic inequality and the school's impact in instilling a sense of failure in its pupils. 'Work, school and leisure' were the key variables:

> Instead of regarding the working class delinquent as a deviant in a conformity-promoting society, it is possible to regard the working class boy as born into a preordained delinquency-promoting situation. (Downes, 1966, p. 260)

Hargreaves, too, failed to find fully fledged delinquents. There were, however 'delinquescent ' boys whose tiresome behaviour in the classroom was related to their labelling as low stream failures.

The importance of these studies and others of this type is primarily that they introduce other factors into the sociological analysis of delinquency, and also confirm Matza's criticism of over-determination. Brake (1985, p. 61) also points out that notions of youth culture developed from these studies as school was increasingly depicted as meaningless to pupils.

Willis (1978) took this analysis of school subcultures and delinquency much further. In studying a Midlands secondary school, he chose to follow and observe 'the lads', members of the anti-authority school subculture. The 'lads' are an unappealing bunch, male, racist, sexist and bullying. They have developed, Willis argues, a subculture with their own values, which is essentially anti-school and anti-authority. But the scope of this is very limited and paradoxical. While at school they enjoy laughs, teasing the 'earholes' and various joint pleasures; their very alienation from school life, their immersion in the macho-solidarity cult, ensure that they will readily accept the manual jobs they go to when they leave. Willis employs some aspects of subcultural analysis, but the distinctiveness of his work lies in the way he links class, school, lived and shared experience in an overall political economy of deviance.

'Street' studies and the Birmingham School

In reviewing developments in subcultural studies of delinquency in the early 1980s, Stan Cohen argued that 'the new theories distinguish three general levels of analysis: structure, culture and biography' (Cohen, 1980, p. v). He defined structure as 'those aspects of society . . . beyond individual control . . . constraints'. The group most vulnerable to these constraints is working–class youth. 'Culture' in fact equals 'subculture', 'the specific, especially symbolic form through which the subordinate group negotiates its position'. 'Biography' refer to the 'pattern and sequence of personal circumstances through which the culture and structure are experienced'. Cohen goes on to examine 'the new work of British post-war youth culture' as a working out of relationships between these levels.

Several ethnographic studies of delinquent 'subcultures' were published in Britain in the 1970s. Phil Cohen (1972) studied the emergence of 'mods' and 'skinheads' in London's East End. These two conspicuous subcultures of style, dress and demeanour, strongly linked in public and police perception with delinquency, are analysed by Cohen as youth's response to social and material problems. Economic changes – the decline of the London docks, among others – had diminished employment prospects, housing policies had dislocated traditional communities. Becoming a skinhead was not a true solution to these crises; it was not a job-creating move (except, of course, for the memorabilia merchants and, perhaps, a few academic sociologists?). Phil Cohen portrays it as a symbolic or 'magical' resolution of hidden conflicts (p. 23).

Paul Corrigan (1979) studied a group of 14–15 year old working-class boys at two schools in Sunderland. Like Cohen, he produces telling ethnographic detail:

Q. What do you do on an average Saturday evening?
P. I knock around in a gang and we get into fights, scraps, you know.
Q. What sort of fights?
P. Well, we meet up with another gang and start chucking milk bottles at them, mainly the 'South Skipton gang'. (Corrigan, 1979, p. 134)

Corrigan too takes a historical materialist perspective in explaining why these boys spend so much time in fighting, in football hooliganism or indeed smashing milk bottles. They do so, he argues, in order to manufacture excitement 'for themselves'. If the boys are given a chance to talk about fights in the context of 'Saturday's bother', it remains archetypally an activity, an activity created in the knowledge that the alternative is, very likely, nothing (p. 134). The boys are bored, argues Corrigan, because their experiences of compulsory schooling are so irrelevant and numbing. Education, far from being a positive good for working-class youth, was merely imposed upon them by the bourgeois state as a means of creating social order and hierarchy in the nineteenth century.

In his critique of these studies Stan Cohen (1980) notes their slide into historicism. The present very specific subcultures are 'explained' by interpreting broad sweeps of past history. This suggests both an inescapable 'march of history' model *and* the same kind of over-determinism criticised by Matza in 'old' subcultural theory. The theoretical analyst in both cases has been blinded, as 'college' boys have so often seemed to be in these contexts by what Stan Cohen has called 'the obvious fascination with these spectacular subcultures' (p. xix). By only studying the *delinquent* subculture, it is only on this 'solution' that evidence exists. Yet not all working-class youth become delinquent. Hardly any girls do so. As Downes and Rocke (1981, p. 135) note,

> the other options open to such boys, the 'college' . . . and the 'corner boy' . . . adaptations were never successfully differentiated causally from the delinquent option. The question 'Why should similarly situated youths sometimes choose delinquency and sometimes the alternatives?' was left open.

The Birmingham School were associated in the main with the Centre of Contemporary Cultural Studies (CCCS) at the University of Birmingham, and produced in the 1970s a range of studies with sufficiently common subject matter and approach to be called a 'school' – something comparatively rare in British social science, where the lone ranger model of the single researcher is much more common. Willis's work on working-class 'lads' has already been cited as perhaps the most fully realised example of the CCCS approach. Others are less sophisticated and satisfactory. One key argument is that of resistance through rituals and symbols: the notion, outlined above in Phil Cohen's work, of style being a way both of expressing and transforming the frustrations of working-class youth. Some of what Stan Cohen called these 'massive exercises of decoding, reading, deciphering and interrogating' work well. Hebdige (1976), for example, presents a convincing interpretation of the Rastafarian subculture, its symbols and history. On the other hand, as Stan Cohen points out, there is the decoding by Hebdige and others of the use of Nazi insignia by punks. Despite appearances, this is not, they claim, an offensive display of white racism or an allusion to past holocausts; rather it is a subtle and ironic gesture, intended to shock and outrage. 'But', as Cohen asks, 'how are we to know this?' (1980, p. xvii).

In other work, the Birmingham School developed complex analyses of power and hegemony in capitalist society, and the position of popular culture and deviant subcultures within that framework (see, for example, Hall *et al.*, 1978). While this work draws on neo-Marxist theory, especially the work of Gramsci, it also represents one example of what might be termed the 'new' sociology or 'new' criminology, and properly belongs in the next chapter. This is perhaps a good point at which to end the discussion of subcultural theory and to sum it up.

Subcultural conclusions: the end of the affair?

Paul Rock, in a very telling dissection of the 'Sociology of Crime' (1979a), argued that sociology has provided most of the innovative source for criminologists who tend to act merely as 'custodians' (pp. 53–4). Many sociologists such as Merton have dabbled in the study of crime:

> they made analytic excursions into deviance for criminologically eccentric purposes . . . such innovators have usually swept in and out of criminology, leaving confusion in their train . . . . Although they posed criminological dilemmas which have remained unanswered, the innovators have not returned to settle them. (Rock, 1979, pp. 54)

This is perhaps an excessively pessimistic generalisation, but the statement does convey an important truth: in explaining crime it is crucial to understand society; to develop criminology it is necessary to study and apply sociology. This is, of course, just what the strain theorists tried to do. That in the end their enterprise failed was not only due to criminological inadequacies but also to the limitations of their sociological base. The limits of both can be usefully summarised under five headings:

1. determinism;
2. selectivity;
3. gender;
4. conformity;
5. anomie.

Determinism

Subcultural theory is an example both of the general classical sociological fallacy of 'over-socialisation' and of the particular over-determination and prediction of crime. The concepts of human nature and of social processes and interactions used are too simplistic, naive and mechanical. Delinquents are depicted as helpless toy figures moved by outside forces, not as human beings with wills of their own. The rich complexities of the Chicago School's researches, though sometimes drawn on heavily (for example by Albert Cohen, 1955) might never have been. As Rock (1979, p. 53) observes, 'every phase of criminology may be depicted as an intellectually discrete episode which borrows little from its predecessors'.

Selectivity

Subcultural theorists were highly selective in the delinquent subcultures they chose to study. The spectacular and the flamboyant, the street-credible and the style-rebel proved far more attractive than what Matza called 'mundane' delinquents. In itself, this selectivity could perhaps be justified: such groups or gangs were accessible. Conceptual (and indeed ideological) problems arose when they were either portrayed as typical (Albert Cohen's original position) or as the possible advance guard of revolutionary change (Corrigan). Such notions ignored any broader sociological representativeness: there was, for instance, a mass of research on other aspects of young people's lives which showed them to be mild, conforming and domesticated (Schofield, 1965; Leonard, 1978). As for delinquency itself, most subcultural studies overpredicted its incidence and ignored the growing evidence of widespread rule-breaking throughout society.

Another blind spot in the model relates to the treatment of other cultures and subcultures within the society. They never seem to be problematic, never need to be explained in the way the delinquent subculture does.

Gender

Gender was a sociological issue which ticked away, like a time bomb in the cellars, for generations. It finally exploded in the 1960s, and the debris is still falling, although many academics still like to pretend there is no plaster in their hair. This is such a major topic that I have devoted a whole chapter to it (see Chapter 5). There are, however, several particular points worth stressing in relation to subcultural theory. For mainstream sociology itself, how gender might be socially constructed or how gender divisions formed by social processes were questions simply not on the agenda before the late 1960s. Acres of print and years of serious discussion were devoted to the definitions and formations of social classes, élites, even the family. Sociologists to a man were all, when it came to gender, biological determinists. It is therefore hardly surprising that gender is missing from this area too, given what we observed earlier about the dependent status of sociological studies of crime on sociology proper.

However, for explanations of crime, gender is a truly critical issue (see Heidensohn, 1985, and Chapter 5). Subcultural theorists for the most part have recognised this; indeed, they make notions of masculinity central to their theories. Albert Cohen (1955), for example, firmly distinguishes boys' delinquency from girls'. Their delinquencies differ, he argues, because they are of different gender; he then defines gender in ways which clearly indicate that he is confusing biological and social determinants – and taking both as unchangeable givens. Cloward and Ohlin do devote several pages to an initially promising discussion of 'masculine identification and delinquent subcultures', but they too are constrained within the particular male WASP (White Anglo-Saxon Protestant) academic subculture of their day. 'Sex differences are not just biological', they declare, 'they also reflect differences in masculinity and femininity' (Cloward and Ohlin, 1960, p. 48). The point, of course, is that we should now want to question whether gender or even sex differences are biological. Cloward and Ohlin also treat 'masculinity' as an unproblematic construct, and while they reject the notion that male delinquency is linked to 'masculine protest' (p. 50), they do insist that 'transition from adolescence to adulthood poses many problems of adjustment for boys in our society' (p. 54).

The pre-feminist innocents of 'old' subculture theory had at least a legitimate excuse for their failure to deal with gender adequately: they lacked a sociology which could supply them with the conceptual tools. Less tolerance can be extended to the later generation of new youth and subculture theorists. Almost all the modern British works discussed earlier in this chapter are limited by their failure to deal adequately with the question of gender. The problem, of course, is that gender is not a question in them:

> Male researchers have focused on boys because of a gender identification with them and colluded with the subjects of their studies to exclude girls from their vision. (Brake, 1985, p. 164)

Brake does go on to discuss subcultures, especially those of a more delinquent kind which emphasise aggression, drinking, fighting and male bonding, and argues that 'these subcultures in some form or other explore and celebrate masculinity' (p. 182). Yet even Brake consistently makes heroic presumptions about 'masculinity'. *Why* does it require support? And why subcultural support? And what of femininity? As always with subcultures, the 'answers' are circular and the real responses have to come from a different sociology, located as yet out of frame.

Conformity

> The logic of subcultural theories predicted with some success, albeit imprecisely, such developments as the emergence of a 'hustling' culture among West Indian youth, and the appeal of extreme authoritarianism among the most disadvantaged white adolescents. (Downes and Rock, 1981, p. 140)

Certainly subcultural theories have played a part in focusing and structuring the analysis of youthful deviance. Where they conspicuously fail is in explaining youthful *conformity*, which is far more characteristic behaviour.

The understanding of delinquency is implausible if it is not paralleled by the explanation of its opposite. Here, sociology did not lack themes or models. Indeed, it can be argued that understanding the bases of social order has been *the* key question during various formative periods in the development of sociology (Parsons, 1937). Undoubtedly, the selectivity I mentioned above played its part in determining the questions asked. If, for example, more of the 'college boys' had been studied, or the girls under the 'old' subculture theorem, we should understand conformity as well as delinquency. If only Willis had given us a sociology of the 'earholes' as well as the lads: after all, political sociologists assiduously explored Tory working-class voters while educational sociologists anatomised the educational achievers from the working class (Jackson and Marsden, 1966).

Implausible anomie

Durkheim originally developed his concept of anomie in relation to his analysis of societal evolution. As societies experienced rapid social change and differentiation, they might also be characterised by a lack of moral regulation, a weakening of social relations and institutions. In their accounts of delinquents' social worlds, many subculture theorists describe situations that are impausibly anomic. The delinquent's social world consists, in these accounts, of his gang and 'their' street corner; his school may feature, though perhaps only through his account of it. It is a scene of Beckett-like sparseness. The delinquent boy has no family, no wider kin; the neighbourhood or city are only painted backdrops to delinquent acts – no community reaction is ever prompted. Girls, as if some gynocide had struck, are wholly absent. 'New' subculture theory paints a fuller picture filled with structures of class, the state and the economy. It is a more vivid portrait, too, with the more especially florid insignia of working-class subcultures well-lit in the foreground. But the rest is fairly dim. Girls are still invisible. Mothers, fathers, family life, the texture and emblems of domestic settings are not depicted. Even the mass media are often given a very limited role, as Stan Cohen points out:

> There is . . . a tendency in some of this work to see the historical development of a style as being wholly internal to the group – with commercialisation and cooption as something which just happens afterwards. (Cohen, 1980, p. xii)

Subcultural analysis, in short, seems to provide the observer with distorting perspectives. Accounts of social worlds are given which are scarcely credible. Presumably all these children have homes, parents, siblings, elderly neighbours, churches and clubs. If they don't, then such information needs to be built into the picture, since it is likely to be significant. These omissions occur in order to highlight other institutions, but since, according to the original model, their regulatory roles are vital, their absence renders the whole account implausible.

Subcultural theory, then, has major limitations and contradictions. It can, however, be said to have had several great strengths. Precisely *because* it was so 'provocative' (Kitsuse and Dietrick, 1959) it was fully debated, tested and explored. Consequently it is one example to contradict Rock's assertion that 'every criminological paradigm consequently tends to consist of a welter of unrelated conjectures, unfinished work and oblique solutions' (1979). Rock goes on in the same article to insist that 'there is little recognition of the mortality of criminological research'. Yet subcultural theory is probably one paradigm, at least as applied to juvenile delinquency, whose day for the moment is done. This is not only because of the critical reappraisals I have so far recounted, but it is also attributable to the major shift in sociological perspectives which we shall explore in the next chapter.

There may well be other factors in the sociology of knowledge which have played their part – the climate for research and research funding, for instance, which has become an increasingly critical one. Or, as McConville puts it in reviewing research on juvenile delinquency:

> Some criminologists, in their analysis of juvenile delinquency in its social setting, so broadened and enlarged their field of study as to raise questions about the usefulness or feasibility of criminological research at all, as an exercise apart from economic, sociological and political analysis'. (McConville, 1981, p. 206)

It is worth remembering that sociology, like delinquency, happens in a real and complex social environment.

It is at least possible to consider developing certain aspects of a delinquency-based model for future use. We would be untrue to our professed aim of maintaining tradition while planning for change if we did not try to do so. I propose an example of work published in the 1980s which might provide a model. Ann Campbell's *The Girls in the Gang* (1984) follows three New York gangs, focusing on a woman member in each and her relationships with other members, her children, family and local community. The political economy of the society and the city were vividly described, as well as the political vacuum left by the lack of a working-class political party and the struggles *between* immigrant groups for dominance (pp. 234–5). Gangs and their alliances fill the gap and provide subcultures and some meaning to life, but no solution: 'Gangs exist not in an anomic vacuum where sex roles are forgotten and anything goes, but in a subculture deeply embedded within the value system of western capitalism' (Campbell, 1984, p. 267).

Girls in the Gang is by no means flawless, but it does escape most of the defects of subcultural studies I mentioned earlier – although there is an over-determinist strain in it. Even if old paradigms fade away, they can be put into storage rather than buried prematurely.

There are just two further themes in this context which should be emphasised: youth as a problem and social policy and delinquency.

Youth as a problem

Pearson (1984) suggested that the history of Britain over the past two hundred years can be rewritten as a 'history of respectable fears' – fears, that is, of lawless, violent youths whose unprecedentedly violent behaviour on the streets or other public places threaten social order, frighten honest citizens and signals 'a moral downfall among the British people of landslide proportions' (Pearson, 1983, p. 207). Taking a series of steps backwards in history, Pearson demonstrates that there has always been a moral panic about youthful, male street crime, accompanied by a nostalgia for 'twenty years ago'.

In the 1980s, riots with a racial component were the 'threat', while in the 1950s, far from peace prevailing, the Teddy Boys were seen as dangerous. Pearson's argument is that permanent 'respectable fears' about working-class youth are translated into a controlling strategy based on the 'social reproduction of an underclass' (p. 217). Pearson never really explains the *origins* of the fears, why they persist through marked periods of social change, or why 'new' moral panics have to be recreated for each generation. Nevertheless, the concept of 'respectable fears' has some relevance for our discussion of delinquency.

Pearson's thesis appears to be that each generation (or the powerful in league with the media in each generation) represents the same continuities to cries of public outrage. In the late twentieth century both in society and in sociology, the 'perpetual problem' of youth is being conceived of in rather different terms. As Brake (1985, p. 192) points out, high rates of youth unemployment, especially amongst ethnic minorities, have changed and diminished the status of young people. In some senses, respectable fears about the potential menace of young people are now so great that they are extended over a range of issues. Smith (1986) suggests, for instance, that in some inner city areas fear of crime has become a 'legitimate' surrogate for racial anxieties. In the same way, juvenile delinquency has, so to speak, moved up the tariff to become the conflated 'crime' that is so feared.

Reporting of crime in the media has become more sensational and at the same time more specific (Hall *et al.*, 1978). There is at any one time a series of moral panics about folk devils (Cohen, 1981), most of which have a youth dimension, for instance, muggers (Hall, *et al.*, 1978), rapists (Stanko, 1986), football hooligans (Williams, *et al.*, 1982) and drug pushers (Young, 1971). Such conceptions are inherently unstable and might well be reassembled into the all-purpose juvenile delinquent at any moment.

Such a figure, at the time of writing, is absent from the sociology of crime. As Parker and Giller point out,

> The novice reader of criminological literature would have had little trouble in detecting a fundamental shift of emphasis within the sociological perspective over the last fifteen years. Titles such as *The Delinquent Solution, The Social Background to Delinquency, Juvenile Delinquency, The Family and the Social Group, Growing up in the City* and *Adolescent Boys of East London*, produced in the fifties and sixties, not only highlighted youth for academic attention but, in particular, their criminality was a focus of primary concern. (Parker and Giller, 1981, p. 231)

In another review of the 'where are we now' type, Stan Cohen (1981, p. 238) described how 'the sociological landscape has been fenced off into separate territories . . . a whole range of sociological connections have now appeared for students of crime and deviance'. These included education and law, but delinquency had disappeared – disappeared, perhaps, at present from sociological discourse, but not of course from a variety of others. What McConville called 'traditional social-psychological projects' have continued (e.g. West and Farrington, 1971, 1973, 1977). Parker and Giller argue in their research review that this work is not wholly impervious to sociological theorising and paradigm shifts, and does 'co-opt' certain sociological ideas and challenges (1981, p. 236).

Of more interest, perhaps, to sociologists (Downes and Rock, 1981, devote a chapter to it) and certainly of great and growing interest to policy-makers (Riley and Shaw, 1985, p. 5) is what is known as 'control' or 'bonding theory'. Control theories, as Downes and Rock point out, have a long and distinguished pedigree, although the conceptual lineage of present day theories is far from clear. Hirschi (1969, p. 132) and his colleagues in the USA have carried out numerous surveys of school-age children in order to show correlations between (self) reported and recorded delinquency and 'bonding' variables such as attachment and commitment to school. Hirschi's thesis is that 'delinquent acts result when an individual's bond to society is weak or broken' (p. 16). There are four elements of the social bond: attachment, commitment, involvement and belief. Hirschi found that strong family attachments *did* protect boys from delinquency.

In Britain, Wilson (1980 and 1982) carried out a series of studies of parental chaperonage of young boys which showed that supervision was a crucial variable in determining delinquency. Riley and Shaw's (1985) study for the Home Office reached slightly more tentative conclusions: 'supervision is not independently related to offending among boys', although it was 'clearly an important influence on girls' delinquency' (p. 48).

These studies are strong on empirical data, weak on conceptual analysis – the Home Office study offers no theory of gender to explain its finding – and especially lack perspective on intent and motivation. Several aspects, however, are important. First, such theories have an appeal for policy-makers – the Home Office study contains a series of prescriptions for parents and others. As we shall see in Chapter 7, these approaches play an important role in helping, and justifying situational methods of crime prevention. There is too what Parker and Giller describe as 'the very volume of their empirical work' which cannot be ignored. Indeed, since it will often be in the public academic domain on tapes and discs, it might well be re-analysed to see if it can yield more profound insights. (The alert student who has completed a research methods course will be well aware of the possible hazards of this enterprise.) Finally, there is no doubt that this conceptually simplistic form of sociological theory raises some serious questions that 'strain' variants did not. How, for example, is social control established and maintained? Why do some individuals or families take part in delinquency and others remain immune? Is the production of conformity in society really a more interesting area to study than the more exotic forms of delinquency? New theories of sociology did begin to explore these questions about the time Hirschi first raised them, as we shall see in the next chapter. But they remain important agenda items. If strain theories had been able more easily to build such concepts into their model, perhaps they would have flourished longer.

Social policy and delinquency

Youth, I suggested earlier, seems a perpetual problem in advanced industrial societies. In the 1950s, for example, there appeared to be a worldwide phenomenon of juvenile delinquency (Rock and Cohen, 1970). Britain had Teddy Boys, in France there were 'blousons noirs', even Japan and Russia experienced distinctive and disturbing behaviour (Fyvel, 1963). (Pearson argues that such panics are manufacturered and that there was no 'real' upsurge in crime rates.) However, what was undoubtedly real was the social policy response. Debates about crime and penal policy in Britain in the following decade were almost all focused on juvenile delinquency (Bottoms, 1974; Manning, 1985). Their outcomes were, among other things, the Children and Young Persons Act 1969 and the setting up of generic personal social services departments under local authority control (in Scotland, Social Work Departments). From these policies flowed considerable consequences, not just for the treatment of juvenile offenders, and indeed other young people, but also for the way in which the issues surrounding juvenile delinquency were conceptualised (Morris *et al.*, 1980; Harris and Webb, 1987).

What is also important is that these developments have generated, are still generating and are likely to go on generating, quite phenomenal amounts of research and writing. The bibliography on intermediate treatment for the period 1968–84 amounts to forty double column pages (Skinner, 1985). Some of this is of the 'informal' kind, some in a serious and worthwhile form. There are now, after all, many people working in teaching, social work and probation who have had sociological and research methods training. Evaluative research is sometimes built into experimental treatment programmes. In the next chapter I shall look at some of the most interesting work that has flowed from the new delinquency industry. It fits there, rather than here, because, as Parker and Giller (1981) predicted, most of such studies, although in some ways like control theories, lie outside the paradigms of academic sociology and has largely 'co-opted' the perspectives of the new theories. I have advertised these so often that it really is time to reconceptualise the old problems and move on.

4 Changing Perspectives on Crime: from Interactionism to Critical Criminology

Hindsight is at once a useful tool and a dangerous weapon. It is easy to look back on an era, knowing what has since happened, and assert confidently that it was in those years that the origins of the welfare state or of the Second World War can be located. It is easy because we have after-knowledge; yet we may be imposing a pattern on unplanned and potentially inconsequential events, which at best distorts and at worst does them real injustice. Danger comes when hindsight is used as a basis for foresight, for predicting future trends on the premises of past ones. In the mid-1970s, for instance, many commentators averred that Britain had become an ungovernable country and faced possible revolution, authoritarian dictatorship or, at the very least, continual constitutional crises. Yet ten years later Britain had a Conservative government in power with a large majority and had successfully fought a war to preserve traditional British interests. The diagnosis and the forecasts had been either over-optimistic or over-pessimistic, depending on your point of view. They were, however, certainly wrong.

Predicted events may not occur. Key pointers, on the other hand, may be ignored. Most accounts of the events of the 1960s dwell on the Paris 'events' of 1968, on the campus uprisings, civil rights and the Vietnam War and its consequences (see, for example, Cockburn and Blackburn, 1969; Quattrocchi and Nairn, 1968). Student activism was seen by many as having the greatest potential both for fundamentally changing the nature of sociology (Gouldner, 1970) and for the much grander task of providing the spearhead of the revolution (Marcuse, 1964). What is perhaps most interesting to observe (and not very hard to explain) is that none of these commentators appeared to have noticed, and certainly failed to predict, the rise of modern, new-wave feminism which has proved so far to be the most enduring and powerful (if indirect) product of the campus activities (Mitchell, 1971 and 1986).

Despite these reservations about interpreting history, it is hard not to read the 1960s as having been a distinctive decade (the 'decade' was probably really 1963–73). Various factors combined to make it so. Many Western countries experienced unprecedented affluence, much of which was channelled into consumer spending but also into real growth in welfare expenditure. There was a relatively large generation of young people who had been born after the Second World War, some of whom entered higher education, which expanded to meet the increase. The social sciences specifically grew at this time, with more student places in universities and polytechnics, more teaching posts and research money, and a broader demand for sociological explanations of puzzling phenomena and social problems (Gouldner, 1970). At the same, the Vietnam War developed into a bitter and terrible conflict which had profound effects both on the geopolitics of South East Asia and on the domestic politics of the United States. Old smouldering injustices of race and religion burst into flames in American cities, in Northern Ireland and in South Africa. It was perhaps the contradiction, the tensions between these contrasting events which fuelled those peculiarly 1960s phenomena such as flower power, student revolts, teach-ins, sit-ins and the whole notion of 'politics of experience'. At another level, and most significantly for our purposes here, these events and the climate they helped generate provided the setting for new theories of deviancy.

New deviancy theories

It was in the expanding, exciting and fraught years of the 1960s that the new sociology of deviance theories first flourished and had wide impact, but their origins lie much further back. Their intellectual and conceptual roots can be found in the theories of Karl Marx, George Herbert Mead and the Chicago School, and in the phenomenology of Alfred Schutz. Some of the key texts of the development were also published well before 1960: Tannenbaum's *Crime and the Community* had appeared in 1938 and Becker's classic essay 'Becoming a Marijuana User', in its original version, in 1953.

The concepts and arguments had thus been available for some time but came together and had their greatest impact in the period under discussion. 'It is not at all clear why interactionism should have come to prominence in the criminology of the 1960s', remark Downes and Rock (1981, p. 141) of one of the main strands of the new theories. I have tried to suggest some reasons why. We should now turn briefly to some of the sources of the new thinking before exploring the ideas themselves, their application and their capacity for development.

First, however, a word about names and titles. Curiously, but perhaps not surprisingly, among theories and writers to whom the use of names and labels was to loom so large, there is little agreement on how to describe the different approaches. Pearson (1975, ch. 3), for example, used the terms 'misfit sociology' and 'misfit sociologies' to describe symbolic interactionism in ethnomethodology and radical criminology, and sees them all 'mysteriously linked . . . to the misfit paradigm' (p. 64). In a lengthy critical and rehabilitating review, Plummer (1979, p. 87), on the other hand, argued that '"labelling" is a perspective, which raises a series of problems and suggest a few themes' and that this perspective linked all the main 'new deviancy' enterprises of the 1960s, despite their very diverse theoretical sources in functionalism (Erikson, 1966) conflict theory (Quinney, 1970) and ethnomethodology (Garfinkel, 1967). In yet another approach (1981, p. 144), Rock and Downes distinguish with rigorous clarity various schools of thought, in symbolic interactionism 'generally if misleadingly termed "labelling theory"', phenomenology and radical criminology. This can all seem very puzzling: which one has the right labels and who has applied them correctly? The answer, of course, is rather like the outcome of the caucus race in Lewis Carroll's *Alice's Adventures in Wonderland* in which everybody won. The purposes of the classifications were to clarify and simplify, and it is best to take what seems the most useful system for one's own ends and not be too fussed about who fits where. (The point of the caucus race was for all the animals and birds to get dry after having been soaked and nearly drowned in the pool of Alice's tears.) As Plummer (1979, p. 87) pointed out, Howard Becker, seen by many as the originator of labelling, does not seem 'at all happy with being identified as a labelling theorist'. I propose to make the following, I hope helpful, distinctions: first of *interaction-*

ism, whence the inspiration of new deviance theory came; then of *critical* criminology which developed somewhat later. Through them both, as Plummer suggested, runs to some extent the *labelling* perspective as a common if multi-coloured and all-purpose thread, a sensitising concept in its truest sense, and not a school. Finally, I shall look at some fascinating studies, many of them historical, which share some of the same origins and which, given their subjects and their emphases, might best be called *new social control theories*.

Founding fathers revisited

All the deviance theories we shall be examining are hybrid in some form: they are derived from more than root-stock, grafted on to another, and reconstructed with inheritance from a multiplicity of 'parents', as bio-engineering can now achieve with designer plants. It is helpful, nevertheless, to recall some of the key concepts and sources from which the theories derive. For interactionism, 'there would seem to be at least two interactionist traditions' (Fisher and Strauss, 1978, p. 458). Both derive from Chicago, the first embodying the ideas of Park and of Thomas. Thomas bequeathed key concepts with his notion of the 'definition of the situation' and his use of human documents. Blumer (1939, p. 81), one of the leading torch bearers of the tradition, formulated a list of 'important contributions which have made *The Polish Peasant* (Thomas's major study of Polish immigrants in the USA [1918–20]) meritorious and which explain the profound influence which it has had on sociology and social psychology'. Blumer headed his list with 'A demonstration of the need of studying the subjective factor in social life', G. H. Mead's social psychology with its concepts of 'significant other', and 'role taking'. Essentially, interactionism was a product of Chicago sociology, albeit with influences from European sociologists such as Simmel (Rock, 1979a).

    The thinking of Alfred Schutz – deftly summarised in Berger and Luckmann's title as '*The Social Construction of Reality*' (1967) – with his concentration 'on the structure of the common-sense world of everyday life' (op. cit., p. 27) as well as his questioning (derived from Husserl) of all taken-for-granted-notions, was critical to the sociological perspective of phenomenology (Wolff, 1978). While this perspective, and new developments within it, formed part of the creative ferment of the 1960s in sociology generally, it had arguably fewer criminological outcomes than other aspects of misfit sociology (Downes and Rock, 1981, p. 166). The particular approach of ethnomethodology in the work of Garfinkel (1967) and Cicourel (1968) which links to this perspective is one part of the story.

Karl Marx played what one can only describe nowadays as a 'surrogate father' role in the conception of critical criminology. Indeed, if it is not indelicate to say so, his contribution remained frozen for many years. Marx himself had little to say about crime and scorned the criminal classes, believing that crime was a product of capitalism which would wither away after revolution. Critical criminology took this insight as axiomatic (Taylor *et al.*, 1975) but then filled in fuller analyses based more on early Marx and his concept of alienation than the later Marx of *Capital*. Much modern neo-Marxist debate has been between various revisionist schools who challenge each other's aproaches. The work of Althusser has been crucial here, mainly, in studies of crime, for the opposition to his views expressed by several writers. Of great and more recent significance has been Michel Foucault, whose 'prophetic' work (Jones and Fowles, 1984, p. 45) has been a seminal influence on a rich seam of studies of social control. Foucault is almost unclassifiable: Harris and Webb (1987, p. 81) insist that he was 'a *Foucaultiste* pure and simple; his method of inquiry is . . . idiosyncratic'. (For attempts to interpret his work see Cousins and Hassim, 1984, and Smart, 1981.)

New deviancy theories thus had a pantheon of respectable and ancient founding fathers. (At the risk of repetition it should be noted that they had no recorded mothers.) Nevertheless, they represented real departures and developments which have had considerable influences both on sociology and in the ways that crime is viewed by various audiences in the wider society. In reviewing the autobiographical accounts of women offenders who disavow their deviant behaviour, I have suggested that

> if they had all read text books on 'labelling' theory in criminology, they could have hardly have made more successful attempts at minimising, rather than amplifying their deviance. (Heidensohn, 1985, p. 19)

One American textbook published in 1970 tried to convey the effect on sociology of the paradigm shift with the following piece of hyperbole:

> A new wave of thought is beginning to sweep over sociology. Aspects of the wave have been given an assortment of names – 'labelling theory', 'ethnomethodology' and 'new symbolic-interactionism' – but these do not cover its entire range of critique and perspective. A new name must be found to cover a concept which presents not only a unique perspective on conventional sociology but is also a radical departure from the conventional. We feel an appropriate name is *The Sociology of the Absurd.* (Lyman and Scott, 1970)

What had happened and how did it change the study of crime and society?

Interactionism

Interactionism has sometimes been called 'social reaction theory' because of its emphasis on society's reactions to the deviant rather than on the deviant him/herself. Becker's formulation, the most quoted definition in the whole sociology of crime and deviance, encapsulates this:

> the central fact about deviance [is that] it is created by society. I do not mean this is the way it is ordinarily understood, in which the causes of deviance are located in the social situation of the deviant or in 'social factors' which prompt his action. I mean, rather, that *social groups create deviance by making the rules whose infraction constitutes deviance* and by applying those rules to particular people and labelling them as outsiders. From this point of view, deviance is *not* a quality of the act the person commits but rather a consequence of the application by others of rules and sanctions to an 'offender'. The deviant is one to whom that label has successfully been applied; deviant behaviour is behaviour that people so label. (Becker, 1963, pp. 8–9, original emphasis)

The contrast Becker made in this statement is important: he polarises two kinds of approach to deviance. In the first, the deviant is the focus, and indeed the problem. His behaviour is inexplicable and meanings are sought in the shape of structural explanations, like the anomie and subcultural theories of the last chapter. In the second, the emphasis moves from the deviant to the society. The societal reaction becomes problematic, not the individual deviant. Rubington and Weinberg (1968, p. 2), introducing an interactionist textbook, set out the differences between the two approaches in terms of the agendas for enquiry they set. If deviance is taken for granted and objectively 'given', the major questions for inquiry become:

— Who is the deviant?
— How did he become a deviant?
— Why does he continue in deviance despite controls brought to bear on him?
— What sociocultural conditions are more likely to produce deviants?
— How may deviants be best controlled?

On the other hand, if deviance is regarded as 'subjectively problematic', then both the set of questions and the whole methodology changes: 'major questions of inquiry are less often formulated by the sociologist than by the persons involved.'

Two interacting perspectives now have to be studied. First, that 'of those who define a person as being a social deviant . . .' to find out

a) What are the circumstances under which a person gets set apart, hence forth to be considered a deviant?
b) How is the person cast into that social role?
c) What actions do others take on the basis of this redefinition of the person.
d) What value positive or negative do they place on the facts of deviance?

The sociologist then adopts the perspective of the person adjudged to be a deviant and considers some questions such as these:

a) How does a person adjudged to be a deviant react to this designation?
b) How does he adopt the deviant role that may be set aside for him?
c) What changes in his group membership result?
d) To what extent does he alter his self conception to accord

> with the deviant role assigned him? (Rubington and Weinberg, 1968, pp. 5–6)

Such an emphasis on the social reaction to deviance as opposed to qualities of the deviant was not new in sociology. Tannenbaum (1938) had noted the process of public labelling in what he called the 'dramatization of evil', arguing that this was the critical feature of the making of criminal careers:

> The young delinquent becomes bad because he is defined as bad and because he is not believed if he is good . . . The community cannot deal with people whom it cannot define. (Tannenbaum, 1938, pp. 19–20)

Lemert (1967) had already begun to refine the notions of interaction, and especially of labelling. He distinguished between *primary deviance*, which is ubiquitous and may not prove significant unless there is a strong social reaction to it, and secondary deviance which results in a label being attached and, eventually, a new identity formed. This could be a complex and above all *uncertain* process. Lemert was always at pains to stress the tentative and undetermined nature of the development of crime. In his study of cheque forgers, he describes an extreme case where the anonymity and 'seclusiveness' required of the successful cheque forger as a way of life eventually destroy his personality: 'he can no longer define himself in relation to others on any basis' (Lemert, 1967, p. 131).

Lemert emphasised the dynamic and problematic nature of becoming deviant as early as 1951, seeing it as the following sequence:

1. primary deviation
2. social penalties
3. further primary deviation
4. stronger penalties and rejections
5. further deviation perhaps with hostilities and resentments beginning to focus on those who are doing the penalizing
6. crisis reached in the tolerance quotient expressed in formal action by the community stigmatizing the deviant
7. strengthening of the deviant conduct as a reaction to the stigmatizing and penalties
8. ultimate acceptance of deviant social status and efforts at

adjustment on the basis of the associated role. (Lemert, 1951, p. 77)

Becker's statement was therefore not in itself the breakthrough. Rather it is important because of the frequency with which it has been cited, criticised and explored. Rubington and Weinberg place it first of all the extracts in successive editions of their *Deviance, The Interactionist Perspective* (1968, 1973), the Genesis of the interactionist bible, or as Pearson (1975, p. 52) describes it, 'the catechism of labelling theory'. Matza (1969, p. 109) accords Becker the key role in making 'the sociological conception of man become thoroughly human'. He then goes on to construct an elaborate coda on the themes of Becker's classic article 'Becoming a Marihuana User'. Matza's discussion, at thirty-three pages long, is nearly twice as long as the original article and almost as long as both Becker's essays on marihuana use and on control (Becker, 1963, pp. 42–58, 59–78). In his first essay, Becker explored, on the basis of some fifty interviews, how one becomes a user of the drug. As he saw it 'instead of the deviant motives leading to the deviant behaviour, it is the other way around; the deviant behaviour in time produces the deviant motivation' (p. 42). Smoking, inhaling and pleasure all have to be learned and be perceived. In exploring the social control of marihuana use, Becker was writing at a time when penalties were severe; nevertheless he suggests that users negotiate and redefine their perceptions of sanctions and controls and replace the conventional views of 'straight' society with an insider's view (p. 78).

Becker's work was therefore seminal. Apart from the major sociological step which Matza described, part of its impact lay in a kind of shock effect – he almost seemed to be saying that the public, or more particularly the rule makers and rule enforcers, whom he called 'moral entrepreneurs', were *responsible* for crime and deviance. Such a view, of course, chimed well with the 1960s climate of challenging the wisdom and even the legitimacy of accepted authorities. One of the most obvious aspects of this was the switch from the more judgmental term 'crime' to the more morally ambiguous 'deviance' – deviance, moreover, defined not according to any intrinsic characteristics of the offences or the offender but by external agencies. Plummer summarised the importance of such an approach:

It highlights the ambiguity of a world no longer divided into a series of neat types . . . the good and the bad . . . the continuity between normality and deviancy is stressed. (Plummer, 1979, p. 96)

In consequence, all kinds of areas at the margins of deviance of a more exotic kind could be studied: mental illness, for example, and how it is produced and regulated by psychiatrists (Scheff, 1966, 1967), or brothel-keeping (Heyl, 1979). Much earlier interactionist work still concentrated, paradoxically, on individual deviants, not on the rule makers or enforcers. Liazos, not a sympathetic critic, described how the highly popular deviance courses in American universities in the 1960s were known as 'Nuts, sluts and perverts' studies. His analysis of eighteen current textbooks in the field showed interactionism to be the dominant perspective in half of them, and yielded cast lists of 'prostitutes, nudists, abortionists, criminals, drug users, homosexuals, the mentally ill, alcoholics and suicides' (Liazos, 1972, p. 40). Liazos suggested that this focus on 'popular and dramatic forms of deviance' (p. 46) illustrates some of the central contradictions of the approach: on the one hand deviance is treated as normal and not pathological, socially constructed and not inborn, yet the very use of the term deviant acts as a 'label' setting both the subjects and the subject matter apart, and, on the whole, still accepting official definitions of deviance. Political deviance is thus ignored or misconstrued, and the crimes of the powerful are not considered (Líazos, 1972, pp. 44–6).

In the longer term, as we shall see later, among the most interesting studies conducted within the interactionist perspective were those which took up the themes of societal reactions to deviance. Although such projects were certainly implicit in Becker's original formulation, it was not until the 1970s that they began to appear. It obviously took some time for the paradigm shift to shift the attention of the paradigm shifters away from deviants and towards the apparatus of social control. Matza, for example, is quoted as confessing (in 1970)

that he had simply not bothered to say that his book *Delinquency and Drift* was an attack on the juvenile court system because he considered it so obvious that it would be 'an insult to the reader'. (Pearson, 1975, p. 106)

Musto explored the way in which cocaine use was gradually

criminalised in early twentieth-century America by the manipulation of scare stories. He suggested (1973) that politics and in particular the divisions between Northern and Southern states and between blacks and whites were central to this process.

In Britain, Stan Cohen observed and recorded a parallel 'moral panic' about the behaviour of Mods and Rockers – two teenage groups – at British seaside resorts in the early 1960s. Cohen argued (1972 and 1980) that there was a postwar 'moral panic' about youth culture, reflecting broader political and socal ills. Young people were cast in the roles of 'folk devils', their relatively unfocused and innocuous behaviour dramatised by media attention and over-zealous reactions from agents of control. He suggested that the media amplified deviance to the public, thus provoking exaggerated responses. For example, he describes warning notes being sounded in seaside-town newspapers, *before* any events had occurred in their area.

Cohen distinguishes between different aspects of, and roles in, the societal reactions to the Mods and Rockers (pp. 158 *et seq.*), although much of his book is taken up with the style and the substance of the Mods and Rockers themselves. In that sense, *Folk Devils and Moral Panics* is a privotal study, marking a transitional phase in the development of deviancy theory. It has all the 1960s hallmarks: youth as a focus, mildly deviant, challenging behaviour made to seem more portentous than it really was, and an emphasis on fashion and style. Sociologically, it is characterised by Cohen's careful ethnography, but also by his detachment and by his attention to wider social structural considerations. Yet it also looks forward to later work (as Cohen himself observes in his preface to the second edition, 1980), especially on control agents, courts and the police (see below).

It is not fair to say of interactionism, as Wood (1984, p. 68) did later of subcultural theory: 'because of the tradition within which I was working, I went time and time again for the male and the spectacular in my ethnography'. Indeed interactionism, while rarely showing interest in female deviance (Leonard, 1982, pp. 80–9) did address some of the more florid aspects of gender in studies of men and boys who committed illegal homosexual acts for pleasure or gain while contriving to maintain their 'straight' male identity (Reiss, 1964 Humphreys, 1970). Nevertheless, there is truth in the assertion that

there is a modest affinity between interactionism and deviance
. . . heroin users, thieves, and prostitutes may draw themselves
apart seeking those who share common experiences, problems
and solutions . . . they create a series of strange groupings whose
peculiarities can stimulate the sensitivities which are indispensable
to interactionalism. . . . observing people doing extraordinary
things, the sociologist can be both provoked and appreciative.
(Downes and Rock, 1981, p. 143)

Interactionism did indeed produce both provocation and appreciation, shifting as it did not merely the persectives, but the places
and the roles of those who study and are studied,

thereby enabling both the foundations for a formal theory of
deviance as a social property and a method for understanding
the routine and the regular through the eyes of the ruptured and
the irregular. (Plummer, 1979, p. 96)

Or as Gouldner, unfairly, suggested, marginal men studying
marginal men (1962). Partly at least because of these vivid and
timely attractions, partly too because it did represent a seismic split
in sociological ways of looking at the world, especially the worlds
of crime and deviance, interactionism has had lasting impact:

'it was interactionism that enlarged the task and complexity of
criminology by insisting on the creative role played by outsiders
in the production of deviance'. (Downes and Rock, 1981, p. 152)

That is not, of course, to say that it has not been criticised for its
limitations as an approach or series of approaches. There are four
main strands to this criticism, although these do not form a
comprehensive whole, since critics' own theoretical bases determine
the foci of their objections. Matters are further complicated by the
definitional difficulties I referred to above, so that some critics (e.g.
Líazos and Plummer) group much of modern deviancy theory
together as a labelling perspective while Downes and Rock make
the subtlest distinctions. The four strands are:

1. interactionism, or more especially labelling, *is not a theory*.
2. interaction discounts or ignores the problem of *causation*
3. interactionism is *relativistic*
4. interactionists ignore the questions of *structure and power*.

Not a theory

Taylor *et al.*, writing from a Marxist point of view, stress that 'the social reaction approach to deviance . . . is a remarkable advance *towards* a fully social theory of deviance' (1973, p. 139, added emphasis). It is in fact an approach rather than a theory, and does not distinguish between causation and description. Gibbs (1966), in an early critique, had also pointed to the vagueness of much interactionist theory. Even Schur (1971), who can be counted as an interactionist, argued that causal analysis was not the appropriate task for labelling theory. Davis (1972) and others have proffered a further variant on this view in arguing that labelling is not a *scientific* theory since it cannot generate testable hypotheses – although Gove (1975) does in fact try to test out just such hypotheses.

Causation

Many writers have criticised interactionism for over-emphasising social reactions to deviance and neglecting causes and motivations (for example Gibbs, 1966; Taylor *et al.*, 1973; and see Plummer, 1979, for a review). Plummer argues that 'no labelling theorist seems to espouse the "label creates behaviour" view' (p. 104). Indeed, he stresses, as does Matza, that it is through this perspective that labelling sociologists 'have generally played a major role in restoring choice and meaning to the deviant's activity' (p. 105).

There are also criticisms of the failure, certainly in early labelling studies, to explain the mechanisms of the process – how labels are made to stick, so to speak. Later writers have refined and sophisticated the concepts so that rejecting labels, or deviance disavowal, is seen as possible (e.g. Cameron, 1964).

Relativism

Numerous commentators have disagreed with Becker's central contention that only society's reaction determines whether an action is seen as deviant or not: 'it flies in the face of empirical reality, where we commonsensically know that some acts are more deviant than others' (Plummer, 1979, p. 96). Taylor *et al.* (1973, p. 147) stress the Weberian point that human actions have meaning and that therefore '*most deviant behaviour is a quality of the act*' (original emphasis).

It has sometimes seemed to some critics as though interactionists, the purpose of whose endeavours was to rout determinism from sociology, are guilty of portraying deviants as the passive playthings of labelling processes (Gouldner, 1970). This can increase the notion of relativism, since moral choices appear to be neutralised and replaced by the whim of outside labellers.

Indeed, this problem was acknowledged by Becker, who addressed at least part of it in a key article, suggestively entitled 'Whose Side Are We On?' (1967). In this he declared that sociology was and must be for the underdog, the victim of power, and that the approach to deviance and crime should be 'appreciative' rather than correctional, in Matza's terms. One of the problems I have with this view, and which I will take up in later chapters, is its narrow conception of who is a victim or being exploited. Actual victims of crimes against their person come nowhere into view.

Power and structure

Perhaps the most serious charge faced by interactionist and labelling perspectives is that they ignore the issues of wider social structure and of power. Becker certainly made clear in his discussion of rule making and rule breaking that questions arose about 'whose rules' were being broken (1963, pp. 17–18). He noted, for instance: 'it is true in many respects that men make the rules for women in our society'; but he took that insight no further. As Laurie Taylor has commented,

> labelling theory only nods towards the labellers, admits their presence, documents their effects, but then fails to demonstrate the social processes which allow them to indulge in such labelling. (Taylor, 1971, p. 195)

Given their own declared stance, it is not surprising that Taylor *et al.* should particularly castigate these approaches for omitting what they term 'the *missing element of power in the creation of deviancy*' (1973, p. 169, original emphasis). But Downes and Rock (1981, p. 161) point out that such concepts belong to a different order of sociology: 'Interactionism produces a rather different imagery of society'.

Of the new theories of deviance which came to prominence in the 1960s, the 'labelling perspective' had the most impact, and I have therefore dwelt on its concepts and some of its weaknesses. It shook sociology and had particularly marked effects on the study of crime (Downes, 1979, p. 13). As Parker and Giller (1981, p. 230) have pointed out, by the early 1980s the agenda for the study of deviance had been radically altered. Interactionist perspectives were not alone in achieving this. Critical or radical criminology had also brought stimulating and challenging ideas into the debate. These have largely been expressed as criticism of other theories. As we have already looked at some of the products of this approach in the last chapter, as space is limited and, indeed, as some of the authors involved moved on fairly rapidly to other approaches, I shall not give as much space to critical criminology as to the other half of the new deviancy theory.

Critical criminology

The turbulent conditions of the 1960s which I outlined above were the fertile ground for many growths. One of the more surprising among intellectuals, after the disillusionment with Stalin and the suppression of the Hungarian uprising in 1956, was a reawakened interest in Marxist and conflict theories of society. In part this reflected the restless search for new ideas and concepts characteristic of that decade; in part, too, there was a rejection of the liberal values and consensus which had prevailed since the Second World War. Undoubtedly, confrontation with university authorities or the police as the result of civil rights activities (Platt, 1975), of student protest (Rock and Heidensohn, 1969) or soft drug use (Young, 1971) served to demystify the view of power and radicalise the politics of some students and academics.

In the United States, several writers have developed radical and critical ideas and proposed a new criminology. Quinney's is the most fully realised vision, having as his focus the capitalist state and its dominant class (Quinney, 1975, pp. 37–8). Quinney builds power into the deviance-defining processes by arguing that these are political acts. The powerful control the powerless, criminal law being seen as a particularly coercive part of the state-control apparatus (Quinney, 1973, p. 87). Platt (1975) also urged a 'new criminology' based on a radical critique of the 'old criminology' and the achievement ultimately of a truly socialist society. He studied the 'creation' of the concept of delinquency and what he called the child-saving movement, which he saw as serving the interests of American capitalism.

Julia and Herman Schwendinger (1978) both studied, and in Julia's case took part in, the work of a rape crisis centre set up in Berkeley in the early 1970s. Their analysis of cultural definitions of rape, of police reactions and of victimisation is informed, as is their other work, by Marxist concepts both of social theory and of praxis, as well as with radical feminist notions. These writers hardly form a school or systematic critique, although their work is interesting evidence of the varied development of this perspective in an intellectual climate less congenial to it than in Europe.

Chambliss is of one of the relatively smaller number of American sociologists who have related the comparatively high levels of crime in American society to the distinctive features of American capitalism, finding racketeering throughout that society. From his detailed observations of underworld life in Seattle, he concluded that corruption was rife in the USA 'from petty crooks to presidents' (Chambliss, 1978). Such work is 'concerned with a relatively uncomplicated application of Marx's most central concepts of crime and crime control' (Downes and Rock, 1981, p. 213), and it is interesting to note that these writers on the whole sharpened their Marxist emphasis during the 1970s.

This may have been attributable to the work of the influential British neo-Marxist writers whose work developed strikingly during that decade. As both Pearson (1975) and Cohen (1981) point out in the original British manifestations of new deviancy theory, especially in the National Deviancy Conference (of which both were key members), both interactionist and neo-Marxist perspectives were joined together, and their respective adherents provided mutual stimulus and an adherence to what Cohen calls 'the master theoretical move' (1981, p. 241). With the publication, however, of *The New Criminology* (Taylor *et al.*, 1973) and *Critical Criminology* (Taylor *et al.*, 1975) divisions became more apparent, although, as we shall see, some of the best and most interesting work within the long and convoluted framework of 'new deviance' draw on both traditions.

In their first book Taylor *et al.* set out to achieve 'a fully social theory of *deviance*' (their subtitle, added emphasis). The attentive reader will have noticed both the change of direction signalled in the title – here comes *criminology* again – and, underneath, so to speak, the hedged bet of the subtitle with its stress on deviance. Most of the book consists of detailed criticisms of previous theories, with only the final chapter stating the authors' requirements for their theory. First, there are seven formal requirements to cover the scope of and sustain the connections between:

1. the wider structural origins of the deviant act + 2. its immediate origins + 3. the actual act – for an account of real *social dynamics* surrounding the actual acts; [then] 4. the immediate origins of social reaction + 5. the wider origins of deviant reaction and 6. the outcome of the social reaction on the deviant's further action and [finally] 7. the nature of the deviant process as a whole. (Taylor *et al.*, 1973, pp. 270–7)

While much of this incorporates, as the illustrations cited by the authors make clear, a great deal from the societal reaction perspective, their final and crucial requirement does not. 'New' criminology, they insist, must return to pure Marxist and normative roots and praxis, 'to a political economy of criminal action, *and of the reaction it excites*' (p. 279, added emphasis). Quite firmly they insist on a moral enterprise that had been alien to most sociologists since Durkheim: the altering entirely of social relationships, indeed of society itself, in order to eradicate crime: 'the abolition of crime *is* possible under certain social arrangements' (p. 281, original emphasis). This sweeping claim is one that has perhaps attracted the most criticism, since it is so utopian and flies in the face of known experience. Taylor *et al.* claim in particular that crime is a product of capitalist society and of capitalist social relations. Yet their only attention to the definition of capitalism is to reiterate Marx's views, with no attempt to acknowledge modern debates about the complex and varied natures of differing industrialised societies. As I have already noted, information on crime in state socialist societies is very limited. However, those studies and observations we do have suggest that these countries experience similar or in some cases worse crime problems than those in the West (Kwasniewski, 1984; Zeldes, 1981). Where they do differ are in reactions to specific local situations or because of the problems of authoritarian regimes:

At the more observable level the massive turning away from the state and party by Poland's post-Solidarity youth has been symbolised by the spawning of a whole kaleidoscope of subcultures . . . such as punks, hippies and even rastafarians! Others take on specific Polish attributes, highlighting a sense of collective malaise. (Kolankiewiecz, 1985, p. 417)

Although Taylor *et al.* argue strenuously for reintegrating criminology with sociology, it as though 'capital', 'class', 'the state' and indeed 'crime' were quite unproblematic concepts which no one had ever sought to define or reconceptualise. In the same vein, their analysis totally lacks a comparative perspective. As David Downes vividly, if wearily, comments:

> critical criminologists too often write as if imperialism was monopolised by capitalist societies, as if the tanks had never rolled into Prague or Budapest, as if people in capitalist societies were utterly dehumanised (except where they are struggling heroically against the bosses). (Downes, 1979, p. 9)

Other Marxists even accused the critical crimonologists of the ultimate heresy – revisionism (Hirst, 1972).

There are many other problems with critical criminology, notably the issue of 'false consciousness' in a particular form applied to criminals. Within this paradigm, criminal behaviour is interpreted as rational and purposive, conscious rebellion against capitalist hegemony. This, of course, involves a peculiar distortion of the motives of petty thieves, sexual offenders, etc. and a massive indifference to the known patterns of victimisation (Downes, 1979; Leonard, 1982).

Critical criminology did not fulfil its aims. Crime-free society and a totally social theory are still unachieved. But the impact of this relatively short list of studies was immense. They filled the gaps in some ways in the interactionist analysis, inserting some structural analyses into the power vacuum there. More importantly, perhaps, they rehabilitated not so much Marx himself as the various neo-Marxisms which flourished in Europe in the 1970s and whose influence can be discerned very clearly in much recent work. The synthesis of neo-Marxist analysis with interactionist insights can be illustrated by some of the best work of the Birmingham School outlined in the last chapter. Willis's *Learning to Labour* (1978) is one example; *Policing the Crisis* (Hall *et al.*, 1978) is another.

In the latter study Hall and his colleagues explore the 'crisis' which developed around 'mugging' in Britain in the 1970s. They trace the background to the 'moral panic' after mugging (not really a crime category at all, but a suspect conflation of several offences), in a style reminiscent of earlier social reaction studies (see above), pointing out how 'black youth' came to be seen as a folk devil and was portrayed by the police and media as the archetypal 'mugger'. What is distinctively 'critical' about their analysis is the way they go on to interpret the politics of mugging. The 'criminality crisis' over mugging was, they argue, contrived. The 'real' crisis for the British state lay in potential conflicts over the economy, class, race and Northern Ireland. In order to prevent the spread of dissidence, a manufactured crisis was created to define away the real one and to deflect and diffuse possible dissidence.

This analysis is persuasive and ingenious in some parts:

> theoretically, the advance made by this book was the attempt to integrate the interactionist insight concerning 'moral panics' with the Marxian insight into the nature of 'crisis' wrought by capitalism in Britain in the early 1970s. (Downes and Rock, 1981, p. 221)

But Hall *et al.*'s depiction of a conspiratorially successful ruling class, accurate in its aims and clear in its achievements, is unproven and implausible. Such syntheses do, nevertheless, suggest possible approaches and help to select items for the research agenda in a fruitful way. While interactionism moved the centre of attention to definitions of the situation by the deviant and those around him, the concepts of critical criminology, especially when cleansed of any self-righteous insistence on moral rectitude, can provide ways of analysing the makers and enforcers of rules about crime and deviance in profitable ways.

Developing syntheses

Mapping the trends and movements in the study of crime can sometimes be like the process of charting the effects of great battles or even major natural disasters. Where has everyone gone? What shock redistributed our population over that terrain? Surveying the impact of new deviancy on the study of crime more than twenty years later is certainly not just a mopping-up activity.

Undoubtedly, the area will never be the same again. Terms such as 'diversion' (from Matza), 'labelling' and 'moral panic' are commonplace discourse in social work text books (Raynor, 1985) and in the practice and making of penal policies and treatment philosophies (Bottoms and Sheffield, 1983). The selection of many new areas for study, especially the police (see Chapter 6), owed much to the 'new' approach in which nothing could be taken for granted.

Developments in the 1980s continued to illustrate the power of these theories and their capacities for growth and further developments. Logically, perhaps (although, as I said at the beginning of this chapter, it is unwise to read too much purpose and organisation retrospectively into our subject) the 'new deviancy' perspectives were then applied to form what we can call 'new social control theory'. The paradigms of both 'labelling' and critical criminology draw our attention towards the control systems and the way they operate.

Thorpe and his colleagues (1980), for example, attempt to interpret the developments in the treatment of young offenders in Britain since 1969 using insights derived from Becker (p. 52) and Foucault (pp. 30–1). They note, ironically, that concepts such as 'labelling' had themselves been influential at certain stages in the development of policies (pp. 58–9) as well as providing ways of analysing them.

A more sustained and sophisticated study of developments in dealing with young offenders is contained in Harris and Webb (1987). Starting from their national survey of the use of supervision orders on young people, they use Foucault's and Donzelot's frameworks to analyse the growth of particular approaches to delinquents. The perspective is firmly historical, as is virtually all the best work of this type. They begin by analysing the emergence of the juvenile justice system during industrialisation,

firstly as a function of the intersecting structures and purposes of the adult criminal justice and child care systems, and secondly as an element in a steady expansion of state control over the working class young. (Harris and Webb, 1987, p. 1)

They identify one of the characteristics of the social control system for juveniles as *confusion*:

everything is almost inextricably intertwined with everything else, with the judges becoming therapists and the therapists judges; nobody's function is precisely circumscribed or monitored nobody's territory clearly staked out. (p. 3)

From macroanalyses, using the excavatory approach of Foucault, they move to a microanlysis of the development of concepts of dealing with young offenders, using biographical and other accounts of the role of social workers and probation officers. While this analysis is not always convincing, it does provide important insights into the treatment of delinquency and leads them to make interesting predictions about trends which

seem likely to exert a decisive influence on the future direction of social control. They are:
1. diversification of penality
2. an increasingly reliance on the experts
3. humanitarianism
4. net widening
5. boundary-blurring. (1987, pp. 161–3).

They concur with Stan Cohen's (1985) contention that far from being a liberal and humane alternative to incarceration, 'community corrections' can be as repressive in its own way.

In his *Visions of Social Control* Cohen drew together, albeit in a critical way, many of the insights discussed in this chapter, to analyse what he called the 'master patterns' (1985, p. 13, *et seq.*) 'of organized social control associated with the birth of the modern state' (p. 4). It is central to Cohen's thesis that his study developed and synthesised the 'new' theories in ways that had not previously been achieved (pp. 6–7). *Visions of Social Control* can be linked to a series of other historical and sociological studies which look at different aspects of the social control 'systems' (e.g. Scull, 1977 and 1984; Cohen and Scull, 1983). The approach to the original concepts is often highly critical and deliberately distancing (see, for instance, Scull, 1984, ch. 1). What is fascinating, however, is the way that these now well-worn ideas are still seen as inspiring new work, stimulating new approaches and analyses.

Many gaps remain in the enfolding story of understanding crime. Gender appears within only some of the frameworks considered in this chapter, although it obviously could do so in all of them and could have done so for a long time past. However, the most striking absence from the accounts of crime rendered through these 'new' perspectives was that very un-1960s figure whom we shall meet later on – the victim of crime.

5 Gender and Crime

Introduction

Since the late 1960s sociology, in common with other social sciences, has been affected by a major change in its assumptions about the world: for the first time, gender is on the agenda. A whole new genre of sociological literature now exists which explores gender divisions in society and the gender aspects of social institutions as diverse as the family (Barrett and Macintosh, 1982), state welfare (Ungerson, 1985), education (Deem, 1978), and politics (Randall, 1982). This has probably been the most significant and certainly the most fruitful development in modern sociology (Giddens, 1987).

The study of crime has also been caught up in the general trend of re-examining gender. There are, however, distinctive characteristics of crime and its analysis which are unique to it. This chapter is about the importance of gender to crime and the need to explore gender in order to understand crime. In it we shall see how far that understanding has gone, what impact it has had on criminology and on related policy issues, and what, in both fields, remains to be done.

In the late twentieth century very many societies have been characterised by perceived shifts in women's roles. I stress 'perceived' because I doubt whether there have been major changes in the distribution of power and resources between men and women. Some images and perceptions have, however, been altered by political action, but above all by research and writing in artistic, literary and social studies. These movements, variously described as 'new wave' or 'modern' feminism, have their roots in the modern

85

women's movement, and in economic changes. These have been described and analysed in depth elsewhere (Coote and Campbell, 1982; Banks, 1981). This fruitful flowering of intellectual endeavour meant that these existed by the 1970s a feminist critique for use in sociology. Oakley (1982) describes it as having two key emphases: that women are 'invisible' in most sociological research and writing or that, where they are considered, they are subject to marginalising and distorting treatment. She suggests that this was due in part to the structure and origins of the academic profession, and also to the pervasive 'ideology of gender'. No field of sociology was softer and riper for feminist harvesting than the study of crime.

Sex and crime

The incidence of recorded crime is strongly linked to sex and to age. So are the rates of self-reported crime and of victim- or observer-recorded offences. All strongly suggest that crime is an activity carried out by young, and young adult, males. Sex crime ratios (that is, the proportions of men and women offending) vary by offence, but of convictions for serious offences in England and Wales in recent years, over 80 per cent have been of males. Shoplifting, often thought of as a 'typically' female crime, is one for which more males than females are convicted in Britain. The most dramatic differences, however, occur in more serious crimes such as robbery and in recidivism rates. Women tend to commit less serious crimes and to do so less often. In consequence, there are far fewer women and girls in custody than there are males: of an incarcerated population of nearly 50,000 in Britain, fewer than 1,500 are female. This pattern, while it varies somewhat over time and place, is remarkably stable. In the USA, as in England and Wales, about 80 per cent of court referrals of delinquency cases are of boys (Cressey and Sutherland, 1978, p. 130), and a survey showed males constituted 97 per cent of all inmates in state correctional institutions – a proportion very close to that in Britain.

Figures from other countries, although they always have to be treated carefully and critically, are consistent with male predominance in crime. They only vary in the degree of that predominance. In India and in Sri Lanka in the 1970s, males made up over 95 per cent of convicted offenders, whereas the male share in many

Western countries is closer to 80 per cent (Cressey, 1978, p. 131). While the female share of criminality has risen slightly in some Western countries in the later twentieth century, this share is still very small.

Attempts to correct this apparently stubbornly stable ratio in recorded crimes by revealing the hidden and secret crimes of women have not been successful. Self-report studies, victim surveys, observational and other studies tend broadly to confirm the picture of crime as a largely male activity (Heidensohn, 1985, ch. 1). Many critics of criminal records have, of course, pointed out that they are not just an *inadequate* and *incomplete* account of all criminal activity, much of which must inevitably remain unobserved and uncounted. They are also fundamentally flawed since they mark police (and public) concern with only certain kinds of deviant acts or actors and not others. Armed robberies, which may net only hundreds of pounds, are carefully logged, publicised and pursued. Perpetrators are given long sentences, as are purveyors of illicit drugs. Yet these, it can be argued, are the crimes of the poor and the powerless. Depredations wrought by white-collar criminals – huge embezzlements, elaborate computer frauds, etc. – are often concealed or only lightly punished (Box, 1983). Undoubtedly, corporate crime is literally big business today, and criminal law is selectively shaped and selectively enforced. Exposing these sections of the submerged 'iceberg' of crime would not, however, increase women's contribution to recorded criminality. On the contrary, as Box points out, if anything, it would *reduce* their share, since they play little or no part in the hierarchy of organised crime syndicates nor indeed in the higher echelons of finance where such coups are possible.

One further point about concealed crime needs to be made at this point. There is little or no evidence of a vast shadowy underworld of female deviance hidden in our midst like the sewers below the city streets. As we have become increasingly aware in modern times, quite the opposite is true. There is a great deal of crime which is carefully hidden from the police, from families, friends and neighbours. Much of this takes the form of domestic violence, the abuse of children both physically and sexually, incest and marital rape. The overwhelming majority of such cases involve men, usually fathers and husbands injuring or abusing their wives and children. As Young puts it,

professional criminals engaged in violent crime [are] a quanti-
tatively minor problem when compared to domestic violence
. . . the one most likely to commit violence is the man of the
house against his wife. (Young, 1986, p. 22)

Mothers do harm their own children and sometimes even collude
in their sexual abuse: nevertheless, 'private' crime seems to be even
more male-dominated than public street crime. No doubt this is
because it is so crucial to male dominance (Stanko, 1984; Walby,
1986). Among the observations made when criminal records were
first kept was that women were far less criminal than men. This is
still true. As a classic text has it,

> Sex status is of greater statistical significance in differentiating
> criminals from non-criminals than any other trait. If you were
> asked to use a single trait to predict which children in a town of
> 10,000 people would become criminals, you would make fewer
> mistakes if you chose sex status as the trait and predicted
> criminality for the males and non-criminality for the females.
> (Sutherland and Cressey, 1978, p. 130)

Sex is therefore a crucial variable, indeed *the* crucial variable in
predicting criminality. You might expect, then, that students of
crime, its causes, consequences and remedies, would have used this
observation frequently in their work of explaining criminality;
that it provides an obvious touchstone for all theories of criminal
behaviour, a vital litmus test for the validity and reliability of all
types of studies; that the remarkable conformity of females, as well
as the sex differences, would stimulate considerable research. You
might reasonably suppose these things but, at least until the late
1960s, you would have been wrong. Some attention had been paid
to sex differences in recorded crime during the twentieth century,
but it was slight, intermittent and profoundly unilluminating.

This is an appropriate moment to make clear the distinction
between sex and gender and to explain how I am using the terms
here. Sex refers to the biological characteristics of males and
females, gender to those masculine and feminine traits associated,
but not exclusively, with men and women and therefore having a
social rather than a physical base. In relation to the recording of
crime, sex and gender are closely congruent, since the law largely
ignores gender in favour of the legally definable category of sex

(although see Edwards, 1984, for a discussion of problems which this can lead to).

Faced with the obvious and persistently low rate of female crime, a few writers constructed theories to explain the phenomenon in terms of the pecularities of female physiology and psychology, Lombroso and Ferrero, Thomas and Pollak were the key figures in this psycho-biological campaign, although the latter two were sociologists. They all argued that women's behaviour was determined by their reproductive system, which generated pathologies and aberrations. Lombroso asserted that criminal women were amoral throwbacks, to whom prostitution was the equivalent of male crime. Thomas, more sociologically, related deviant women to their social and community positions, but still stressed their emotional and psychic 'wishes' and disturbances. Pollak declared that women were inherently more devious than men, being blessed or cursed with the ability to fake orgasms and the need to conceal menstruation and pregnancy. As a result, he argued, women could and did conceal a mass of offences from scrutiny and detection. Crude biological determinism characterises all these writers. They also, of course, massively overpredict female crime. We should expect far more women than men to be criminally involved. Lombroso did link male crime to physiology, but his theories were soon discredited and biological approaches replaced by psychological or sociological ones for male offenders. Long after this, female criminals were still subject to 'biology is destiny' forms of explanation (Heidensohn, 1985).

What is striking about sociological studies of crime for much of this century is the extent to which they ignored the gender gap and also avoided discussing female crime. Leonard (1982) has described as 'dismal' the history of the sociological study of female crime, and she illustrates the inadequacies of all the major schools and theories in dealing both with women and gender. Thus 'the application of anomie theory . . . clearly illustrates this theory only applies to men and mainly to the goal of financial success' (Leonard, 1982, p. 61), while 'differential association does not explain why the situation of men and women varies so profoundly . . . regarding . . . crime' (p. 61); and again, 'subcultural theory [is] aimed implicitly or explicity at males' (p. 138). In short, Leonard indicts the whole modern sociological enterprise as bankrupt because of its failure to consider gender and crime.

Why was there this failure to examine an obvious, and even obviously helpful, issue? I think (and have recounted more fully in Heidensohn, 1985) that there were several major features of the sociology of crime which contributed to this failure. They have all now been somewhat altered, which makes this topic a particularly apposite and interesting one for the main theme of this book. The study of crime, like all major subjects in the social and other sciences, was dominated by men. It is no accident, as Oakley (1982) points out, that we talk of the 'founding *fathers*' of sociology, and she stresses how this has determined what is studied and by whom in the discipline. Participant studies of gangs of delinquent boys such as Whyte's *Street Corner Society* (1955) or Downes's *Delinquent Solution* (1966) were possible because the young, male researchers could identify with their subjects and merge with their lifestyles. In a study in Glasgow, Patrick (1973) concealed his middle-class identity in order to study violent gangs at first hand. It would have been very hard for a woman to carry out such a study; more important, however, male authors could *not* study women and girls for the same reason, and nor did they seem to wish to.

Careful attention to the detail of studies such as those in subcultural theory reveals that there was certainly awareness of the gender dimension in crime. Albert Cohen's subculture theory is based on assumptions about masculine gender and what impact this has on boys' delinquency. Cohen (1955), however, equates sex wholly with gender and only discusses masculinity. No doubt male hegemony ensured that such issues were not addressed or discussed.

Male power in academia (and in the whole apparatus of criminal justice and social control) was widespread and pervasive. This is true for almost all subjects and not just the study of crime. Criminology has had three unique aspects, at least in their combination and interaction to it. Many (male) academics and other students of crime have developed a kind of hero worship of the delinquent as romantic rebel, working-class revolutionary, or streetwise star. Stan Cohen admits to 'the obvious fascination with these spectacular subcultures' (Cohen, 1980, p. xix), while Taylor and his colleagues describe the syndrome as 'an identification by powerless intellectuals with deviants who appeared more successful in controlling events' (Taylor *et al.*, 1975). The machismo cult of the delinquent as hero reinforced the emphasis on male crime, especially urban working-class delinquency, and of course helped to exclude by 'crowding out' interest in female crime.

There was in any case a further difficulty since, given women's low and unspectacular crime rates, they were harder to find and study because they were so rare. Further, it seems clear that female offenders fear the stigma and the loss of reputation associated with their offences more than their male counterparts (Heidensohn, 1985), and this makes them even more elusive as subjects.

One of the most critical reasons for avoiding gender in the study of crime seems to be the best reason for confronting it: the crucial nature of gender for theory. As we have seen, gender is the single most important variable in criminality. It can therefore become the benchmark for measuring and testing all theory (Heidensohn, 1987). In practice, most theories of crime – especially those in the sociology of deviance – *are* based on assumptions about gender. However, those assumptions are merely asserted, not examined; they are generally only explored in relation to masculinity; and where they do outline feminine behaviour, they do so in a clumsy and oversimplified way. Merton and Cohen take for granted that masculinity is concerned with economic roles and that delinquency in males results from failures in these. Femininity is equated with female sexuality by Cohen and Sutherland and Cressey. That teenage boys may suffer crises of sexuality or that girls also require command over resources to live are unexplored issues. It was in this climate that, perhaps not surprisingly, a new feminist criminology began to flower.

Feminist perspectives

I have already described the shift in sociological paradigms in the 1960s and 1970s which promoted gender as an important topic for analysis. The feminist critique of the study of crime had from its beginning two main aspects. These were, first, that women were largely invisible in the literature on crime, and second, that when they did appear it was to be portrayed in ways which distorted and marginalised their experience (Heidensohn, 1968; 1985). These two features inevitably led to a third: the avoidance of gender as an issue, so that theories of male criminality were presented as theories of all criminality. Feminist criminology began, then, very much as a critique of mainstream male criminology. The answer seemed to be to try for a rapid drive for scholarly equality: 'what seems to be needed in the study of female deviance is a crash programme of research which telescopes decades of comparable studies of males' (Heidensohn, 1968, p. 171). As an afterthought it did also seem 'that further study of female deviance in depth may involve some challenging of underlying assumptions about male deviance' (p. 175).

I should now like to look at the extent to which feminist criminology succeeded in reconstructing mainstream studies and whether it has offered new ones. The story has developed in rather interesting and surprising ways. It provides a useful case study of the benefits and problems that are generated when we try to adapt sociology for the world which is changing about us.

First a note about feminism. There are nowadays many intellectual forms of feminism: radical, Marxist, bourgeois amd libertarian. There are also various political approaches related to these theories. However, one of the essential traits that the modern women's movement has in all its forms is an emphasis against authority, categorisation and 'putting down'. I have therefore assumed that feminist criminologists are those who so identify themselves. However, I have also tried to make clear any obvious inconsistencies and to highlight distinctive approaches when they occur.

One of the main contributions of feminist criminologists was the inevitable one for pioneers for clearing ground of old lumber and of mapping and reappraising existing terrain. The classical criminological theories of Lombroso and Ferrero and Thomas outlined above have all been subjected to rigorous critiques to demonstrate their theoretical limitations (Klein, 1976; Smart, 1977) as well as their detrimental influence on the treatment of women offenders. 'In the nutshell of Lombroso and Ferrero's theory of 1895 . . . are all the elements of a penology for women which persists [in] misogynous themes' (Carlen, 1985, p. 3). Smart (1977) showed the influence of Thomas's work, which focused on personal and psychological factors in the treatment of female offenders. This leads to an emphasis on their being expected to live and be trained for a conventional 'well adjusted' feminine lifestyle in prison.

All offenders have at various times been subject to regimes based on ill-conceived or outmoded notions. It has been the distinctive fate of female criminals for much of the twentieth century to be the target of treatments which were as dated as the 'miasma' theory of infection. A second generation of psycho-biological determinists followed Lombroso *et al.* in insisting on physiological bases for female criminality (Cowie *et al.*, 1968; Richardson, 1969). These views and the long shadows they cast on female criminality were carefully and patiently analysed within the new perspective – an enterprise which has had to be sustained. Dobash *et al.* (1986, p. 129), for example, suggest that

> the Holloway Project Group only wished to consult research supporting their preconceived ideas and these appear to continue in the vein of psychological and physiological explanations that had come to dominate the thinking at that time.

The Project Group was an official body planning the redevelopment of the women's prison and 'that time' was the early 1970s.

The first achievement, then, of the new gender-awareness in the study of crime was to reappraise and largely to refute those elders of the discipline (and their heirs) who had studied female crime. Their verdict was that more stereotypes had been reinforced than serious enlightenment shed.

Most critics of the older mainstream work also addressed more modern studies to see if they could contribute insights into understanding the gender gap or female crime. Many of the same criticisms have been applied to newer theories as to the old. Leonard (1982), in a comprehensive analysis of major schools, shows how they variously render women invisible, marginal or confine their views of females to narrow categories of deviant behaviour. Even when, as with interactionist or critical criminological theorists, the writers are deliberately aiming for new approaches to crime and deviance, gender is ignored. Millman (1982) pointed out the contradictions in Howard Becker's classic study of becoming a marihuana user. Becker based his work on his own experiences as a jazz musician, and his approach is of the sympathetic participant faithfully recording his subjects directly – his male subjects, that is, because when it comes to their wives, only the husbands views are sought: 'Howard Becker certainly never asked the wives of jazz musicians what *they* thought about their husbands' occupations, much less quoted them as authorities on the subject' (Millman, 1982, p. 260).

The criticisms of mainstream criminology offered by feminists have been extensive. They include the central paradigms and assumptions of the subject and challenges to all major theories and methodologies. How well have mainstream writers responded? Have they made gender and female criminality central issues?

The impact of the feminist critique

Not so very long ago, students searching textbooks on crime for references to either gender or women would find few or none. That is no longer so, although there has been no comprehensive revolution; criminology has not yet been born again. Rather we can point to three broad kinds of response which illustrate but do not exhaust some of the possible range within the main currents. These three are:

1. the detailed and lengthy statistical analysis of sex crime ratios and their significance;
2. the 'cosmetic touches' approach in which token references to gender are applied to create a more appropriate impression, while the inner one remains unchanged;
3. some examples of at least partial rethinking.

(In a later section we shall see how the work of feminist criminologists has continued and the new directions it has taken.)

Sex, crime and statistics

Men's excessive contribution to criminality has been observed for almost as long as crime has been recorded. It has led to the focus of most studies of crime being in practice on men. Yet very little attention has been devoted to trying to explain links between sex and crime. Instead, as in so many activities, male activity rates are taken as the norm, and it is women's which, when they diverge, have seemed strange.

Since the 1970s there has been considerable research and debate on sex–crime ratios – that is, the respective contribution of men and women to recorded crime rates, and the trends within them. While the first feminist critiques pointed out women's relative social conformity (Heidensohn, 1968), by the mid-1970s a new approach was offered: the so-called 'liberation causes crime' argument. Voiced most fully in the works of Adler and Simon, this view was based on apparent observations of both a *faster rising* female rate of crime and a *change in the nature* of female crime both related to women's emancipation. Adler, for example, argued that women's crime rates had been going up more quickly than men's and that women criminals were moving into new illicit fields, such as violent crime, just as they were finding their place in conventional careers. Liberation was leading women to be bank robbers as well as bankers (Adler, 1975).

Adler's own work has been much criticised methodologically as well as for its assumptions about women's 'achievements' and for its impact (Smart, 1979; Box, 1983; Chesney-Lind, 1980). Yet ironically it is around this theme that a considerable debate has focused, putting female criminality into mainstream discussion.

Numerous researchers have explored the extent of the undisclosed female share of crime through self-report studies and observer-based accounts (Gold, 1970; Smith and Visher, 1980). Others have tried to test Adler's hypothesis that there is a link between the rise of the women's movement and increases in recorded female crime. On the first issue, results do not suggest that there is more hidden female than male crime. On the second, while it is very difficult to test methodologically – how do you measure female emancipation? – Steffensmeier (1978, p. 580) concluded:

> The new female criminal is more a social invention than an empirical reality . . . the proposed relationship between the women's movement and crime is indeed tenuous and even vacuous.

Box (1983) and Box and Hale (1983) suggest an alternative view that women's crime is linked to other socio-economic factors, including male crime rates and women's increasing economic marginalisation.

The considerable concentration on this part of the gender agenda conveys several instructive messages. On the one hand, this is a notable example of an issue which has engaged the attention of feminist writers (Smart, 1979; Roberts Chapman, 1980) and mainstream criminologists such as Austin (1981) and involved them in debate with each other. The topic may have been taken seriously in this way because it could be treated in a somewhat discrete and compartmentalised fashion. There have been no broader discussions of gender and comparative crime rates. This separation is reflected, for instance, in a modern textbook which places gender and crime last in a series of patterns of crime and deals there with this debate rather than integrating it into the section on measuring crime (Marsh, 1986, p. 53). Another significant feature of this issue and the way it has been taken up is its methodological character. Much of the research has been directed at ways of measuring women's liberation or of finding means to study 'hidden' female crime (Box, 1983). Thus the emphasis has been on technical and 'scientific' matters (Austin, 1981, p. 372; Box and Hale, 1983) rather than on values and assumptions. There is a final, crucial point to stress. Most of the evidence would not appear to support the 'liberation equals crime' or 'new female criminal' concepts, and they are seen by many as unfortunate diversions down a dead-end road. The currency of new ideas does not, however, depend only on whether or not they are minted of true steel. The notion of the 'new female criminal' has not only been widely spread in the mass media in such headlines as a 'new, aggressive, liberated criminality in women' (*Sunday Times*), but has also led to something of a moral panic against women offenders (Chesney-Lind, 1980).

Cosmetic touches

For the most part sociologists studying crime have hardly begun to take gender seriously as an issue in their work, to make it, as it clearly needs to be, a central strand in their approach. Despite two decades of a systematic critique, a few retain a lofty disdain and ignore the problem. Others tend to grant the need for some acknowledgement of the issue in either bold and brazen fashion or more shamefacedly. Neither takes on board the full importance of the issues.

Several British writers have been much less receptive than Americans to issues of gender and seem happy to assert that 'we have . . . ignored women . . . our notion of "the working class kid" is a male one. We have no excuse except ignorance' (Corrigan and Frith, 1976, p. 239). Cressey on the other hand, introduced the tenth edition of a classic text thus:

> I have neutered *Criminology* . . . it is incorrect to accept the common practice of referring to all police officers as *policemen* and all judges . . . prosecutors and criminologists as 'he'. I made

this error in previous editions because I am a product of my cultural environment. (Cressey, 1978, p. viii)

Rethinking gender and crime

Only a few writers have worked through the full implications of the messages about gender and crime: that masculinity is at least as much a problem to be analysed and explained as femininity. In fact logically it is an even greater problem, since it is masculinity which is associated with crime and delinquency, whereas femininity is linked to conformity.

Willis (1977, 1978) is often cited as one author who analyses the gender component in subcultures of working-class 'lads' with some sensitivity; while admiring them he also observes their racist and sexist aspects and how ultimately oppressive they are to their own members. But Willis is highly selective in his focus on the 'lads' and takes for granted not only their version of masculinity, but also of femininity. Brake in his recent work (1985) treats gender as a problem to be explained for both females and males, although even he devotes more space to the issue in relation to the former and calls his chapter on gender 'The Invisible *Girl* – the Culture of Femininity versus Masculinism'. Nevertheless he does explore some important gender-related issues, such as that between sub-cultures and kinds of work, and hints at some of the costs and damage of masculinism and machismo – to gay youth, for example. While this is a helpful and thoughtful analysis in many ways, Brake does not link his approach in this chapter to others where he deals with delinquency, racism, etc., in which gender appears again taken-for-granted and unproblematic.

Wood, in an article ambiguously called 'Groping Towards Sexism', examines the contradictions and weaknesses of masculinity and how these can lead to violence and fantasies about rape in a class of secondary school 'drop outs'. He is particularly interesting on his own role as observer and recorder and 'my effective identification with the boys' (1984, p. 68). Auld and his colleagues link gender, heroin use and the irregular economy in their analysis of the contemporary drug scene in Britain. They observe, as few writers have, the use of male power to exclude women from illegal as well as other activities:

the impediments to girls getting involved with heavy drugs are not purely cultural ones related to stereotyping but are also brazenly economic, insofar as males tend to monopolize the opportunities thrown up within the irregular economy amongst themselves. (Auld *et al.*, 1986, p. 177)

In what is again a first, or at least an early, sighting in this kind of subcultural study, they link sex roles not only to the lifestyle and drug use of young men on the streets and in sexual encounters, but also suggest that younger male drug users may actually have families, especially mothers, with whom they interact. Auld *et al.* do not treat their notion of masculine gender as problematic, nor do they comment on, although they describe, the contradictions inherent in it. Their views on prevention and control policy in relation to male behaviour are also very coy. They stress the way in which traditional sexual divisions both lead to a particular pattern of drug use and are used to sustain it, but they stop well short of challenging those patterns and merely urge 'a sensitivity . . . to sexual divisions' (p. 185).

One of the most important gender issues raised in recent years has concerned the sex of the victim and of the perpetrator of violent crime. By and large, as we have already seen, the feminist critics have not succeeded in directly putting gender into the main currents of criminological thought. But if the academy has been slow to respond, the polity and public opinion have reacted more rapidly and considerably. Campaigns to promote awareness of and to seek help for battered wives and rape victims, and more recently the victims of sexual abuse in the family and of sexual harassment at work have all met with some degree of public response and even policy changes (Pizzey, 1973; Wilson, 1983; Brownmiller, 1973; Toner, 1982; Stanko, 1984). Women's Aid Refuges have been given some, albeit meagre, public funding, and police responses to rape victims have been rethought (Blair, 1985). The feminist analysis which lies behind most of these campaigns has not, on the whole, been widely accepted, stressing as it does the patriarchal attitudes which both are widespread in society and support and justify male violence to women and children. It is the politics and images of these campaigns, not their theories, which have had impact (Randall and Rose, 1984). However, at least one American study suggests that the women's movement has led to a gentler and less sexist handling of rape victims in the US criminal justice system (Robin, 1977).

Criminologists, too, who have turned Nelsonian telescopes on the signals from feminist criminology have acknowledged at least the concern with the gender of victims of crime and also the gender of those who most fear becoming victims (see Chapter 7). Young (1986, p. 27) notes 'the pioneering work of feminist criminologists both in the field of women as victim and as offenders'. It would be wrong to claim that the huge modern interest in victims and victimology grew exclusively from this source, but it has clearly been an influence, not least perhaps because having *political* force, such concerns might attract research funds and approval (Rock, 1988a).

A separate sphere

Concern with gender is thus slowly seeping rather than flowing into the mainstream of the study of crime. There have, however, been notable flows from the tributaries. The first achievements of the feminist critics of the sociology of crime, as of other areas in sociology, was to point to the neglect of gender as a variable and the absence of studies of women in the subject. Most of the original work by these critics consisted in developing and explaining these criticisms (Heidensohn, 1985). For a time it seemed that, given the failure of established criminology to respond, there might be no further progress.

The 1980s, though, have seen important new developments which should point the routes to new directions and territories. From a now burgeoning and well-established crop I would pick out three especially fruitful topics:

1. important contributions to the ethnography of female criminality;
2. gender and criminal justice;
3. gender-based crimes.

Studies of female crime

Women criminals were long invisible and silent in studies of crime. Partly that was due to the male bias of researchers, but also, in a more fundamental sense, they *were* invisible and elusive. Since women committed so little crime, how could they be studied? The rich and varied ethnography of male crime, especially urban working-class street crime, had no counterpart. Full-scale folk myths are still lacking, but things have changed. Students can now read a growing range of authentic accounts of female crime.

Campbell (1981, 1985), for example, has published two major studies of delinquent girls in gangs which overturn a number of sterotypes about girls' inability to fight and to join groups, and confirm Shacklady Smith's pioneering work in the 1970s. A particularly noteworthy aspect of Campbell's work is that her first study looked at delinquent girls in Britain and her second the USA, and thus provides a comparative record. She is critical of much earlier writing on girls and gangs and the obsession of many writers with girls' sexuality. In her depiction of the lives of Connie, Weeza, Sun Africa and their gangs she provides both rich description and cogent analysis:

> that's usually girls fighting, pulling hair and scratching . . . I don't like pain. If I'm getting pain, I'm going to make sure you're going to stop. She grabbed my hair and I got so pissed and I went and grabbed her hair and I started banging her head . . . she ruined my hair style because once I combed it, I don't want nobody touching it. (Campbell, 1984, pp. 147–8)

The girls in the gang are not, Campbell maintains, part of a revolutionary change. They are still under the control of their men, their concerns conventional – to have a stable man, beautiful children and a suburban apartment.

Eleanor Miller (1986) studied a group of women street hustlers in Milwaukee, Wisconsin. Like Campbell, she provides vivid portraits of the lives and work of her subjects:

> The reason most women does crimes is mens. I think it's more prostitutes you know. Everybody's gettin' into the street life. Everybody's runnin' around. He's a pimp; she's a whore. (Miller, 1986, p. 165)

Miller also relates the closed, illicit world of illegal work in which these women live to their poverty, family responsibilities and their exploitation by men (pp. 177–8). In particular, she challenges Adler and Simon's views on rising crime to suggest that links between low incomes, race and family networks are much more significant than 'liberation' in drawing young women to participate in crime.

Women's low rates of participation in crime partly explain their low visibility in studies of it. Another reason has been their especial fear of the stigma attached to criminalisation and hence their reluctance to be publicly identified with deviance. It has always been very difficult to find autobiographical accounts of women offenders' careers (Heidensohn, 1985). Again this is an area that has changed considerably. Carlen's (1983) pioneering work with women in a Scottish prison gave, among other things, stark and immediate portraits of the lives of women offenders in and outside prison. This was followed by *Criminal Women* – the stories, edited by Carlen, of a group of ex-offenders told in their own ways and emphasising their un-stereotypical career patterns as fairly serious offenders. A further volume will deal with Carlen's most recent research on women's criminal careers. Two other studies of imprisoned women – Dobash and Dobash (1986) and Mandaraka-Sheppard (1986) – also contain personal accounts of their careers by incarcerated women offenders.

Gender and justice

Many of the feminist writers who were critical of conventional criminology and its treatment of female offenders and of gender and crime have moved on to focus on gender and the criminal justice system, and they have been joined by others whose research in this area has been within a broadly feminist framework.

Work in this field has been very extensive, and it is helpful to pick out key themes and illustrate them from the work of several authors. Three major themes stand out as illustrating, though not wholly covering, the range of the work achieved:
1. chivalry and the courts and police;
2. prison and penal policies;
3. questions of philosophy and justice.

1. Chivalry
Generations of criminologists have believed with Mannheim (1940, p. 343) that 'the female offender – if punished – meets on the whole with greater leniency on the part of the courts than the male'. It is probably still believed to be so by many people.

Several writers have tested the 'chivalry' hypothesis by comparing differential sentences on women and men and also examining the language and behaviour of participants in court proceedings. Chivalry is one of the main strands of Eaton's (1986) work, and she reviews most other studies in this field, including the work of Nagel *et al.* (1980 and 1981) and Moulds (1980) in the USA. This work *appears* to show women receiving less severe sentences than men, yet seriousness of crimes and length of record were not controlled. From Eaton's own study in a London magistrates' court she concludes: 'within its own terms Hillbury Court treats men and women equally when they appear in similar circumstances' (p. 97). However, in practice this rarely happens because of the substantial inequalities experienced *outside* the court. It is specifically within the family that sexual inequalities are experienced and expressed, and Eaton argues that magistrates make use of familial ideology as the basis of summary justice. Both men and women are treated in this way and thus inequalities are reproduced.

Edwards (1984) has examined similar issues in her series of studies of criminal justice. In her research on magistrates' courts in London and Manchester and in the Manchester Crown Court, she concludes that women offenders were often 'medicalised', to their detriment, by the courts, and that 'Women defendants are on trial both for their legal infractions and for their defiance of appropriate feminity and gender roles' (p. 216).

Iles (1986) has noted similar trends in the treatment of women political criminals on trial for terrorist acts, although she agrees with Eaton that there was no difference in sentencing outcomes – only in the court and media presentation of women, which defined them in narrowly sexualised ways (but also see Allen, 1987, for another view).

Many writers in this field have concluded that women coming before the criminal courts experience the double bind – that of 'double deviance' and of 'double jeopardy'. Courts are unused to dealing with female offenders who rarely come before them. Women are thus seen both as rule breakers and role defiant, and may be treated accordingly. Young girls are overprotected, their lives interfered with and made the focus of intrusion for lesser delinquent acts than boys (Webb, 1984) or merely for sexual behaviour permitted in males and adult females (Chesney-Lind, 1980). Adult women receive punitive remands (Dell, 1971; Heidensohn, 1981) and prostitutes are subject to stigma and lack of basic civic rights (Edwards, 1984; McLeod, 1982). Many criminal women feel that they are unjustly treated by mainly male judges, police, etc.: 'Their contracts with the criminal justice system fostered neither respect nor fear, but quite often indigation, anger and disdain' E. Miller, 1986, p. 167).

'Double jeopardy' occurs when women, who are often subject to additional informal systems of social control and social justice, also face the formal legal apparatus of the courts. It is clear that women already experience sanctions other than those of official agencies (Heidensohn, 1985, ch. IX). Thus the stigma involved in the loss of reputation to women is profound and damaging: their identity is, literally, spoiled. Since men, or sometimes other women, control this, it can be used to punish and control women. Lees (1986) describes how adolescent boys control the behaviour of girls in this way. Carlen's (1983) respondents described to her the beatings they received from their husbands. Scutt has also reported on the outraged feelings of women facing male justice in the courts (Heidensohn, 1986). Chivalry, in short, appears to be a medieval concept neither practised nor cherished by the courts today.

2. Prisons and penal policy

The penal treatment of women was among the first issues discussed in modern debates about women and crime (Ward and Kassebaum, 1966; Giallombardo, 1966; Smith, 1962). A wide range of writers agreed that the very few women who actually went to prison suffered because of their rarity, since facilities tended to be fewer, limited in scope, and less accessible. Moreover, regimes designed for men were persistently ill-adapted to women, who thus received unnecessary and undeserved punishment (Smith, 1962; Heidensohn, 1969, 1975).

More recent writings have extended the range of this work and also pointed to important gender issues within social control. Carlen (1985), Mandaraka-Sheppard (1980) and the Dobashes (1986) all stress the distinctively petty and heavily controlling systems in women's prisons. They also note the emphasis on domesticity in the regimes for women in prison and how gender stereotypes are reinforced so that women who have failed in and been failed by conventional domestic life learn homemaking skills when what they lack are education and training to make them economically independent. Genders and Player (1986) have drawn attention to a similar anomaly in the treatment of young women in prison who are intended to socialise with 'mature' and motherly older prisoners. Such an approach would not be acceptable for men.

Many writers have pointed to the differential treatment of the male perpetrator and the female victim of crime, especially violent crime. Rape has been a particular focus of such studies (and of protests over light sentences) (Smart, 1977; Toner, 1982; Balir, 1984; Adler, 1987).

3. Philosophy and justice

As more research and writing on gender and justice has been carried out, it has become increasingly necessary to discuss and determine what justice in this context means. Does it require strict equality between the sexes? How might that be achieved? For example, most policemen, judges and court officials are males. Most developments in this field have been in civil justice and concern sex discrimination, but interesting work has been done on the sociology of the magistrates' court (Carlen, 1976), on 'welfarism' in juvenile justice and its implications for young women (Webb, 1984), and on the implications of alternative strategies for changing the laws on prostitution (Matthews, 1986). In the United States civil rights legislation has been used extensively in 'class action' law suits to improve prison conditions for women. There have also been analyses and discussions of equality and women's rights, for example of their right to defend themselves reported in the *Women's Rights Law Review* (L. E. A. Walker, 1987). In all of them, aspects of gender and justice are considered. Increasingly, feminist writers have linked these issues to civil and family law matters with which they interact (Smart, 1984; Brophy and Smart, 1985). Along with these and other writers, I have suggested that alternative models of gender justice might be explored, rather as juvenile justice constitutes a partially distinct system (Heidensohn, 1986).

Gender and crime

I have already mentioned in this chapter the success achieved by feminists in exposing 'hidden crimes' against women. As I suggested, campaigns to render these problems visible and even to attract some help for their victims have had some impact. But the impact has generally been bought at a cost – often a literal cost, since public money was required to fund help, and in order to obtain it crucial findings were muted. As Morgan (1985, p. 65) puts it, 'The problem [of wife battering] was first identified by feminists as a manifestation of gender domination'.

Gendered crime is 'real' crime

'Have you stopped beating your wife?' is, in English humour, a traditional joke-query at which audiences are meant to laugh. Such laughter helps to conceal the true extent, enormity and damage of gendered crime. By 'gendered crime' I mean those offences committed mainly by men against women and children in which they use power or force and in which traditional gender roles are played. This definition includes wife–beating, rape and sexual assaults, sexual abuse and harassment. (Physical abuse of children is also, of course, carried out by women against their children.)

Numerous surveys have shown how violent crimes against women are grossly underreported. In their study of 129 women in Leeds, Hanmer and Saunders (1984, p. 32) found that 'over half reported one or more experiences of violence to themselves in the past year'. (This is in marked contrast to the *British Crime Survey*'s results – see Chapter 7.) In her research in San Francisco, Russell (1987) found an incidence of rape twenty-four times higher than that reported by the FBI in their Uniform Crime Reports.

Not only are such offences far more widespread than official records suggest, but it is clear that the harm they cause is deep and long lasting. It is physically and psychologically destructive, but reporting incest, for example, involves the betrayal of trust and fear of destroying the family. Renvoize (1982) presents a series of accounts of incest victims and notes their fears, stigma and the life-long harm they often suffered.

Sex and social control

It has been commonplace in criminology to see sex-linked crimes as crimes of faulty or inappropriate sexuality (or sometimes appropriate but inopportune or unfortunate as in certain rape cases). West *et al.* (1978) suggest that rapists suffer from faulty upbringing which has damaged their masculinity. Feminist critics have, however, insisted that sex-linked crimes are power, not sexually, based. Dobash and Dobash (1970, p. 93) conclude from their work in Scotland:

differential marital responsibility and authority give the husband both the perceived right and the obligation to control his wife's behaviour and thus the means to justify beating her.

Wilson (1983, p. 78) has analysed rape in a similar fashion: 'Rape is an act of violence against women. It is a hostile and sadistic act. It is a violation of a women's autonomy and a negation of her independence'.

In important analyses Stanko and Walby both link male violence towards women with economic inequality between the sexes. Stanko (1984) comprehensively relates all 'intimate intrusions' forced by men on women to women's powerlessness and their struggle for survival. Walby (1986, pp. 60–3) specifically links male violence with patriarchal structures in the economy and the state which empower men and dispossess women.

Agencies ignore or condone male violence

Most of the surveys already reported show that official agencies are very reluctant to protect women from male violence. The police have been notoriously reluctant to intervene in cases of domestic violence: 'officers are very unlikely to make an arrest when the offender has used violence against his wife' (Dobash and Dobash, 1979, p. 207). Stanko quotes an American prosecutor:

> Take a felonious assault case involving a domestic quarrel. Does this deserve to be tried by a 12 man jury? No. We are much better off if they kiss and make up rather than if we put him in jail. (Stanko, 1984, p. 129)

Adler's work on rape cases tried before the Central Criminal Court in London suggests that, despite Parliament's intentions, rape victims are not well-protected by the law of anonymity, nor are their characters spared. She also found jurors reluctant to convict in such cases and bleakly concludes that women are still very reluctant to report rape (Adler, 1982).

Fear of attack as a form of control

Numerous studies testify to the immense fear of crime experienced by women, especially older women and particularly in the inner city. Successive *British Crime Surveys* have found notable gender differences in fears of crime (Hough and Mayhew, 1983). Clarke and Lewis (1982) found elderly women in the inner city to be much more fearful than elderly men. Figures from two London studies make the point starkly (see Tables 5.1 and 5.2).

Table 5.1   Percentage of respondents who have felt unsafe in their own homes

	Male	Female
Islington Crime Survey	17	36
Broad Water Farm	22	44

Source: Young (1986)

Table 5.2   Percentage of respondents who often or always avoid going out after dark because of fear of crime

	Male	Female
Islington Crime Survey	14	54
Broad Water Farm	14	57

Source: Young (1986)

As the author of the paper observes, 'fear of crime on Broad Water Farm is therefore a serious problem and *its impact on women approaches curfew levels*. But it is not atypical for inner city areas as a whole' (Young, 1986, p. 29).

A paradoxical effect of some victim and fear of crime studies is that they focus attention on street crime and attacks by strangers. Clearly anxieties about such offences are real among women and seriously limit their freedom of movement and inhibit their behaviour. They can be analysed as an aspect of the complex of checks and controls which constrain female behaviour in our society (Heidensohn, 1985). Yet, as we have already seen, violence to women is more prevalent in the home than outside it. There too it can produce fears and be used as a crude form of discipline and domination. As Stanko suggests,

This attention to violence committed by strangers obscures the possible fear producing effects of violence within the home and mitigates against the inclusion of intimate familial violence, largely perpetrated against women and girls, from being considered serious crime. By retaining the ideology of the safe home, we retain a major contributor to women's subordinate status within a gender stratified society. (Stanko, 1988)

Theories of male dominance
From a sociologist's perspective the most interesting and valuable insights generated by research in this area are those which enhance theoretical perspectives. In seeking to explain male violence to women a variety of explanations have been offered which not only illuminate these dark corners of human experience but also lead to rethinking assumptions about the family, socialisation and forms of social control.

Brownmiller (1973, p. 15) contends that 'rape and fear of rape are used as a weapon of control by men over women as a conscious process of intimidation by which all men keep all women in a state of fear'. Hanmer's more sophisticated analysis suggests that male violence to women is the basis of patriarchal dominance. By using it, or by threatening to, men ensure that only that 'the central institutions . . . of power, prestige or influence where the most significant transactions of the community are carried out are effectively closed to women' (Hanmer, 1977, p. 20), but they also gain women's domestic services and support. Patriarchy, in short, rests on violent, coercive support. Walby, however, disagrees and argues:

> Men's violence against women is not a necessary basis for other patriarchal structures, but it does help to sustain them. Violence does, both directly and indirectly, have effects on women's behaviour, especially in the curtailment of movement. (Walby, 1986, p. 66)

She maintains that

> men's violence against women is particularly facilitated by women's weak material position . . . and by the unwillingness of the patriarchal state to enforce the criminal law when men are the aggressors and women the victims. (1986, p. 65)

Research on gender-based violence, especially in the domestic setting, has affected concepts of the family. Families can hardly be characterised as 'havens in a heartless world' (Lasch, 1977) if the safe home is a myth for many women and children. Nor can the notion of the 'symmetrical family' (Young and Wilmott, 1973) be easily sustained in the face of such evidence of gender inequalities (Morgan, 1985, p. 90).

Most of this conceptual analysis and some of the related research is excluded, as Morgan (1985) suggests, from public debate about violent crime. Gender is forgotten, or trivialised as an issue, or else only seen as a simple, biological explanation and not a problem. Yet the range of material we already have, together with growing public concern and awareness of such issues (*London Evening Standard*, 3 February 1987; *Sunday Times*, 1 February 1987) indicate that this will not always be a hidden agenda item. Education, health and illness are all related to gender – but none more crucially than crime, where gender is the most vital of variables. As we have seen, this message has already been understood by some criminologists who have begun to address the issue in their work.

If anything, academics have been slower than professionals, the police and the public in appreciating the importance of gender, even if the latter groups have sometimes responded in partial and stereotyped ways. It is clear that feminist criticisms and campaigns, together with the work of other very different activists, have highlighted and made visible gender dimensions to crimes such as wife battering, the sexual abuse of children and rape (Robin, 1977). They have also achieved some modest changes in policies: for example, more sensitive handling of rape victims.

Awareness of gender issues has clearly also played its part in the changed emphasis on the rights of the victim and the moves towards reparation and conciliation. This is not the only origin of such changes, but it has played its part. Schemes to prevent and control crime through better planned and lit housing estates, women-only taxi services and self-defence classes, are all associated with growing fears of and for women as potential victims of crime.

Policy responses remain piecemeal to this issue, and mainstream criminology is only beginning to have its consciousness roused. There are, however, considerable developments to record in the understanding of women and crime and the relationships between feminine gender and criminality. The findings of the research set out above and that of related work suggests at least five major insights derived from studying female criminality.

Economic rationality

Female offenders are as likely as males to be motivated by economic needs to commit crime. If anything, it is poverty, theirs and their children's, which leads them to property crime and offences connected with prostitution.

Variety
Women are not specialists in crime. They commit almost all forms – they fight, steal, kill and lead terrorists groups. Their *potential* for deviance may be as great as men's, their actual *depredations* far fewer. This suggests that gender-linked factors intervene to curb and gentle the possibilities of female criminality.

Stigma
Women and girls often feel deeply damaged by criminalising stigma, the consequent harm to their lives often proving irreparable.

The double bind
Courts and other agencies treat women as deviant twice over: they have broken criminal law and social expectations of proper female behaviour. Further, since women are also subject to fuller informal sanctions and punishments than men, they experience 'double jeopardy' when they have to confront the public system of criminal justice.

Crime, conformity and femininity
Socialisation into the feminine gender role appears inevitably to involve a much higher degree of social conformity than does the masculine role. 'Boys will be boys' implies licence to deviate and stray, but 'Sugar and spice *and all things nice*: that's what little girls are made of'.

Our knowledge of female criminality and of feminine socialisation has therefore developed enormously through the gender-based paradigm shift in sociology. The next stage might be to apply these insights to male crime – 'real' crime, after all – and to masculinity. Why do societies tolerate the costs and damages associated with certain forms of 'masculine' behaviour? Do solutions to crime and delinquency lie in socialising boys and young men and controlling, for example, their public freedom in ways which appear to be acceptable, and prove effective, for girls and women? There are obvious problems and dangers in such approaches, but looking at gender and crime leads us to raise them. To end this chapter, consider only an obvious irony: whenever a horrific rape or sexual murder occurs the police urge women to stay at home. It would be at least as rational to keep all men under curfew.

Conclusions

If sociology is to contribute to the future understanding of crime, it must take on board and use fully the concept of gender. This observation is true of many areas of sociological interest – of social mobility for example. But so far this has neither been an acceptable perspective for the state nor one which could be assimilated into public policy, and therefore individualised and medicalised models have replaced it:

> In constructing a non-threatening image of the problem of wife-battering the state has eliminated the need for enquiries into the condition of women in contemporary society. (Morgan, 1985, p. 73)

It is vital, therefore, to rescue and present some of the important insights and findings in this area in their unneutered forms, since these are often lost or ignored in public debate. Again, this is a field in which many have researched and key results and analyses can most helpfully be picked out.

6 Policing, Crime and Social Order

DOGBERRY: You are thought here to be the most senseless and fit man for the constable of the watch; therefore bear you the lantern. This is your charge; you shall comprehend all vagrom men; you are to bid any man stand, in the prince's name.
SECOND WATCH: How if a' will not stand?
DOGBERRY: Why, then, take no note of him, but let him go; and presently call the rest of the watch together and thank God you are rid of a knave.
(*Much Ado About Nothing*, Act III, scene iii)

As the above quotation suggests, the concept of what Kinsey, Lea and Young (1986) have called 'minimal policing' was already a familiar one in Elizabethan England. Maintaining 'law and order' or the 'civil peace', or controlling the dangerous classes, have, as we have seen already, been constant items on the agenda both of public debate and, when it began to develop as a discipline, sociology itself. There were, it could be said in sweeping summary, a major and a subsidiary agenda for the subject. First, there were all the central projects of the 'founding fathers', Marx, Durkheim and Weber, directed at explaining and understanding the development of society and its institutions, especially of industrial society and its character-istic institutions of class, power structures and status systems.

Second, drawing on this sociological tradition (Nisbet, 1966), sometimes in very distinctive ways, has been an underworld of work on crime and deviance. So far in this book I have tried to illustrate how this kind of sociology has developed: not in any smooth and upward progress, as in a Whig version of history, but rather in a series of tenuously related stirrings. These can, read backwards, be rendered into a shape and coherence which their participants would not at the time have recognised.

Pattern and coherence of a kind can, nevertheless, be discerned, *and* forms of learning and discarding. The process has been a curious blend both of a kind of sociological Darwinism – the survival of the fittest theories – and a Lamarckian one of passing on acquired characteristics to the next generation. That is not to say, of course, that there are no sociological equivalents of stone-age man, surviving in the intellectual equivalent of a remote rain forest, using theories and conceptual tools long outmoded everywhere else. There are, on the other hand, sociological Mr Toads who, like the anti-hero of *The Wind in the Willows*, regularly discard and forget one favoured approach and replace it with a passionate commitment to whatever is new, fast moving and exciting. Between these extremes, the subject has been jerkily promoted, with some key shifts occurring from time to time which register high on everyone's Richter scale. The 'new deviancy' theories of the 1960s were part of one such major change, altering the whole study of crime, both in concepts and subject matter. The feminist studies of the 1970s was another whose impact is so far only partial, although it has been marked by its focusing attention on victims and on fears of crime and their consequences. These changes sprang from developments within sociology which both reflected and were part of social and cultural developments in the mid–twentieth century.

In this chapter and the next I want to turn to two areas of great and growing interest in the study of crime: policing and prevention. On the whole, the very considerable new research on and moral concern for these issues in which sociologists, along with other social scientists, have been involved, have not sprung from sources inside the discipline. Instead, the sources and the pressures have been external:

Policing has moved into the centre of political debate and controversy in Britain in the last twenty years . . . stimulated by this, there has been an efflorescence of writing and research about the police . . . what characterises almost all this work, whatever its provenance, is an *over-riding concern with current policy and political issues*. Little attention is paid in most current work to the project of furthering a deeper theoretical understanding of policing . . . the debate has been dominated by immediate problems. (Reiner and Shapland, 1987, p. 1, added emphasis)

While, as we shall see, there are certain crucial theoretical differences, much the same could be said about crime prevention.

While sociological studies of the police have been part of a response to a dramatically portrayed crisis, they have not wholly lacked theoretical dimensions. Indeed, the above quotation introduces a selection of articles whose 'main purpose . . . is to encourage the development of a deeper theoretical analysis of policing' (p. 2). Nevertheless, the distinctive nature of studies of policing, especially as they have appeared in Britain, requires a somewhat different approach and framework from that adopted in previous chapters. Instead of following through the development of key sociological ideas in work and crime and evaluating their results for theoretical and empirical studies, I shall explore three central issues which have their origins in sociological discourse on social control and can provide a taxonomy for classifying 'what is now an impressively large volume of research' (Reiner, 1985, p. xii). The questions raised by these issues, and for which we can find some partial answers in the recent 'explosion' of policing studies are:

1. *Why police* (noun)? Why have this sort of social control, these agents of control? What is their effect on crime?
2. *Why police* (verb)? Why is policing conducted in the manner that it is? Has it changed? Is it subject to political pressures? Or social change? What have these matters to do with crime?
3. *Who controls* this crucial form of social control? Who manages the police and their 'war on crime'? To whom are they accountable? Are there alternatives?

This is a necessarily arbitrary framework but on which will prove, I hope, helpful in making sense of a dynamic and controversial area of social research which is certain to continue and indeed to grow in importance in the future.

Which police?

First, however, a note on which police are, for the most part, considered here. British and American police developments and developments in police research in the two nations differ markedly.

'Crisis' and 'concern' are terms that have only been used in mainland Britain since the 1970s; as we shall see later on, the 'our-policemen-are-wonderful' myth was sustained for quite a long period in the twentieth century: 'the police . . . were regarded as perhaps the most unproblematic of the major institutions of government in Britain' (Lustgarten, 1987, p. 23).

In the United States of America, on the other hand, no such honeymoon period has ever really existed. In an older, standard criminology text, the main section on the American police begins: 'The system of which the police are a part is honeycombed with corruption, graft, and partisan politics' (Barnes and Teeters, 1951, p. 245), and goes on to consider, complete with horrific details, the 'third degree' interrogation methods, and the 'general charge lodged against American police [of] their cruelty in making arrests and in attempting to get confessions from suspects or evidence from witnesses' (p. 250). In consequence, American research on policing has a much longer history, although there too there has been much development in modern times (see, for example, Cressey, 1978 for a survey). American studies therefore have often been the stimulus to later British ones: 'American research . . . the brilliant work of Westley, Skolnick, Reiss and Bittner for example, has its pay-off when brought to British policing' (Holdaway, 1979, p. 3).

While several authors treat the 'classic formulation of the Anglo-American police mandate' (Manning, 1979, p. 42) as a unity with a common origin, it has clearly very different later outcomes (and this view of its origins has been regarded as increasingly problematic – see Brogden, 1987, and below). The emphasis therefore in this review will be on Britain and British studies, with references, where appropriate, to American research. This makes for some coherence, as these studies have been published in a clear if crisis-torn context. The organisation and administration of policing in the USA is extremely complex and fragmented, with some 40,000 'forces' at federal and state levels. This contrasts with England and Wales, where there are forty-three separate forces, including the Metropolitan and the City of London police forces.

'Police' in the context of this chapter, as in both common parlance and in academic studies, refers to the work and staff of those forces. That is, of course, a narrow definition. The term derives from the broader concept of the good government of civil society and how that is achieved (Alderson, 1983, p. 163). In more modern times

> it is found being used to describe the civil force to which is
> entrusted the task of maintaining public order and enforcement
> of law for the prevention and punishment of its breaches and
> detecting crime. (Alderson, 1983, p. 163)

It should be stressed that the police are by no means the only
official agency involved in these tasks (the role of informal control
is discussed in this chapter and elsewhere in this book). The
Customs and Excise service, for instance, has wide powers and
plays an important role in policing drug use. Historically it was
organised and bureaucratised *before* the Metropolitan Police and
even acted as a model for the introduction of that innovation:

> The success in England of the Excise service, a highly effective
> and non-penal tax bureaucracy, increased confidence that a
> salaried government service could be made to fulfil the adminis-
> trative goals set for it. (Styles, 1987, p. 22)

Numerous other regulatory inspectorates exist, many with powers
to inspect, control and enforce legally backed sanctions, but they,
like HM Customs and Excise, have attracted little public attention
and hardly any research. For two interesting exceptions see Carson's
(1970) work on the Factory Inspectorate and Hutter's (1986) study
of three regulatory inspectorates, part of which is reported in 'An
Inspector Calls'. A host of other agents and agencies are almost
invisible, socially and sociologically – for example, private security
and crime investigating bodies, debt recovery and credit-control
firms, and store detectives – although they have very considerable
powers and functions.

> Among all the forms of organisation and procedures that combine
> to control behaviour the police have a limited, yet decisive, role
> to play. (Smith and Gray, 1985, p. 9)

Part of the reason for the focus on the police to the virtual exclusion
of other bodies lies in that 'decisive' role. As Smith and Gray
illustrate in the discussion of paying gas bills, from which this
quote comes,

> as long as most people conform at least when some pressure has
> been brought to bear on them by other agents, the police can
> effectively deal with the few remaining cases. They are *the last*

resort in a long process of social control. (Smith and Gray, 1985, p. 10)

The police, in other words, are the thin, blue bottom line, ruled round the edge of social order.

However, their position is also distinctive because of the symbolism they embody: 'The occupation espouses and displays the most salient indicators of attachment to the state: the most sacred of secular symbols are worn on the uniform' (Manning, 1979, p. 44). Or, as Reiner less cryptically put it:

The police are an integral aspect of the presentation of society as governed by the rule of law . . . the architects of the British police tradition were concerned to construct an image of the bobby as both effective and *the embodiment of impersonal rational-legal authority*. (Reiner, 1985, p. 136, added emphasis)

Manning (1979, p. 45) also pointed out, as did Cain (1973), the social isolation of police officers from the rest of society because of organisational as well as community constraints. These features combine to make the police a distinctive high-profile agency on which societal and sociological attention is most likely to focus.

The changed context of policing

There were, however, a series of other developments during the 1970s and 1980s which, taken together, make the symbolic role as well as the operational role of the police in maintaining social order more problematic than they have been since the rise of the 'new police' in the nineteenth century (Reiner, 1985, ch. 2).

Scandals and corruption

Historically, the first of these developments began with mounting concern over scandals and corruption, especially in Scotland Yard, concerning bribery, drugs and pornography. There had been previous sensational cases, for example one involving the planting of 'half bricks' as 'evidence' in demonstrators' pockets, but 'what was most shocking was the revelation of the systematic, institutionalised and widespread network of corruption' (Reiner, 1985, p. 65). Such scandals continued to surface, despite major purges and reforms (Mark, 1978), with similar allegations and occasionally fresh ones concerning the fraudulent manipulation of crime records or conspiracies to hush up other scandals.

Rising crime and urban riots

Throughout the 1970s and 1980s key measures of police effectiveness were seen to move very much to their disfavour. Crime rates, presented and recorded by the police themselves, not only rose fairly steadily, but 'clear-up rates', the classic measure of effectiveness, *declined* at the same time (Kinsey *et al.*, 1986, p. 1). These events occurred at a time when expenditure on police and policing was both increasing *absolutely*, at a faster rate than on welfare services and taking a greater share of national resources (Heal *et al.*, 1985, p. 1). Obviously the public credibility gap between claims and achievement widened considerably. It became a chasm, for a time at least, following the two periods of inner-city rioting in Bristol, Liverpool and the London suburb of Brixton in the early 1980s, and in Handsworth (Birmingham), Brixton and the Broad Water Farm housing estate in inner London in 1985. In all these events, police actions played an initial part (Scarman, 1986; Gifford, 1986), and their escalation into dramatic and violent confrontations and even death showed not merely civil disorder on the mainland, but the police's failure to prevent and contain that disorder.

Race relations

Urban riots were the most extreme manifestation of social conflict and of specific conflicts between the police and some groups of citizens. Most of all it is clear that there 'has been a catastrophic deterioration of relations with the black community' (Reiner, 1985, p. 81). 'The gulf between police and young blacks . . . is the most menacing and most intractable' (Harrison, 1983, p. 364).

Many factors have contributed to this situation: the riots themselves; the events that led up to them and their aftermaths; scandals involving police brutality, real and alleged; deaths or injury in custody or in cases where innocent relatives were harmed while the police pursued suspects; the harassment and overpolicing of certain black communities and yet the failure to deal with racial attacks; evidence of racial stereotyping among police officers. All these have played their part in forming a situation where police–community relations with some black groups have been very poor and where the wider social audience can perceive the police to have performed badly.

The miners' strike

While the police's law and order mandate could be said to have failed in keeping crime rates down and managing relations with ethnic youth, their handling of the miners' strike in 1984–5 was at once as problematic and as divisive. In a crude sense, the police could be said to have 'won' in the miners' strike since the dispute was eventually settled and coal supplies and the services dependent upon them continued in a way which they had not done in previous disputes. But the policing of the strike, portrayed as were the riots, in the media as a dramatic confrontation with the forces of law and order, polarised some groups and attitudes and made divisive conflicts over order, policing, accountability, democracy etc. very apparent. For some commentators at least, events at Orgreave, Amforth etc. intensified policing and politicised it in new and dangerous ways (Scraton, 1985; Fine and Miller (eds), 1986).

Technological changes

Less dramatic than riots and strikes but nevertheless considerable in their impact on the public, were various changes of a technical and administrative kind – personal radios, computers etc. whose combined effect was to distance the police from public contact. Technical advances, for example, brought the notorious Unit Beat System into being (Alderson, 1979). More recently attempts have been made to replace it (Brown and Iles, 1985), but it is hard to wean police from what Hough (1987, p. 74) called 'the technological fix'.

The media and Irish reflections

Two final aspects of the changes in public perceptions and acceptance of the police during the 1970s and 1980s should be stressed. One concerns mass media reactions to crime stories. It is clear from research that the media now sensationalise crime stories (Chibnall,

1979; Smith, 1984) in ways that overdramatise them and lead to increased fears of crime. Some of this has been managed by the police (Chibnall, 1979; Reiner, 1985), but manipulation is a tool which can cut two ways, and there are indications that media stories add considerably to the amplification of deviance and crime in ways which bear heavily on police time and resources.

Finally, one feature of the changed context of modern British policing has not been stressed often, if at all: the implications of events in Northern Ireland for law and order in general and policing in particular in the rest of the United Kingdom. Hillyard (1986, p. 356), in reviewing Reiner's book (1985), suggested that 'this parochialism, which is characteristic of other law and order texts . . . is misplaced and the importance of Ireland to past and recent developments in Britain goes very much further [than Reiner allows].'

Northern Ireland presents both an image of a disordered society in which riot, murder and community conflict are commonplace, and that of a heavily policed society in which a police force (with military backing which grew and then declined during the period), armed and equipped in ways not yet acceptable on the mainland, strove to master civil strife and unrest. This situation, and its forceful representation in media images, has been a potent, if underresearched force in destabilising traditional notions of policing.

The wider context

Britain in the late twentieth century is arguably a more polarised society than it was at mid-century. Unemployment and poverty are rife; so are wealth and good fortune. Immense contrasts are obvious, for example in inner-city areas where competition for scarce housing brings together the old working class and the new managerial and professional groups. Policing a polarised, conflict-prone society, given that policing has largely to be based on consent, becomes more difficult for the police and is more resented by the citizenry.

These, then, are some of the social and historical reasons why policing became a much debated issue in the 1970s and 1980s. We can now turn to the response sociologists have made to this crisis and see how far their contributions clarify and illuminate the debate. The growth of work in this field has been quite remarkable. Writing in 1979, Holdaway (1979, p. 1) could legitimately argue that 'the

British police have remained largely hidden from sociological gaze.' He went on to suggest that the 'new deviance' and 'new criminology' approaches should have led to many more studies of the police:

> If . . . 'social control leads to deviance' is taken as a tenable and rich premise for studying deviance, then one would expect exponents of this position to place considerable emphasis on the police in their research.

Yet this had not happened:

> appreciation was with the deviant underdog, the dilemma of the prisoner rather than the prison officer. . . . There is a certain irony here, for the much needed revisionists of criminology found themselves giving as much attention to the deviant as to those they sought to correct. (Holdaway, 1979, p. 2)

Within seven years, however, there had been major changes:

> Not only have the police themselves been brought from the shadows to the centre of attention, but they have also been close to the centres of conflict and social change in society at large. . . . There has been an enormous increase in the number of official and unofficial reports, assessments and comments on policing, public order and crime. (Smith, 1986, p. viii)

Among these outpourings there has been a considerable sociological literature: participant observational studies, including some by serving policemen (Punch, 1979 and 1983; Holdaway, 1983); studies of police activities and attitudes (Smith and Gray, 1983; Jones, 1986); action research and evaluative studies (Blair, 1985; Heal *et al.*, 1985; Southgate, 1986); and socio-historical accounts (Philips, 1977 and 1983; Philip Cohen 1981). There have also been numerous critical accounts of policing (Bunyan, 1977; Hain, 1980; Scraton, 1985; Fine and Millar, 1986). Indeed, such a vast range of studies has engendered reviews and appraisals to guide readers through its complexities and contradictions (Johnson, 1981; Reiner, 1985; Reiner and Shapland, 1987).

In drawing out the insights which this work has to offer, as we fill out our portrait of the way sociologists have depicted crime, it is worth stressing several points. First, we need to remember the critical context of contemporary policing and police research:

Little attention is paid in most current work to the project of furthering a deeper theoretical understanding of policing . . . a major reason for the lack of theoretical advance is the way the debate has been dominated by immediate problems. It is difficult to develop a coherent framework for longterm theoretical development whilst being engaged in the thick of battle over specific instances or media 'crises'. (Reiner and Shapland, 1987, p. 1)

Much of the research is of a committed, perhaps even a partisan, kind, and the debates around it have political content and relevance. Debate, as we have already seen, is generally a sign of health and growth in social science, an indication that there is still life in theories and concepts. Discussions over policing issues are still in relatively early stages and are likely to develop considerably.

I suggested earlier that the police should not be thought of as the only formal agency of social control, let alone the only social control agency. It is partly due to their distinctive role, especially in relation to crime, but partly also to the contemporary crisis in confidence in the police, that they have been uniquely highlighted. Clearly, no sensibly constructed theorising about social order, social control and crime would *start* with the police. For that reason, I shall begin our exploration of the sociology of modern policing by placing it in its proper context of an understanding of the maintenance of social order and the production of conformity.

Why police?

I have already suggested in earlier chapters of this book that the history of sociological thought can be read as largely concerned with the problem of social order:

The fundamental ideas of European sociology are best understood as responses to the problem of order created by the beginning of the nineteenth century by the collapse of the old regime under the blows of industrialism and revolutionary democracy. (Nisbet, 1966, p. 21)

The work of the 'founding fathers' (Marx, Durkheim, Weber, Toennies, Simmel, etc.) can be interpreted as projects to explain the massive social changes they observed and to try to predict and create a new moral order or restore and recreate some modified semblance of the old (Nisbet, 1966, pp. 18–19). Certain key themes and concepts developed by the classical sociologists have continued to be central to the discipline ever since.

The most fundamental and far reaching of sociology's unit ideas is community . . . – the rediscovered symbolism of community . . . the ties of community – real or imagined, traditional or contrived – *come to form the image of the good society.* Community becomes the means of denoting legitimacy in associations as diverse as state, church, trade unions, revolutionary movement, profession and cooperative. (Nisbet, 1966, p. 47)

While, as Nisbet persuasively argues, the concept of 'community' was central to the thinking of all the great traditional sociologists, it was in the work of Durkheim that it was used with most originality and power. For Durkheim, the community has 'prior reality': it is from the community, not the individual, that states and rates are hence produced – suicide and religious belief, for example. Society, then, became the source of morality and social control for Durkheim. While Durkheim did not fully develop his remarkable and tantalising views on the normality and inevitability of crime, he did in *Suicide* extensively explore remedies to prevent that particular social ill, and in doing so provided an enormously influential analysis of, and recipe for, social control of deviant behaviour:

the only remedy for the ill is to restore enough consistency to social groups for them to obtain a firmer grip on the individual, and for him to feel himself bound to them. He must feel himself more solidary with a collective existence which precedes him in time, which survives him, and which encompasses him at all points. (Durkheim, 1952, pp. 373–4)

The influence of Durkheim's concept of social order and the steps necessary to re-establish it chiefly through strengthening key social groups, has been profound (Thompson, 1982, p. 145). The effects have been especially marked in some areas of the sociology of crime and deviance where his analysis of the sources of social solidarity and control have been taken seriously (Erikson, 1966). As we have noted before, this kind of usage tends to be highly selective; Durkheim himself was concerned with the nature of the state and with politics and was not inherently conservative or authoritarian (Giddens, 1971).

Durkheim's sociology was not a conservative hankering after a
return to the stability of the past, nor was it a manifestation of
an authoritarian urge to subjugate the individual to society . . .
there could be no going back to the mechanical solidarity of
simpler societies in which the individual was subordinated to the
collective conscience, based on uniformity . . . ideals of moral
individualism could only be fulfilled if society was organized in
such a way as to enable the individual to govern himself, that is
to control the appetites and be free to realize his potential and to
assist others to do the same. Solidary groups and group ethics
were required. (Thompson, 1982, p. 147)

That social order is maintained through a combination of social
and moral presssures, with power and individual autonomy as key
intervening variables, is one of the important insights in the heritage
of sociology. It leads us on to further questioning. Why and under
what conditions does order break down? Why especially does crime
take place? Why are coercive measures, such as policing, penal
policies etc. introduced? Are there alternatives? Durkheim himself,
as we saw earlier, believed that criminality was inherent in a healthy
society, and Erikson (1966), in a historical study of sixteenth-
century Massachusetts, suggested that pursuing and punishing
heresy and witchcraft could reinforce the bonds and mark out the
moral boundaries of a society. Durkheim also believed, as the
quotation from *Suicide* indicates, that social and moral order could
be repaired and improved through social groupings. These included
the family religion and occupational groups but not, Durkheim was
adamant, the nation state, which was too remote and meaningless
(Durkheim, 1952, p. 374).

Yet, of course, what we find in all advanced societies is that
formal, publicly run policing agencies take over certain key aspects
of the maintenance of social order, especially where crime is
concerned. Questions of the kind I suggested above have not until
fairly recently been asked by sociologists. Indeed, it has been
policemen themselves, especially those committed to the philosophy
of 'community policing' who have drawn, selectively, on his ideas:
'Durkheimians to a man – they pledged themselves implicitly
and sometimes explicitly, to the restoration of yesterday's moral
community' (Brown and Howes, 1975, p. 2). What we shall find
in practice are only certain answers to some of the queries I raised.

A fully developed sociology of social control should one day be able to offer us more, and we should not forget them while we examine the responses we do have. That such issues can now be seen as relevant issues at all owes a good deal to the modern questioning of the assumptions about the role and the nature of the police force in modern Britain.

Why did policing develop in Britain as it did?

Conventional histories describe the development of policing in Britain and the USA as very different from most European systems, which were often characterised by dual forces of civil and military or quasi military types (as in France, Spain and Italy), by specialised squads and forces for 'high policing' (as in France – see Brogden, 1987) or riot control (as in the Netherlands – see Punch, 1979), and in particular by much earlier and far less benign interventions by the state. In these conventional accounts, described by Reiner (1985) as the 'cop-sided view of history', professional policing is described as growing naturally

> as an inevitable and unequivocally beneficent institution . . . which had been developed by English pragmatic genius as a response to fearsome threats to social order and civilised existence. (Reiner, 1985, p. 9)

In these histories (for example, Reith, 1956; Critchley, 1978) social order in pre-industrial Britain was seen as maintained by the traditional system of constables and the watch (of which Dogberry and Verges in *Much Ado About Nothing* were typical). These forces derived their power from the community rather than central government. They were only replaced when the growing complexities of life and of crime in the eighteenth century and the inadequacies of the amateur response, together with certain crucial riots and disturbances, forced reform in the shape of Sir Robert Peel's Metropolitan (London) Police Act of 1829.

Reiner (1985, ch. I) has interrogated 'these views of the development of policing in Britain under a range of headings concerning the need for the "new" police, their social impact and the powers that controlled them'. He notes the functionalist nature of such accounts:

the irresistible force of industrialisation and its control problems, meeting the immovable object of stubborn English commitment to liberty, could result in only one outcome – the British bobby. (Reiner, 1985, p. 19).

Such accounts have, however, been increasingly challenged by modern research in what Reiner calls 'revisionist' accounts:

> in this the police are seen as a means . . . of maintaining the dominance of a ruling class against the interests and opposition of the various sections of the working class who constitute the majority of the population. (Reiner, 1985, p. 10)

In a useful comparative analysis, Reiner sets out the findings of more recent and more sophisticated historical studies which provide alternative views. In particular, these accounts suggest that popular acceptance of and trust in the police were far from complete. Philip Cohen (1981) described continued conflict in the working–class district of Islington in North London during the nineteenth and well into the twentieth century, with only the focus of the conflict changing. Brogden (1982) discerned a similar inheritance of antipathy to the police in Liverpool passed on from riots in Victorian times to Toxteth in the 1980s, while Scraton draws on a wide range of such accounts (his analysis appeared after Reiner's and is not discussed there) to argue that there is in Britain a 'controversial tradition of the police . . . commonly held assumptions that the police have a well-established history of policing by consent is (sic) a myth' (Scraton, 1985, p. 38).

Reiner argues that although providing a considerable advance on orthodox theories, revisionism is also flawed by teleology and by a widely assumed conflict model of society as opposed to the cohesion of the conservative views (Reiner, 1985, p. 82). He then attempts an interesting synthesis of these differing views (for some reviews of this 'controversial' approach see Brogden *et al.*, 1986; Hillyard, 1986). Reiner asserts that

> the ultimate question is whether a complex modern industrial society could exist without some sort of police force, in the minimal sense of a body of people mandated to intervene in situations potentially requiring the exercise of legitimate force. (p. 32)

He concludes that 'it seems utopian to suppose that we could do without a police force in any conceivable large-scale and complex industrial social order whether or not it was capitalist' (p. 33). However, Reiner argues (p. 33) that there was nothing necessary or inevitable about developments in Britain. Alternatives might, within limits, have been possible: for example, the Metropolitan Police *could* have had a different form of political control and accountability – say to a locally elected body, not the Home Secretary – had the relevant Act been passed by a later parliament after the Reform Act. Following this Reiner suggests that the origins of British policing have to be seen as the creation, maintenance and negotiation of a particular tradition 'embedded in a social order riven by structured bases of conflict, not fundamental integration' (p. 47).

Such matters are not just the stuff of erudite debate about the past between sociologists and social historians (see Styles, 1987, for an example of the latter taking the former to task). They are highly relevant today, for now and for the future, because they relate to discussions about the *legitimacy* of police authority, about their designated *roles* in society and how these may have changed, and the *kinds* of police and *forms* of policing consequently adopted. These are relevant issues, not only for sociologists trying to understand how society is controlled or crime policed, but also for a variety of other actors.

Lord Scarman, for example, in his report on 'the Brixton disturbances' of 1981, explicitly called on the (supposed) tradition of consensual policing in Britain and on the (apparently) unproblematic nature of their function:

> The function of our police has been authoritatively defined as 'The prevention of crime . . . the protection of life and property, the preservation of public tranquillity' . . . the primary duty of the police is to maintain 'the Queen's peace', which has been described as 'the normal state of society', for in civilized society, normality is a state of public tranquillity. (Scarman, 1986, pp. 102–3) [the first quotation cited by Scarman is from Mayne's instructions to the 'New Police of the Metropolis' in 1829, the second from Newsam's account of the Home Office, 1955.])

Beliefs about *why* we have police and what they are for are most powerful, for reasons we shall shortly consider, within the police force itself. That they may not in fact be shared by other groups in society is an important conclusion derived from modern social research, and one which has consequences for strategies such as community policing and situational crime prevention (see Chapter 7), and also for much wider issues such as the policing of industrial disputes on political protest.

Legitimacy

From his analysis of historical accounts and his own sociological perspective, Reiner concludes that the British police did achieve a period of prolonged legitimacy (from 1856 to 1981) based on consensus policing. This was a constructed consent, and

> was the product of specific aspects of police organisational policy. It was also helped by (and helped) the process whereby the working class, the main source of initial hostility to the new police, came to be incorporated into the political and economic institutions of British society. (Reiner, 1985, p. 51)

Manning had argued that, while there were parallels in the history of policing in Britain and the USA,

> England manifests a greater degree of ethnic and cultural homogeneity . . . political consensus led in England to the joint-national-local showing of control of policing . . . the degree of defence to authority and consensus concerning the domain of law appear to be greater in England. (Manning, 1979, p. 43)

Contradicting this view, Reiner argues:

> the opposite is the case. The architects of the benign and dignified English police image, Peel, Rowan and Mayne, adopted the policies they did because of *the strength of opposition to the very existence of the police*. (Reiner, 1985, p. 51)

Miller (1979, p. 14), while painting a picture of Victorian England less riven by conflict than this, also argued that 'the police tradition cannot be explained as the result of a consensual society. The London police were born and matured in a period of often intense social conflict.'

Reiner lists eight factors which he claims led to the British police achieving the classic and near-sacred Weberian transformation from power to authority: 'Police *power* i.e. the capacity to inflict legal sanctions including force, had been transmuted into *authority* power which is accepted as at least minimally legitimate' (Reiner, 1985, p. 51). The eight factors are:

1. bureaucratic organisation
2. the rule of law
3. the strategy of minimal force
4. non-partisanship
5. the service role
6. preventive policing
7. police effectiveness
8. incorporation of the working class.

The first seven were all aspects of police policy, consciously used to achieve legitimacy; only the last was part of the 'changing social, economic and political context' (Reiner, 1985, p. 61) and thus beyond direct police control. It is central to Reiner's argument that the decline in police legitimacy which occurred from the 1950s onwards was due to failings and disasters in each of these areas, with the alienation of the black community as the final and most catastrophic (p. 81).

In a later chapter, Reiner makes a fascinating analysis of the way mass media images of the police affect perceptions of them and have consequences for their legitimacy and authority. Police–public encounters are, he points out, with a relatively small and powerless group 'at the base of the social hierarchy' (p. 137). For the rest, especially women and older men, media presentations form the basis of their perceptions and attitudes. Analysing films, detective stories and television series, Reiner finds 'Both the "factual" and "fictional" presentations of the police broadly legitimate the police role in presenting them as necessary and for the most part effective', although he does discern certain distinct trends. The long era of consensus was reflected in police fiction, but changes in the 1960s in turn led to a renewed politicisation, while by the 1980s the reassertion of legitimacy was once again a recurrent theme. The extraordinary number of television police series featuring women police officers in the 1980s might, for example, be seen as associating the controversial image which the police had by then acquired with 'feminine' qualities suggesting virtue, order and decency. Reiner's analysis of the achievement and decline of police legitimacy is by no means definitive. It does, however, show how an important topic can be illuminated by research.

What kind of police?

The police are no longer a closed book to sociologists. Researchers have ridden in panda cars (Smith and Gray, 1983), gone on drugs raids and homicide cases (Punch, 1979) and even observed the elusive CID (Criminal Investigation Department) (Chatterton, 1976). Some police *are* sociologists and some sociologists were police. What does all this research tell us about the police, what kinds of people they are, and why? Since the police have both considerable powers – for example, to arrest, to search for stolen goods, to deprive citizens of their liberty – and legitimacy to do these tasks, it is obviously important to know to whom such powers have been entrusted.

An occupational culture

All accounts agree that the British police (and USA forces, too – see Reiss, 1971; Skolnick, 1969) are characterised by a distinctive and powerful occupational culture. The Home Office's own research studies acknowledge its existence and indeed the limitations it imposes on police work:

> the occupational culture favours a law enforcement approach to policing over a broader social problem-solving approach. This in turn leads to stereotyping and the labelling of people in terms of the way they impinge upon the job of law enforcement or detract from its pursuit. (Southgate, 1986, p. 56)

In this particular study, although the characteristics of 'cop culture' (Reiner, 1985) are not spelt out, the scripts of a series of police–public encounters give dramatic and graphic accounts of some aspects attributed to conventional police culture, especially racial prejudice (Southgate, 1986, pp. 90 and 119).

Participant researchers have acknowledged the strength of police culture and found that it even affected them and their work. Smith and Gray (1983, p. 298) found it necessary to recuperate from time to time and to restore the sense of our own identity (the norms of working groups are so powerful that they soon begin to impose themselves on the researcher as well as the official in the group).

Punch, too, confesses:

I over-identified perhaps too readily and this doubtless endangered my research role. For the patrol group is a cohesive social unit and the policeman's world is full of seductive interest so that it is all too easy to 'go native'. (Punch, 1979, p. 16)

Exactly the same term was used by Holdaway in his thoughtful and sensitive account of his covert research at 'Hilton' police station. As both a serving police sergeant and a research sociologist, he was well acquainted with the system and its culture, while holding different values himself. He described the pressures to conform, and his own resistance to them. After a drunken driver had dashed out of the charge room and had been returned he noted:

The rules of the occupational culture direct that a loss of police control like this should be redressed by physical contact, but I did not offer that contact, and my colleagues saw that I did not. In this way I began to define the limits of their and my tolerance. (Holdaway, 1983, p. 7)

Holdaway observed that:

The risk of 'going native' was always present . . . but when I became too involved in policing I was often pulled back by a particularly distasteful event . . . [once] after hearing a conversation about race relations, I wrote in my diary: I . . . want nothing to do with such sentiments . . . underneath these policemen are ruthless and racist. (Holdaway, 1983, p. 10)

After completing his research, Holdaway left the police force and became an academic.

We come, then, to that situation nicely described by Holdaway as when 'sociologists first asked the police that piercing research question, "Hello, hello, what's going on here then?"' (p. 16).

Studies in the USA in the early 1970s documented certain aspects of an occupational culture among policemen. Westley (1970) found the police to be hostile, abrasive and even violent to the public, especially to black citizens. Such apparently illegal behaviour seemed to be possible because, in a situation fraught with anxiety, threats and danger, the lowest level of officers forged their own rough and tough tools for urban survival. Skolnick (1966) drew on Westley's work, and in a much larger study concluded too that there was a 'working personality' encouraged in policemen, focused on two elements of danger and authority. Again, the favoured traits are courage, secrecy, suspicion, loyalty, assertiveness and authoritarianism. One of the first comparable British studies was Maureen Cain's of policemen and their community roles in Birmingham and in rural Suffolk. Cain (1973) described the police as isolated and creating their own group norms to cope with various features of their jobs.

The working group of constables was of primary importance in defining their own policing role and notions of normal policing. The pursuit of crime and criminals were normal and 'authentic', so too were illegal acts of violence and control which furthered those ends. Secrecy and group loyalty were crucial to maintaining the group, as was 'easing behaviour' for the quiet times (Cain, 1973, pp. 45–76).

Holdaway (1983, p. 19) criticised the social construction of the 'symbolic assailant' described by Skolnick, pointing out that the latter accepted officers' own definitions of danger and hostility from the public. Box (1983, p. 95) is slightly more inclined, as are the above authors, to accept the police's own definitions of their roles and situation. He does, however, point out that the relative isolation of the police and the persistence of their 'subculture' prevents them testing out, and modifying, their theories about public attitudes and behaviour.

A number of later studies both flesh out more fully the picture of the occupational culture and situate it clearly in its police and social setting. They also relate it to documented police activities and public expectations. In their studies of police and people in London (commissioned, incidentally, by the Metropolitan Police) Smith and Gray (1983, p. 336) observed a series of 'informally understood objectives and norms and showed how they influence the general pattern of policing and the detail of police behaviour'.

Since patrolling is rather aimless and boring, 'a considerable amount of police behaviour can best be understood as a search for some *interest, excitement or sensation*' (p. 338, emphasis added). Car chases, pursuing criminals, even violence were seen as antidotes to this. Boring patrols were *not* seen as appropriate, but the police culture did clearly define 'good' policing in terms of a series of polarities: between 'good arrests', 'good villains' (sic) and 'good results' as opposed to 'rubbish' (pp. 346–50). 'Good' policing meant crime work and, above all, arresting serious professional criminals. Gray (Smith and Gray, p. 348) observed the respect with which three PCs treated just such a 'good cat burglar' and the reflected status aura they acquired from him. Their observation held for uniformed officers, but the CID had somewhat different values, including what they described as 'the cultivation of a special idea of manliness that [has] little to do with achieving results, in terms of practical police work' (p. 349). 'Rubbish' police work was typified by domestic disputes and disturbances which the officers thought were not their provenance or concern (p. 349). 'Being seen to be dominant and not being seen to lose face' (p. 351) were highly valued in the working groups observed by Smith and Gray. They recount several examples of officers asserting their dominance (pp. 351–5). However, they also point out that there is a contradiction between 'the high value placed on dominance and a lack of the skills needed to achieve it legitimately' (p. 351) – that is, the manipulative and psychological skills which are generally the most successful in such situations. Like the earlier researchers, the Policy Studies Institute study found that group solidarity was extremely strong. This was manifested in rapid responses to support calls for urgent assistance to colleagues (p. 355) and also, more significantly, in attitudes to discipline. Internal informal discipline by peers was preferred to external sanctions: 'Control from within the group was not only less damaging to the officers concerned, but also less threatening to the group as a whole' (p. 356)

Among the most significant parts of the account of police culture given by Smith and Gray is their depiction of its strongly machismo atmosphere, especially as manifested in the CID. They record four key elements in this atmosphere: alcohol, violence, sex and a lack of human sympathy. 'Drinking seems to have a great importance in the lives of police officers' (p. 363), and clubs and pubs were major foci of *work* for CID officers and of recreation for uniform officers. Not to drink was seen as unprofessional (p. 365) and unmanly, and one of the researchers was tested out in a drinking ritual at the start of the study. Police drinking sessions were the setting for frequent expressions of the other values of the macho culture:

> There was a great deal of conversation about sex, in very gross language, in which the men were always conquerors and the women 'slags' and 'whores' . . . This talk about sex, women and drink was interspersed with descriptions of violent incidents that the PCs had witnessed, heard about or taken part in. (p. 369)

Talk of violence was one way of expressing 'the central meaning of the job for most police officers – the exercise of authority and force . . . is for them the main symbol of authority and power' (p. 369).

Although some 9 per cent of the lower rank officers were female at the time of the study, and despite the fact that, following the Sex Discrimination Act 1975 police forces have to be integrated and non-discriminatory (Jones, 1986), Smith and Gray discerned 'a "cult of masculinity" which also has a strong influence on policemen's behaviour towards women, towards victims of sexual offences and towards sexual offenders' (p. 372). As well as making work difficult for policewomen (pp. 376–7) such attitudes can hamper the work of policemen themselves. Smith and Gray observed, for example, that many calls answered by the police were not to the preferred crime-and-conflict scenarios but to ones, such as domestic disturbances, disputes with neighbours, deaths and suicides or episodes of mental illness, where help, sympathy and advice were required. Here police culture was deficient, denigrating such contacts and providing only negative evaluations of the skills needed to manage them. 'The denigration of women implicit in canteen talk is also a devaluing of qualities associated with women that are actually required in much police work' (p. 373).

A further dimension of police culture which was extensively documented in the PSI studies was racialism. Although Smith and Gray insist that the grossly racist attitudes and abuse they heard did not always lead to racist behaviour towards black people (p. 404), they do nevertheless record several cases of racist influence on cases (p. 388 *et seq.*) These cases involved both stopping and arresting black people for alleged crimes and the handling of allegedly racist attacks on black people.

In reviewing his own contribution and that of a wide range of studies to depicting 'cop culture', Reiner lists a broadly similar set of headings. He too identified a 'machismo syndrome' (1978, p. 161) with its concomitants of racial prejudice and sexism and focus on excitement. But Reiner goes further in arguing that excitement and action are linked to, and made more significant by, the policeman's sense of mission – 'he is one of the good guys' (1985, p. 89). Isolation and solidarity are also, in Reiner's view, characteristic of the bases of 'cop culture', as are both pragmatism (p. 103) and conservatism (p. 97). In considering these elements he does stress that there are considerable variations in styles 'of individual police perspective around the core elements of the culture' (1985, p. 103). From a variety of studies Renier (1985, pp. 105–6) synthesises four distinct types:

1. the 'bobby' – the ordinary copper
2. the 'new centurion' – the street-wise crusader against crime and disorder
3. the 'uniform carrier' – the lazy cynic
4. the 'professional' – ambitious and career-conscious.

From *'Inside the British Police'*, Holdaway (1983) delineated the way in which the officers at the Hilton police station socially constructed their own culture. This had similar focal concerns: 'action and excitement, the control of space and persons held in custody, the use of force' (p. 134), and racism – all of which are similar to other accounts. Holdaway, though suggests a subtler reading of the stories, jokes and reactionary attitudes as a narrative or myth which helps to make sense of a disordered world:

> All of these anecdotes, stories and jokes feed and sustain the occupational culture because they stand between the officers and groups in Hilton who can try to call them to account. They may be true; they may sometimes be false. Accuracy is not the point of narrative, which selects and reigns particular experiences of policing at Hilton to sustain the world of the lower ranks. (Holdaway, 1983, p. 154)

Despite his appreciative analysis, Holdaway finally insists that reform of the police will only come about through addressing the problems of the lower ranks and their culture and changing them: 'The tightly bound culture of the lower ranks has to be broken into; the ritual sanctity of police policy has to be demystified' (p. 175).

Jones (1986) reported a study of the police force of pseudonymous 'Medshire' in which police culture, especially its macho aspects, had considerable impact on the police themselves – that is, on the female officers of the force. She described as 'folklore' and 'ritual arguments' the set of assumptions and beliefs used to justify informal selection barriers to female applicants and officers. These centred around arguments about 'the "unfeminine" "nature of police work"' (Jones, 1986, p. 133 *et seq.*), the physical stamina required, and the risks involved in the job (pp. 148–51). *Appearing* to have authority was seen as crucial, too, as were beliefs about innate differences in emotionality. In recruiting to the police, 'the "mark of affinity" argument would seem to have a compelling relevance to the police service, given the masculine occupational subculture' (p. 131).

In Jones's book, which is essentially an analysis of the formal equality required of the police service contrasted with the formidable structural and cultural inequalities practised within it, she frequently points to the mismatch of the 'cop culture' myth and the mundane reality of the police world (ch. VII). Hers is one of many voices which have pointed out just how different from the 'chasing criminals' folklore is daily life in a police station. First, and most obviously, a mass of research shows that most calls to the police – 80 per cent in one study (Reiss, 1971) – do not relate to crime at all, but to calls for help. Punch and Naylor (1973) found in their study of three small Essex towns that 'service' calls ranged from 50 per cent to over 70 per cent of all those received by the police during a study period. In other studies 'crime incidents' represented only about one third (34 to 36 per cent) of all the incidents attended by police patrols (Hough, 1985, p. 11). Another third of incidents were of a social service type. These findings, and many similar ones (Smith and Gray, 1983; Holdaway, 1983) support Punch's contention that the police are a 'secret social service' (1979, p. 6).

This aspect of police work has in various ways been acknowledged, although without apparently denting the macho image of real policing. The movement for 'community policing', for example, is clearly related to welfare and moral goals and is aimed in Alderson's 'central concept' at 'motivating the good in society' (Moore and Browning, 1981, p. 10). That the police are not well equipped for their secret social service role and that they may be blinkered by their own expectations and culture, are points well illustrated in a

Home Office study (Southgate, 1986), which presents the scripts
of some stereotypical and clumsy police–public encounters which
are meant to form the basis of new skills training for the police
and to emphasise the commitment to 'the importance of the human
dimension of policing skills in training' (Home Office, 1985).

'Shifting the focus from crime' (Hough, 1987, p. 77) in this way
is one means by which, Hough suggests, a further aspect of the
police-as-crime-controllers notion might be tackled. For as he
(pp. 71–3) and others (Morris and Heal, 1981; Clarke and Hough,
1984) have pointed out, research demonstrates 'that the police have
a more limited *capability* for crime control than is generally assumed'
(p. 70).

Thus the police do not chase out most crime: 85 to 90 per cent
of offences are brought to them by reports from victims, witnesses,
etc. (Clarke and Hough, 1984, p. 3). At the same time, most crime
actually goes unreported and unrecorded (Hough and Mayhew,
1983 and 1985). Even when crimes are known to the police, they
are not actually very effective at clearing them up – only some 9.5
offences per officer per annum – and rates of clear-up have been
falling as crime rates have risen (Kinsey *et al.*, 1986, pp. 25–8). In
view of all this evidence, it is pertinent to ask why the occupational
culture of the police remains so wedded to an image of policing
that is neither valid nor achievable, as disillusioned managerial
studies have also shown (Clarke and Hough, 1984; Reiner, 1985;
Hough, 1987).

Following Skolnick, Reiner (1985, p. 109) argues that the culture
develops from 'similar elements in the police role in any advanced
industrial liberal democracy, notably authority and danger.' Yet
this belies the findings already quoted above, that police work is
more likely to be peace-keeping than crime chasing, social service
than social conflict, and mundane and boring than active and
exciting. It can be dangerous, if seductive, to accept the functionalist
notions implied in the notion of subcultural fit, as we saw in
Chapter 3; just because we have certain kinds of people acting as
our police and they develop a distinctive protective and supportive
subculture, it does not follow, morally or socially, that this situation
has to continue. Part, at least, of the modern crisis in policing must
have its roots in the internal workings of the police, their culture
and their organisational forms and the conflicts these help to
engender or sustain (Box, 1983; Scraton, 1985) with certain sectors

of the public. Smith and Gray (1983) and Jones (1986) pointed out that the emphasis on macho culture in the police and the exclusion and marginalisation of policewomen and 'feminine' qualities was counter-productive. This has in some measure been recognised in changes in the handling of rape cases (Blair, 1985), where considerable public concern (Toner, 1982) and pressure were manifested (but see Chambers and Millar, 1987).

Accountability and control

I began the sociological account of policing outlined in this chapter by noting its roots in recent crises. Exploring this account can help us understand those crises better, although it will not necessarily give clear guidelines for solving them. Some issues can be clarified a little. The debate about the 'crisis in policing' has tended to revolve around issues to do with the control and accountability of the police. Several scenarios can be discerned, all of which, if fully enacted, would have very different consequences for policing. Among the most widely discussed are:

1. The threat of the police state
2. The police-alienation problem
3. Community policing as a solution:
   (a) the police version
   (b) the partnership model
4. Professional policing
5. Law and order models

It should be noted that these are all simplified models, and more could be elicited (Reiner, 1985).

The threat of the police state

According to this view of present and future policing (Scraton, 1985; Scraton and Gordon, 1984) Britain is dominated by a class-based system of criminal justice and social control, promoted *for* the interests of the well-to-do and *against* those of the poor (Scraton, 1985, p. 162). The police are not accountable democratically and are moving inexorably towards a national police force. The solutions to the perceived menace of a police state lie either in major social changes, an end to poverty, inequality, etc., or more mundanely in popular and democratic scrutiny and monitoring of police work (Scraton, p. 169). There is much scepticism in this scenario about democratic accountability and local crime control, although it is not quite clear (a) how different 'monitoring' is from these approaches, or (b) how it can be made effective without other means of communication and accountability.

Police alienation

Within the 'new left realist' scenario of Kinsey, Lea and Young *et al.* (1984, 1985, 1986) the police are seen as having mismanaged their relations with the public, especially in the inner cities and as a result of withdrawing from foot patrols. Crime is recognised as a 'real' problem in working–class areas, for which the solution is a combination of 'minimalist' but effective policing, locally initiated.

Community policing

As formulated by Alderson (1979) and Moore and Brown (1981) this involved a shift to *proactive* policing, community *consultation* and enquiry (but not control), and the redevelopment of local informal social controls. Central to the notion is the idea of policing as a

> negotiated contract between the public and the police so that they both identify that the maintenance of law is a cooperative rather than a delegated responsibility. (Moore and Brown, 1981, p. 116)

Shapland and Vagg (1987) identify an alternative model, based on their surveys of public demands, in which there could be a partnership between police and public 'in which public views about policing would be acknowledged to have weight in determining the scope and manner of policing, and in which decision making would be a joint enterprise' (p. 61). This would constrain local police far more than at present and involve a need for 'the police to give up at least some of their symbolic ownership of disorder and crime to the public' (p. 63).

Professional policing

This view, espoused by senior police officers and by Lord Scarman (1981) and set out in Reiner (1985, pp. 206–12) involves reasserting police legitimacy by improving the craft skills and the achievements of the police – for instance, in crime clear-up rates, better management, etc. – in ways that are deemed responsive to public demand and public disquiet. Research is also to be used instructively to locate problems and improve training and skills.

Law and order

In a scenario popular with tabloid newspapers, among others, as well as some of the police themselves, the police would be given wider powers to control and/or detect crime. Popular indignation over certain kinds of crime would be reflected in the severity of punishment and the discretion accorded to police in the handling of cases.

Social order and policing

In order to explore the implications of any of these, and the alternatives which can be envisaged, we need to return to some of the basic questions and understandings about social order and the policing of that order with which we began. For example, we need to recall what social order is and how it is achieved and maintained. Thus, ideas about community policing must be set against a knowledge of what communities are, whether they can be said to exist and where, how acceptable their control is, and so on. In his provocative and seminal work on neighbours, Philip Abrams (whose work is summarised in Bulmer, 1986) doubted the existence today of 'caring communities', especially in precisely those areas of old, run-down inner cities where crime is most prevalent.

We must remember, too, how small the role of the police is in the production of social order and query if when that is the apparent goal of policing, we have the right forces properly socialised and equipped for the task. Crises have thrown spotlights on to the police, but theirs is not a solo act; many others play important parts which have been too little explored so far. It is crucial, too, to stress how small a part in the police remit crime control itself plays, and to consider the consequences of this. Should it be more or less central? Are there alternative ways of handling crime? The Crown Prosecution Service, for example, has already taken away certain tasks and responsibilities.

Finally, we have to look at policing in its broader context or contexts. Its social history can, as we have seen, provide vital keys to understanding its present. The social structures of both the wider society and the police organisation itself are central to interpreting and predicting the development of policing. McBarnet (1979), for example, has argued that legal frameworks, not the occupational culture, determine the use and abuse of police discretion. Whichever interpretation is used ultimately has very different consequences for any model of police accountability. Issues such as local and national cultures, especially changes in values and sensitive matters such as race and religion, also need to be explored. I can do little more here than set out an agenda for future research, grounded in some of the key problems of the present, but going well beyond them to topics central both to the sociological tradition and the concerns of a troubled society.

The wider context

I have deliberately kept to examples of Anglo-American policing in this chapter so that the subject matter can remain manageable. It should be stressed, however, that the points about the sociology of order and of community control are relevant to all societies. Anthropologists have had much to say, often in a Durkheimian fashion, about maintaining order in pre-industrial societies (Malinowski, 1926; Douglas, 1970). It seems that those societies which have lower official crime rates are those with high levels of solidarity and pressures to conform, such as Japan or Switzerland (Clinard, 1978). On the other hand, stress which develops from economic and social upheavals is blamed for rising rates of crime and disorder (Box, 1987). One US study predicts rising rates of domestic violence and of rape in Third World countries as economic development produces changes in the social system which will threaten men's dominance over their wives (Bowker, 1985). Maintaining order and all the related issues of why and how to police are therefore likely to be both common to many societies and to become more prevalent with economic growth and social change.

Policing problems are distinctive in their local historical and cultural forms. Several nations have faced major postwar problems over confidence in the agencies of law and order because of wartime co-operation with occupying forces, as in France and Denmark after the Second World War. Legitimacy has also been a major problem in West Germany, in South Africa and in Ireland. Corruption of the police is regarded as a serious issue in societies as diverse as some Latin American and Eastern bloc countries. Elsewhere, the existence of several different policing agencies – civil and military in Italy and Spain, local and federal in the USA and West Germany – pose particular problems. While diversity is marked, there are clear common threads of legitimacy, control and authority linking these situations.

7 Social Responses to Crime: Control, Prevention and Victim Support

Finding a common and coherent thread running through the sociology of crime was, I argued in Chapter 1, a task beyond even the fairytale heroine who has to spin golden silk by morning or face death in the story of *Rumpelstiltskin*. Nevertheless, we can put the range of sociological understanding to considerable use. First, sociology provides *accounts* and descriptions: sociologists describe situations, such as those in family life or at work. They also analyse those situations in relation to one another: sociologists have shown, for example, how family background is related to educational achievement. We might call this the landscape-with-figures aspect of sociology. Second, and more contentiously, sociological findings can be used in certain social situations. Some of these may be in social policies: the findings mentioned above influenced a series of initiatives in pre-school provision in the USA and in Britain in the 1960s and 1970s in order to compensate children for the relative disadvantages of their family backgrounds. This aspect we might call 'applied sociology'. (It is important to remember that applying sociology can be a highly political and politicised act, something perhaps not suggested by this innocuous term.) In this chapter I shall examine both the landscape of crime portrayed by sociologists, including the most modern perspectives, and a range of applications in the policy field. Not all of the latter have strictly sociological antecedents, but where they do not they can be seen as parts of wider projects which do.

Most of the sociology textbooks on my shelves have the word 'society' in their title (as, of course, does this one). This suggests, at least by implication, and often by overt claim, that they give an account of society, or that part of it relevant to class, or industrialisation. Studies of crime could not be exempted from this claim, from *Street Corner Society* (Whyte, 1955) via *Crime in a Complex Society* (Knudten, 1970) to *Women, Crime and Society* (Leonard, 1982). Numerous titles seem at any rate to offer us a view of crime in or with society. How successfully have they done so?

In preceding chapters we saw how it was possible to put together a picture of crime in society by drawing on a series of loosely structured key developments in the discipline and assessing their contributions. The Chicago School gave us an urban sociology in which it was possible to locate crime, city gangs and social disorganisation; anomie and subcultural theories focused attention on male juvenile delinquents in criminogenic settings; new deviancy theories switched perspectives from the controlled to the controllers, a perspective partially determining at least the range of studies of the police. Now it is important to remember here a distinction made by Cressey (Sutherland and Cressey, 1978) about the sociology of crime, in which he follows Durkheimian notions and distinguishes those aspects of theories which explain and predict *patterns* of social behaviour – such as crime rates – from those which explain why particular *individuals* become criminal. Cressey argued that adequate theories must deal with both aspects and that there must be consistency between them. Albert Cohen insisted that the latter is really a *psychological* not a sociological problem, even though the answers 'are obviously closely related' (Cohen, 1966, p. 46).

From these comments and from what we know generally about sociological explanation, we might expect that most sociology of crime would indeed have been about 'the properties of the culture or social structure to which we attribute the pattern of deviance' (Cohen, 1966, p. 47) – characteristics, that is, of systems and institutions, processes and interactions. We might, in short, expect the sociologist-as-artist to have produced architectural landscapes, engineering drawings, even to show us how crime is generated and controlled. Yet, as the earlier chapters show, that is not so. By and large, sociologists have produced *portraits* of offenders, or at any rate of certain kinds of the more notable and depictable offenders. Sociology's ancestral home has a rogue's gallery as one of the main parts of its inheritance.

This is of course something of an exaggeration: it is possible to find examples of studies which focus on communities or on institutions, the latter especially in the work done on social control in the 1970s and 1980s. Even so, there have been clear tendencies to focus on offenders, not the offended, on delinquents and not their delinquencies, their audiences or their settings. I think there are two reasons for this: one can best be attributed to the sociologists' search for excitement. Sociologists of crime have often helped, in their choice of subjects, to glamourise deviance; it is not always true to say that 'where journalists are interested in the dramatic, sociologists are interested in the routine' (Dingwall, 1982, p. 617). This has not necessarily been merely a matter of taste; it has also had social reform purposes. Bennett (1981) argued that the gathering and *publication* of oral histories of delinquent careers occurred only under certain social and historical conditions and were used to advocate, and persuade public opinion towards, social reforms. One of the most interesting parts of Bennett's argument is his citing of negative cases, of researchers such as Healy and Alinsky who collected stories from delinquents but did not publish them. Healy, Bennett argues, did not aim to address public but only professional opinion, while Alinsky sought social change through political, not academic, channels.

The other, and much more important, influence on the study of crime, and not just its study by sociologists, has been the long shadow cast by positivism. Indeed, some of the key debates in criminology, especially in areas affecting penal philosophy (Wootton, 1959) have involved positivist and classical or neoclassical concepts of crime and criminals. Taylor and his colleagues (1973, p. 10) indeed argue that

since the end of the nineteenth century, courtroom and penal practice has been dominated by a neoclassical model, whilst most psychological and sociological studies of criminal and deviant action have been carried out within a more or less positivist framework.

Many of the concepts and their consequences discussed in this chapter reflect these models and the tensions they generate. One of its main themes is discerned changes in the relative prominence of these models and it is worth spending a little time on clarifying this important distinction.

Classical, neoclassical and positivist criminology

Writing in the middle of the twentieth century, the authors of a distinguished text could approvingly report a revolution achieved by the 'Italian or Positive School of Criminology' (Lombroso, Ferri and Garofalo):

> all were in agreement that the problem involved scientific understanding and treatment of the offender rather than a discussion of penalties. They transferred the emphasis from the crime to the criminal – a great contribution. Prior to the work and writings of these pioneers, free will and moral responsibility were universally accepted in accounting for crime. It remained for the Italian school to shatter this fallacy among most students of crime causation. (Barnes and Teeters, 1951, p. 143)

What Barnes and Teeters were referring to here was an important, though by no means final or total, change. The first, or classical, revolution in the study of crime, is widely attributed to the enormously influential work of Cesare Beccaria, who in his *Essay on Crimes and Punishment* (1764) set out a series of key principles. Beccaria based his programme of reform on three key assumptions about human nature and society and three consequent ones about preventing crime and punishing it. In characteristic 'enlightenment' fashion, he assumed that human beings were rational and responsible for their own actions while at the same time having propensities to commit crime if not checked. He viewed society as being based upon a social contract which permitted, among other things, the state to punish wrongdoers, and finally his values were utilitarian. As a consequence, he urged the replacement of the cruel, complex and archaic criminal justice systems of his day by ones based on rationality:

1. a rational *measure* of crime as equal to the social injury it caused, and not to its status as a sin, for example,
2. the rational *prevention* of crime through clear and sensible laws and procedures;
3. rational *punishment* of crime by speedy trials and penalties *appropriate to the offence* – e.g. property offences should always lead to fines in order to discourage crime

This work had both immediate and lasting impact. It

achieved instant popularity, and it played a central role in developing concepts of law and crime in both the American and French Revolutions. . . . Every history of penal reform stresses its influence throughout Europe and how Beccaria and Bentham became the founders of what would remain for a century the main western school of criminology. (Jenkins, 1984, pp. 112–21)

What was novel in Beccaria's work was his emphasis on volition and rationality, individual responsibility and the possibilities of 'systems' of deterrence and punishment. Clearly, there are many flaws in such an approach – for example, the insistence that all crime is rational action. There are also contradictions: some criminals, the wholly destitute, for instance, may have reasonable grounds such as hunger for theft, so how can the state punish them? Yet its influence was not only widespread on penal codes from Prussia to Pennsylvania, but persists in the recurring concern with criminal *acts* and with issues such as deterrence (which I want to address later in this chapter). In the article already cited, Jenkins reassesses Beccaria's radicalism, insisting that his influence was profound precisely because

his modest, limited and conservative tract was widely seized upon because it filled an urgent social need . . . Beccaria's work stands as a conservative monument, the first great effort to cure crime without curing the society which produced it. (Jenkins, 1984, pp. 112 and 128)

Nevertheless, Jenkins notes the renaissance of classical ideas in the late twentieth century:

Beccaria . . . argued that fixed and predictable sentences were the best way to ensure an element of certainty for promoting deterrence. After a century of positivism and the rehabilitative ideal, such ideas have once again come into vogue . . . classicism is a central issue both for the history of criminology and for its contemporary development. (p. 112)

The positivist revolution so applauded by Barnes and Teeters followed various 'neoclassical' attempts to modify Beccarian principles. Thus the Victorian British penal system, characterised by Garland (1985, p. 14) as 'precisely' classical, had, by the end of the century, excluded children, madmen and others from the definition of responsible criminal (Garland, p. 15). It was the switch to positivism, pioneered in the work of Lombroso, which was to bring about an even more dramatic and influential change. Lombroso and his colleagues focused on individual offenders and their traits, in Lombroso's case the supposedly scientifically measured physical differences between captive populations of prisoners and non-criminal controls. Lombroso's work was relatively soon shown to be statistically inadequate, and his assumptions about atavism etc. ludicrous (Mannheim, 1965). Again, however, by the shift of focus he accomplished, his work had influence, not only beyond its merit, but in fields, such as the sociological study of deviance, in which it would seem an alien transplant. The persistence of the positivist paradigm is one of the most marked features of twentieth-century social science, and it played an important part in the study of crime.

> Positivism saw its role as the systematic elimination of the free will 'metaphysics' of the classical school – and its replacement by a science of society, taking on for itself the task of the eradication of crime. (Taylor *et al.*, 1973, p. 10)

It is not hard to see what some of the attractions of positivism could be. There is the striving for science – for the accuracy, methods and measurement of the natural scientists and for their achievements and acclaim. For criminologists, who are rarely without some wish to apply their knowledge, there is the added temptation that findings with the status of scientific data are beyond doubt and also beyond politics; they can form a more certain base for change and hence for power. Nevertheless, there have always been tensions within sociology between proponents of 'scientific' methods and other more humanistic approaches. Bulmer (1984, Chapters 9 and 10) provides a fascinating account of such tensions in the Chicago School and how they came to be, literally, carved in stone. We have already seen how both disorganisation and subculture theories suffered from positivistic defects: from tendencies to overpredict crime, to treat delinquent subjects like puppets and not as individual actors with wills to whom action had meaning. The critique of such approaches came, as we have seen, from within the discipline, and while it was in part a break with older traditions and can be so presented, it reflected an alternative view which had a long history.

I now want to look at the pivotal, if elusive, work of David Matza, which both traces the reaction against positivism I have described and is also part of it. We have already looked at some of Matza's contributions in Chapters 3 and 4. I shall then review the work of E. H. Sutherland and his successors in the study of white-collar crime. Both Matza and Sutherland stand in their own right as contributors to the sociological inheritance. Within the work of both of these can also be found threads which link them to some of the most recent work on the study of crime and make possible fuller and closer portrayal.

Matza and naturalism

David Matza's work is at once sensitive, penetrating and elusive. His ideas are not entirely consistent and he can prove disarming: 'what in hell *did* I think when writing those two books?' (Weis, 1971). In two books (1964 and 1969) and a much reprinted article (Matza and Sykes, 1961) he expressed ideas which changed considerably not only the ways in which sociologists looked at crime, but also had considerable impact on the ways in which delinquents were treated:

> he helped to open up . . . a Pandora's Box whose contents – the emphasis on free will, the argument that all prior theorising had 'overpredicted' delinquency, the rejection of the attempt to differentiate deviants from non deviants as a fruitful mode of enquiry – swamped the neat boundaries between this subculture and that which were the hallmark of existing approaches. (Downes and Rock, 1981, p. 116)

Matza's prime concern in his own work is naturalism, being as true, as authentic, as possible:

> the commitment of naturalism, as I conceive it, is *to phenomena and their nature, not to* science or any other system of standards . . . so conceived naturalism stands against all forms of philosophical generalization. Its loyalty is *to the world* with whatever measure of variety or universality happens to inhere in it. (Matza, 1969, pp. 3–5, original emphasis)

In his earlier work on delinquent subcultures Matza (with Sykes,

1964) stressed the mundane nature of delinquents and their commitment to accepted social values, commitments only loosened by the 'techniques of neutralisation' which loosened social bonds and conventional values, albeit temporarily. Delinquents in Matza's view *drift* into delinquency, they have choices, they can be diverted, although they are not free: 'drift is a gradual process of movement, unperceived by the actor' (1964, p. 29). As Taylor *et al.*, 1973, p. 180) point out, Matza's delinquents are far from free; they are in many ways as controlled, as socialised as the puppets of subcultural theory. But it is Matza's critique of that theory, rather than his own attempt, which has been so markedly significant.

In his later work, *Becoming Deviant* (although it could more accurately have been entitled *Becoming Criminal* – see Taylor, *et al.*, p. 188, Matza (1969, p. 38) first traced the growth of naturalism through the Chicago School, functionalist theory and what he called the neo-Chicagoans – Lemert, Goffman and Becker. For Matza the process of becoming deviant is a matter of choice and of stages which the individual himself (sic) processes:

> the process of becoming deviant made little human sense without understanding the philosophical inner life of the subject as he bestows meaning on the events and materials that beset him. (1969, p. 176)

Crucial to these meanings are the concepts of affiliation and signification. Affiliation is the first stage in which the person is drawn to deviance, although Matza does not really explain why. Later comes signification: 'convicted and imprisoned, he is committed to a world in which his identity will henceforth be cast retrospectively', although even then for Matza, 'the process of becoming deviant remains open. Reconsideration continues; remission remains an observable actuality' (1969, p. 196).

Matza reminded a generation that criminals might well be just like everyone else and not manipulated marionettes, dancing on the strings of some invisible puppet-master. They might also think and feel, weigh options, accept and reject identities. Matza's approach is naturalistic only as far as deviants are concerned; 'adults' and others exist in his pages, as does 'the state', but they are not treated naturalistically. Nor, despite his frequent references to images, pictures and surrealism, did Matza ever widen the canvas. He suggested that it might, so to speak, remain permanently

variations in crime rates dis-
observers' (p. 95).

umerous tests and revisions of
erland and Cressey, 1978). For
mportant because its sociological
n formulation, gives scope for
e wider perspective on crime to

nd as a bounded area is, as we have
ntentious issue. Not all the writers
e on definitions or boundaries. Some
topics, such as juvenile delinquency,
se of their careers, have considerably
Conventionally, criminologists have
violations – murder, theft, assault –
as criminal in many societies. The effect
of course, to focus on the offences of
Sutherland proposed a radical step by
s by high-status persons in pursuit of their
cated and studied as crime because (a) these
l, and (b) they do attract legal sanctions,
hes (Sutherland, 1961, p. 31). (Sutherland
efinition of white-collar crime – see Suther-
n et al., 1956. The one I have used here is
on the topic.)
examined some 980 administrative findings
against 70 large American corporations and
he pattern of offending and 'recidivism'. Thus
of the corporations had some 50 decisions
it, and the average 'form' was 14. Some 158 of
ally 'crimes' and so recorded in criminal courts,
tresses that most control of corporate behaviour
l means (pp. 19–26). Sutherland's view that cor-
s 'real crime' proved contentious, and many writers
validity (Tappan, 1947; Geis, 1962), while others

clusion of crimes in business practices, of professional
l of organised crime in the study of criminology is
have very definite revolutionary consequences. When

makes understandable most of the
covered by various researchers and
Sutherland's theory stimulated
it (Short, 1958; Glaser, 1956; Sut
later generations his work remains
character, though 'unfinished'
development, and because of th
which Sutherland applied it.

Defining crime as a concept
already discovered, a highly c
we have looked at would agre
have focused only on certain
while others, during the cou
altered their own emphases
concentrated on the visible
which are widely regarded
of such concentration is,
the weak and powerless
advocating that violation
occupations should be tr
acts are socially harmf
albeit administrative o
did not give a single d
land, 1940, and Coh
from his major study
Sutherland (1961)
and legal decisions
found a considerab
the most crimina
registered against
the 980 were actu
but Sutherland s
was by informa
porate crime wa
questioned its
acknowledged

to
as
one
Finall
sociolo
which h
studies.

Sutherla
social-psych
it was clearly
variety of situ
basic premises o
that it is learned i
becomes delinquen
to violation of law
law (Sutherland and
the text Cressey gave an
noting its confusing pre
were relatively modest –
society was useful: 'As an

that the in
crime, an
bound to

ordinary crimes are lumped with these other sorts of crimes not ordinarily reported and acted upon, it is clear that we have a different gradient of behaviour or a different circle of behaviour to study and explain. (Reckless, 1961, p. 216)

Sutherland himself suggested that the behaviour of white-collar criminals, respectable people not suffering from poverty or psychological disturbance, invalidated theories which linked such pathological causes with crime. It had, instead, to be seen as normal, rational action (1940, pp. 10–11). In addition, he argued, the theories of crime should include white-collar crime as crime and seek to explain it. These were crucial points, but at the time and for some years to come they were not heeded: 'Sutherland's . . . study . . . did, at the time, constitute a rich legacy to bequeath to criminology. Sadly it was a legacy scorned by its putative beneficiaries' (Box, 1983, p. 18). As Box goes on to demonstrate, this was true until the 1970s, when two external sets of factors changed the agenda. First came consumerism – in the particular American form of Naderism – which revealed major threats to life and limb being sold as cars 'unsafe at any speed'. Then there were the revelations of Watergate, the scandal which toppled President Nixon: 'there was a renewed interest in crimes committed in the good name of major corporations' (Box, 1983, p. 18).

Box distinguishes between crimes for and crimes against corporations, and further between those and criminal corporations set up solely for criminal purposes (p. 22). He insists that corporate crime is real crime in that it can kill and maim, and defines as criminal acts of omission, such as failure to repair ships or fence off dangerous machinery (pp. 20–3). It is a more serious phenomenon, too, he argues, because costs of fraud, etc. are much greater and risks are higher, if less obvious: 'whether we are consumers of citizens, we stand more chance of being robbed by persons who roam corporate suites than we do by those who roam public streets' (p. 31).

Box interprets corporate crimes, as did Sutherland, as rational action: 'Executives who commit corporate crime are not coerced into it, they do not necessarily have to go along with the advice or instructions of superiors' (p. 43). Nevertheless, he applies subcultural theory and Matza and Sykes techniques of neutralisation to corporate delinquents (pp. 54–56), but concludes that corporate criminals differ from juvenile delinquents in their 'greater opportunity to commit their favoured types of crimes, but they have the capacity to influence which of their behaviours will be regarded as crimes in the first place' (p. 63).

Box usefully summarises a great deal of research which has explored and extended Sutherland's rather vague model; he also rehearses the arguments about the use of the concept and the way in which it can be used to enlarge and reorientate sociologists' concern with crime. In particular, he insists, corporate crime should be a priority:

> on which type of crime ought we to be concentrating? Surely the deleterious consequences street crime has on our sense of community pale beside the way in which corporate crime fractures the economic and political system – concern should focus first on understanding 'how it is possible for corporate crime to be endemic in our "law and order" society' and second and hopefully flowing from this understanding 'how can it be contained or regulated'? (Box, 1983, pp. 32–34)

A challenging agenda has been set here. Although, as we shall see, the shift in priorities advocated by Box certainly did not take place at once, both research and public awareness of such issues has grown considerably. Mann (1985), for example, carried out an ethnographic study of the way American defence lawyers work to protect their white-collar clients, in particular by controlling the key information – accounts, company papers, etc. – in the case. Clinard who, as a disciple of Sutherland's, had continued to publish in this field over many years, produced a study of corporate ethics and crime (1983) in which he showed that it was the attitudes of top management which led to a criminogenic atmosphere in the corporation. Braithwaite (1984) examined corporate crime in the pharmaceutical industry and revealed a tale of bribery, price fixing and some terrifying examples of companies pushing drugs which were often not fully tested, especially in the Third World. In a similar field, Vaughan (1983) analysed a complex fraud perpetrated by staff of a large firm on the US system of medicare, which was charged twice for patients' drugs. Indeed, according to Henry, the 1980s saw a

> new wave of rediscovery . . . which has finally turned the subject-matter of criminology on its head. Instead of being tools of the powerful serving to measure and modulate the largely

pathetic crimes of the poor, criminologists have turned people's evidence, blowing the whistle on the far more lethally potent, socially pernicious and economically draining crimes of the powerful. (Henry, 1985, p. 70)

Well, yes and no. There have certainly been marked developments in this direction, and it is still a powerful paradigm with considerable scope for further development. There have, too, been a number of scandals which have focused on high-status deviance in bureaucracies. 'Watergate' gave not only a name to a scandal, but to a concept of high-level chicanery. Later events during Ronald Reagan's second term involving illegal arms deals were immediately labelled 'Irangate' by the media. The late 1980s saw major city scandals in both Britain and the USA as changes in business practice led to allegations of 'insider dealing' and vast frauds involving millions of dollars and pounds, by apparently respectable business executives. Box's agenda is likely to be extended and further explored and to have plenty of future material with which to do both.

Corporate crime as defined by Sutherland and his successors has proved a narrow, if ultimately fruitful area. In another related vein, and following similar assumptions both about rational behaviour and organisational constraints, has been a range of studies on workplace and work-related crime. Unlike the corporate crime studies which are for the most part American-inspired and based, this genre has been distinctively British, both in its anthropological orientation and in the location of most of its studies. The research cited on white-collar crime, and particularly that on corporate crime, focused particularly on middle and higher level managers in large organisations, and on a range of activities many of which were not infractions of criminal codes. Underlying much of this work are tensions and contradictions not entirely resolved about what is 'normal' and what is 'deviant' and/or 'criminal'. Braithwaite (1984, p. 2), for instance, sees the executives involved in dubious practices in their industry as ordinary men led to do extraordinary things. It is central to Box's argument that corporate crime causes both serious 'avoidable' social harm and that it is a product of the structure of capitalist society – at once destructive and supportive of the same system. On the other hand, the occupational crime writers emphasise that crime at work is normal (Ditton, 1977), ubiquitous (Henry, 1978; Sien, 1987), and central both to the financial reward system of many jobs (Ditton, 1977) and to their wider meaning for many workers: 'the normal crimes of normal people in the normal circumstances of their work . . . activities that are *an accepted part of everyday jobs.* (Mars, 1982, p. 1)

While this group of studies do differ, and there is a shading off into work on the 'hidden' or 'black' economy (Pahl, 1984; Gershuny, 1970), certain common characteristics are evident which are worth noting as we build up our understanding of crime in society. First, most of the activities they record – cheating by bread roundsmen, checkout girls and bar managers – are illegal, indeed criminal, since they involve theft or fraud and yet are almost never recorded or prosecuted. A cashier remarked to Mars:

> 'I used to fiddle twenty or twenty-five pounds a day . . . what's so surprising to me is that most managers don't know what's happening. They're very bothered by what they call "petty pilferage" – taking stuff off the shelves. They've no idea of till fiddles.' (Mars, 1982, p. 67)

Such a considerable amount of hidden crime has implications for definitions of crime and responses to it. It is, of course, almost certain to be missed in crime surveys.

Secondly, all these studies record not only the near-universal spread of crimes at work, but also their importance both in increasing real wages and in adding to social status when, for example, television sets 'off the back of a lorry' are sold to acquaintances in pubs (Henry and Mars, 1978). A further important point stressed by Mars is the close relationship between certain occupations and their 'matching crimes'. He proposes a typology of jobs and crimes which is a function of two measures of structure – grid and group solidarity (Douglas, 1970) – in various jobs. He identifies donkeys, wolves, hawks and vultures. 'Donkeys', such as the supermarket checkout girl quoted above, are tightly constrained by rules, hours of work, etc. (grid), yet they are isolated from their fellow employees. Wolves, on the other hand, have strength both in grid and group, operate in packs, as dockers, say, and plan well-organised disappearances of cargoes. Hawks, in contrast, are weak on both, and are found among salesmen and bent businessmen. In this category wider social conditions, such as technical innovation and rapid social change, aid the growth of such fixers.

Vultures, like wolves, have strong collective work groups, which aid fraud and fiddling, but have more autonomy because they are less supervised – as roundsmen, say – than wolves in carrying out their activities (Mars, 1982, pp. 28–33). Mars's discussion focuses on the social and occupational factors which generate employee theft and fraud. In conclusion he argues that these are parts of entrepreneurial activity, an alternative economy which should be tapped and used, not ignored or marginalised (p. 228).

All the perspectives on crime considered so far in this chapter have one central feature in common. This is

> something . . . absent in much sociological writing. This something we could loosely call *a sense of agency*. In several of the leading perspectives in sociology, human beings do not appear as the makers of their own history, but rather as the hapless playthings of social forces which they neither control nor understand. (Giddens, 1987, pp. 203–4, emphasis added)

Giddens describes here the state of sociology in general, but what he says is highly relevant to much sociological writing about crime. I have suggested already that this can be partly attributed to the strong positivist influences that shaped the study of crime right across the social sciences from the rise of the Italian School until the 1960s. The criminal and not the crime became the subject of study. Even the conceptual revolution of the 'new' theories did not, as we saw in Chapter 4, bring about dramatic shifts in this perspective. Although 'the controllers', or some of them, did become objects of research, the offences themselves still tended to remain unexplored. In part this was because 'appreciation' and 'naturalism' led, somewhat paradoxically, to getting close to the criminal and hearing his or her story: this achieved the same effect as positivism, albeit within another perspective. There was, too, a tendency to focus on 'victimless' crimes (Schur, 1965) such as illicit drug use, or to deny that there was any 'real crime' committed at all. The latter notion was central to various studies of 'moral panics' (Cohen, 1980; Pearson, 1983). While painting portraits of offenders, or some street scenes of their milieux, remained for some time the dominant trend in the study of crime, things were changing. An alternative perspective had always survived, if not flourished, within criminology; partly classical in its rational assumptions, partly informed by sociological analysis, criminal behaviour is not, within thìs approach, intrinsically a problem. Criminal behaviour is seen as rational purposive, goal-oriented and welfare-maximising. It is not, as it tends to be perceived within the positivist tradition, irrational, puzzling or exotic. Criminals are not merely 'other'; they can be, and perhaps are, ourselves.

If criminals are seen as people who make rational and perhaps informed choices, then certain consequences follow in understanding crime and also in depicting the offence. Such consequences have not on the whole been possible within the positivist model:

> the central focus of enquiry in positivist criminology . . . in its . . . sociological variants – has been the criminal offender . . . deterministic conceptions of the origins of criminal behaviour have . . . given rise to a view of the *offender-as-victim*. (Phipps, 1986, p. 96–7, original emphasis)

Phipps argues that seeing the offender-as-victim crowds out interest in studying the victim. In radical sociology, in particular, he suggests there were two stages of development which inhibited the growth of such interest. First, there was the 'misfit' sociology phase when the existence of victims was denied and the 'offender was [held to be] a victim of criminalisation and labelling by the powerful or of bias in law enforcement' (Phipps, 1986, p. 109). In the second, more consciously Marxist, phase 'the denial of the victim was further compounded by a conception of crime which held it to be an expression of political opposition to the contradictions of capitalism' (p. 110).

It is not possible to explain satisfactorily social scientists' relative lack of interest in victims of crime and the impact of crime. I have already suggested that the dominant conceptual framework limited vision, but this is a necessary, not a sufficient, condition. Alternative perspectives existed, as I have indicated; they were simply not explored.

Phipps (1983, p. 112) lists several reasons to explain the neglect of victims of crime compared with other victims of inequality and exploitation. These include the dilemma of divided loyalties – those who do harm are weak themselves – and what he calls 'confused moralism' – a lack of humanism in radical criminology. More tellingly, from the point of view of this book, Phipps notes the relative isolation from mainstream social science of the study of crime (p. 112) and hence the failure both to generate new concepts and to redefine the old ones. Finally, he notes the distancing of radical criminology from empirical, especially quantitative, work on crime – throwing out the sociological baby with the statistical bath water. Phipps makes quite a persuasive case, although he slides over some issues. For example, he notes that 'the most important contributions to a radical consideration of victims have come from feminist writers on rape and sexual assault, and violence against women and children' (p. 110), but draws none of the obvious conclusions from this.

I would emphasise several further points about the academic organisation of the study of crime and its proponents. I have already noted several times the 'search for excitement' that for a long time seemed to characterise those college boys who studied 'corner boys'. Looking at victims would have been much duller and marred the fun. Other organisational factors in the funding and use of research probably played a role, too (Rock, 1988a). In Britain, for instance, much research money for studies of crime and the criminal justice system is dispersed by the Home Office which, especially after 1972, retained few other responsibilities in the social policy field. Research on the sociology of vulnerability, which has led to a complex (and contested) construction of the 'victimising' effects of poverty (Townsend, 1979), sickness (DHSS, 1980) and disability (Topliss, 1978) were all directed from elsewhere. Such an institutional explanation does not, however, fit the American experience. There it may well have been the pattern and development of academic life which proved critical. The British approach to social policy in which the sociological anatomising of poverty and other forms of disadvantage flourished has no counterpart in the USA (Mishra, 1981, pp. 32–3). Rather, applied sociology has been directed through a 'social problems' approach where perpetrators – criminals, alcoholics, prostitutes, etc. – rather than victims were the foci of concern (Becker, 1967). It is interesting that two different systems had broadly similar outcomes, and that it was in the USA that changes in perspective began (Marris and Rein, 1967).

These must remain surmises. Whatever the reasons for the sustained neglect, changes did occur, but this time they came from outside the social sciences proper, although they have had considerable impact on them. In turn, social research has contributed considerably to their development and to their achieving credibility. From the early 1960s on, we can discern the beginning of three linked, yet distinct, concerns which mark a shifting of focus towards the victims of crime and the impact of crime on society. It is helpful to distinguish, although we shall find their boundaries blurring from time to time, three key new themes:

1. the 'new victimology';
2. the study of the 'fear of crime';
3. research and theories on situational crime prevention.

New victimology

It would be quite wrong to say that victims of crime had never been studied before the 1960s. Indeed, the indefatigable Hermann Mannheim (1965, p. 745) listed more than a dozen references already published by 1965 in various languages. These studies, however, were almost all of the psychodynamics of criminal–victim interaction, especially in violent crimes against the person. One early sociological study of homicide in Philadelphia emphasised the close personal relationships of murderer and victim (Wolfgang, 1959, p. 204), and these led Wolfgang to use the term 'victim precipitated homicide' to describe those cases where the victim (often with a more violent history than the killer) was 'the first to commence the interplay of resort to physical violence' (Wolfgang, p. 252).

Such studies tended either directly to 'blame the victim' (Amir, 1971) or to produce that effect, especially in some accounts of women and girls who were sexually molested or assaulted. Particular pathologies of 'disturbance' or 'neurosis' were attributed to the victims (Mannheim, 1965, p. 674). Alternatively, they were depicted as 'normal' but submissive (Gibbens and Prince, 1963). Victim typologies constructed on the bases of such research (Von Hentig, 1949; Mendelsohn, 1956) all tended to focus on the psychodynamics of criminal–victim interaction, especially in sex offences, and to treat as pathological both offender and victim. Since the empirical research was often clinically based, there were few if any comparative controls in such studies. One cannot help asking, for example, if 'submissiveness' has not been a generally valued feminine trait in sexual relations and not just a distinctive characteristic of victims of sexual offences?

What I have called the 'new victimology' did not really develop from these roots; indeed it is characterised by some crucial differences from them. The definitive history of its development has yet to be written (Rock, 1988b). What we can do is to trace what has happened in this development and consider some of the reasons for it and the impact it has had on the study of crime.

By the end of the 1970s elements of a victim movement could be identified in many Western countries, notably the USA and Britain, and these led to international declarations of support for state compensation for victims. Shapland *et al.* (1985, p. 2) identify 'four strands of the "victim movement" – victim aid and assistance, victim experiences with the criminal justice system, state compensation and reparation by offenders'. Although such phenomena could be found worldwide by the mid-1980s, they appear to have had diverse origins and the same end results: victim support schemes, for example originated from quite different sources in different countries (Rock, 1986 and 1988b).

New Zealand in 1963 and Britain in 1964 introduced compensation schemes for the victims of violent crime. Rock (1988) argues that the Criminal Injuries Compensation Scheme in Britain had two sources: liberal reformers 'who used it as a device to forestall the anger of victims cheated of their right to punishment in an increasingly rehabilitative age', and another, quite different group 'who regarded compensation as a simple extention of welfare insurance'. Rock notes two crucial points about these early schemes. First, victims themselves were quite arbitrarily constructed for the purposes of legislation, they were not consulted, and their characteristics were not known or examined. Shapland and her colleagues (1985, ch. 7) found in their study of 276 victims in Coventry and Northampton that, while many of their subjects did desire compensation, there was a more general wish: 'this is their wish for respect and appreciation – their wish for recognition as an important and necessary participant in the criminal justice system' (p. 176). In fact victims 'preferred compensation from offenders rather than from the state' (p. 177). A system for making compensation orders at the time of sentence or as a sentence now exists.

The second point Rock stresses is that, once the initial policy on compensation has been achieved, it was not followed up: 'there was a silence for some ten years'. Meantime, however, there was a great deal of noise in the USA which led to a further stage in this story.

The study of the fear of crime

Rates and riots in the USA

Concern with the inadequacies of criminal statistics is long-standing and widespread among academics and policy-makers, as we saw in Chapter 1. For several distinct reasons, such concern came to a head in the USA in the 1960s. First, the diffuse and complex nature of criminal justice administration there had always been reflected in crime data of a particularly limited kind: the *Uniform Crime Reports* published since 1930 by the Department of Justice are only based on a *sample* of law enforcement agencies whose participation is voluntary (Sutherland and Cressey, 1978, p. 35). These records came under increasing criticism during the 1960s, from both positivists who wished to see more rigorous and careful collection of data (Sellin and Wolfgang, 1964) and from phenomenologists and interactionists whose new perspectives led to more fundamental challenges to the ways in which such records were constructed and collected. Cicourel, observing the juvenile justice system as a participant, found that it was not juveniles' own behaviour, nor the conditions in the cities he studied, but 'organisational policies . . . via the background expectations of [police] officers' (Cicourel, 1968, p. 330) that determined which young people were defined and processed as delinquent.

While scepticism about recording crime rose, so too did concern about it, not least as a result of riots in the urban ghettos and more general anxiety about rising crime. All these influences came into play during the 1960s and were part of the background of the founding of President Lyndon Johnson's Crime Commission in 1965 (Phipps, 1986, p. 99). This body in turn commissioned a series of crime surveys to provide better data to aid in the fight against crime. These surveys, and later reports from the Riot Commission (Biderman, 1967; Ennis, 1967; Advisory Commission, 1968) revealed and measured the amount of hidden crime and the degree of victimisation. As a summary account made clear,

> there is much crime in America, more than ever is reported, far more than ever is solved. . . . Every American is, in a sense, a victim of crime. Violence and theft have not only injured, often irreparably, hundreds of thousands of citizens, but have directly affected everyone. (Winslow, 1968, p. 1)

In fact, as this report went on to show, victimisation rates *differed*: everyone was affected, but by no means equally. For instance,

> rather striking variations in the risk of victimisation for different types of crime appear among different income levels in the population . . . risks of victimisation from forcible rape, robbery and burglary, are clearly concentrated in the lowest income group and decrease steadily at higher income levels. (Winslow, 1968, p. 9)

Sociological analysis of victimisation had found its moment.

Crime surveys and victims of crime

The 'revelation' of victimisation and the depiction of victims as having certain social characteristics, had at least two important effects for the study of crime. It was one of the factors justifying the mounting of a regular National Crime Survey in the USA from 1972, and the start of such a programme in Britain and other countries. While learning more about victims is not the only reason for carrying out regular crime surveys – another major one is as a corrective to police records – it has nevertheless clearly been an important one:

> most crime surveys are not restricted to counting crime but are also an invaluable source of new information and the risks and consequences of victimisation. (Hough and Mayhew, 1983, p. 3)

There is a further important point. Because of the nature of modern crime surveys, which use a technique of sampling private households and questioning adult respondents about their experiences of crime, personal victimisation inevitably becomes the focus of the survey. 'Victimless' crimes, and most of the types of occupational activities discussed earlier, are excluded by definition from crime surveys. As Hough and Mayhew (1983, p. 3) point out, it is hardly surprising that 'some have gone so far as to suggest the new-found concern for victims of crime is a result, as much as a cause, of surveys of victimisation'.

In fact, as several accounts make clear, revealing and describing victims in crime surveys was only one of several factors to influence the growth of the victim movement whose strands were outlined above. Different types of victim movements grew from distinct stock in various countries, although the example of the USA, where the movement began, provided a model, often much adapted, for others.

> In the United States, where the 'victim movement' was born in a welter of political activity, closely linked to other issues such as women's rights, the main debates and associated actions have revolved around the position and the rights of the victim in relation to both the offender and the criminal justice system. (Maguire and Corbett, 1987)

In Canada, which lacked a popular victim movement, policies for victim support schemes were introduced from above by the federal government, while in Britain a low-profile, locally-based victim support system developed (Rock, 1986, 1987; Maguire and Corbett, 1987). The British system is described and evaluated by Maguire and Corbett as having

> no political aims or 'hidden agendas' . . . Their primary objective was very simple: to act as a 'good neighbour', or perhaps 'good Samaritan' to people who had suffered at the hands of thief or assailant. (p. 2)

Most of Maguire and Corbett's study consists of an account and evaluation of the victim support system in Britain. They do, however, make some suggestions to explain 'this almost unprecedented speed of growth in the voluntary organisation'. These include the charismatic nature of the leadership, the parallel growth of 'an internationally campaigning "victim" movement'. Most critically, though,

> 'Victims Support has also developed within a social and political climate increasingly sympathetic to victims of crime, a *climate which it has both fed and fed upon*. Rising crime rates, doubts about the effectiveness of the criminal justice system, greater knowledge about the effects of crime on individuals, publicity about the treatment of victims by the police and courts . . . have all served to push victims into the arena of public debate. (Maguire and Corbett, 1987, p. 3, added emphasis)

Rock (1988) sees developments in Britain as having had rather less purpose: 'the British history has been the shapeless artefact of many minds'. This was true of the victim movement, which deliberately kept a low profile in order not to become involved in moral panics or persecutions of offenders. Later, 'Administration has imposed definition', and hence 'the dominance of the Home Office mandate in the criminal justice system has led to the identification of a particular clump of activities as the politics of victims'. These include compensation for criminal injuries, reparation and victim support. Such activities, as Rock notes, form part of the Home Office's own set of strategic objectives for criminal justice to 'help victims'. New victimology has played an important part in altering such strategies for criminal justice systems: 'concern with the victim has become a powerful motif in contemporary western societal responses to crime' (Bottoms, 1983).

Such changes have, in themselves, produced considerable changes in direction and emphasis in the conduct of research for criminal policy (Clarke, 1983; Rock 1988a) through sponsorship and in-house research. They have also had wider impact on the study of crime. Social science is, as Giddens points out, fundamentally 'recursive':

> Sociological observers depend upon lay concepts to generate accurate descriptions of social processes; and agents regularly appropriate theories and concepts of social science within their behaviour, thus potentially changing its character. (Giddens, 1987, pp. 30–1)

This has clearly happened with what one might describe as one of the key 'designer concepts' of the 1980s – crime victimisation. Much sociological endeavour has been expended in responding to its considerable impact. For the rest of this chapter I intend to turn to three areas of impact: (a) surveys of crime, (b) the public response to crime and (c) the consequent 'new agenda' of fear of crime and crime prevention.

Crime surveys

The background history of crime surveys was briefly outlined above. They now appear to be an established element of the criminological enterprise. The USA has conducted an annual survey since 1972. Canada, Australia, Holland and Ireland have also carried out such studies, and they have also become a regular exercise in Britain (Hough and Mayhew, 1985).

The first major British study was carried out in three areas of inner London in 1973 by Sparks and his colleagues (1977) and was designed to explore the possibilities of the method. A key feature was a test of reliability, so respondents' answers were checked against police files to see whether they were prepared to tell an interviewer about an already reported crime – over 90 per cent of known incidents were reported. While this was an exploratory study, about whose findings on a low response rate the authors are repeatedly cautious, it was significant in a number of ways. Its broader aims embraced the study of criminal victimisation, perceptions of crime, and attitudes to criminal justice. These became, and have remained, the foci of the growing range of British studies of this type. The agenda for later work was set in a number of areas. Dissatisfaction among victims about the way the police handled cases was noted in this study, and it was reflected in many later studies on the police (see Chapter 6) and in Shapland *et al.*'s (1985) study of victims' experience of the criminal justice system.

The authors of *Surveying Victims* (Sparks *et al.*, 1977) made some attempts to theorise both victimisation and societal reactions to crime. In one sense they assisted at the birth of a new version of positivism, with the victim, not the criminal, now being measured and assessed for a portrait. Their opportunity or life-style model, describing the risks associated with being young, sociable and make, is even almost like earlier pictures of delinquents. On the other hand, their findings challenged another kind of orthodoxy, that of critical criminology, where working-class attitudes to property crime had been seen as more tolerant than those of the property-owning middle class. There was little difference in class attitudes. Indeed,

> persons with relatively little wealth and property are more likely to take a dim view of their property being stolen, than those who have more to lose, and who can thus better afford to lose it. (Sparks *et al.*, 1977, p. 188)

Again, this point has been widely debated and further researched in much subsequent work, especially that associated with 'left realist' criminology.

The most obvious point about such large and expensive national studies is that they provide a great deal of additional information for researchers. Conventional criminal statistics, as we saw in Chapter 1, are collected for administrative purposes by the police and other agencies. For reasons discussed earlier, such records have to be treated as particularly suspect and peculiarly inaccessible:

> unlike social scientists working in other areas of social concern, criminologists have had very little control over the data essential to their endeavours . . . criminology has [been] based . . . on data whose collection and compilation it does not control. (Phipps, 1986, p. 99)

Crime surveys, although carried out also for policy and administrative purposes by government bodies – 'The British Crime Survey is itself a form of criminal statistics' (Bottomley and Pease, 1986, p. 31) – are managed by social scientists, and the material they generate is made available and can be analysed in much more satisfactory ways.

> The British Crime Survey . . . represents a revolution in criminal statistics in that the data on which it is based is readily available to anyone with access to a mainframe computer . . . the direct access to data and the ways in which it is possible to manipulate it . . . is a significant development. In a real sense the Crime Survey demystifies the picture of crime. (Bottomley and Pease, 1986, p. 31)

Or, as Rock (1988) less lyrically and more succinctly puts it, 'crime surveys have redefined policing, victiminisation and the politics of crime'.

Such enthusiasm has not been without its critics. I have already noted that crime surveys have, so far at least, generally been victim, rather than depredation or damage, surveys. Coleman's work, discussed in Chapter 2, is one example of how the latter might be approached. Self-report studies have also been used to 'correct' the dark figure of unknown and unrecorded crime. Each method has attractions and limitations of its own, although some of the flaws could be corrected through critique and dialogue between social scientists: 'the research staff of the Home Office Research and Planning Unit are now of much the same age and background as the academic sociologists of deviance' (Rock, 1988).

Feminists, for example, have been critical of the limitations of the survey as a means of reporting domestic violence or rape

(Stanko, 1987). The authors of the first report on the British survey noted:

A small minority (10%) of assault victims were women who had been assaulted by their present or previous husbands or boyfriends. This proportion may well be an underestimate. Many such victims may be unprepared to report incidents of this nature to an interviewer. . . . Indeed, *their assailant may be in the same room at the time of interview*. (Hough and Mayhew, 1983, p. 21, emphasis added)

Studies cited in Chapter 5 showed a considerably higher level of unreported domestic and sexual victimisation (e.g. Stanko, 1984 and 1987; Russell, 1984; Hanmer and Saunders, 1984). It should be possible for the managers of crime surveys to overcome some of the more obvious flaws in approach.

One effect of the publication of crime surveys has been to stimulate others to produce parallel or corrective studies, especially local ones, or ones geared towards the victimisation of certain ethnic groups or women. Bottoms *et al.* conducted a local crime survey in seven small residential districts in Sheffield. Their findings suggest that very detailed local studies can be worthwhile, since

adjacent areas . . . can appear . . . to be very similar and can even be almost identical demographically . . . yet they can have very different crime rates, and can be perceived by their residents as presenting very different levels of social problems . . . official statistics or crime surveys produced on a larger–area basis . . . can be misleading because they can miss important within–area variations. (Bottoms *et al.*, 1987, p. 151)

An important feature of crime surveys is that they can be repeated and findings compared and developed over time. In this way a sociological picture of victimisation is built up. The *National Crime Survey* in America, for instance, shows vulnerability to criminal victimisation to be distributed in rather similar patterns to other kinds of deprivation. Black and Hispanic people were victims more often than whites, although intra–racial crime was more common than inter–racial. Higher rates of victimisation were associated with poverty, inner–city residence and large families (US Department of Justice, 1983). Two broad types of conclusion are drawn from the British surveys. First, the findings can be used to augment and provide a corrective to criminal statistics. It is clear that there is a large 'dark figure' of unreported and unrecorded crime, although its dimensions are as complex as the double helix of DNA. Sparks *et al.* (1977), for example, found a ratio of eleven to one unrecorded to recorded offences in their inner London study. The first *British Crime Survey* found an overall ratio of four to one, but while there was a near complete reporting of car thefts, 'the survey indicated twice as many burglaries as were recorded by the police; nearly five times as much wounding; twelve as much theft from the person' (Hough and Mayhew, 1983, p. 10). The patterns of risks thus recorded can be interpreted in a number of ways, but the emphasis in all the Home Office studies of the data has been 'on the relative rarity of serious criminal victimisation' (Gottfredson, 1984, p. 30). This has been expressed in the following way:

> the survey showed that a 'statistically average' person aged 16 or over can expect: an assault resulting in injury once every century, a robbery once every five centuries (not attempts). (Hough and Mayhew, 1983, p. 15)

As we shall see, in looking at fear of crime these findings are open to several interpretations.

Indeed, the BCS data show that while the 'statistically average' person has only minimal chance of being robbed or injured by a criminal, 'individual lifestyles affect the chances of personal and household victimisation' (Gottfredson, 1984, p. 30). These lifestyle factors include: 'going out in the evening (particularly at the weekend) and heavy drinking . . . working out of the home, going to school and travelling on public transport' (Gottfredson, p. 31).

Again this model has been challenged because of its focus on street crime rather than domestic risks (Stanko, 1987), and its implied tendency to blame the victim and ignore crime in the suites but not on the streets (Downes, 1979; Box, 1983). An alternative to the 'lifestyle' concept is that of the 'opportunity' theory, which suggests that risk of crime is related to the interaction between offenders, targets and what are described as protectors or guardians (Cohen and Felson, 1979).

One of the most vital effects of the development of crime surveys has been the challenge and the stimulus to theory they have provided. I suggested earlier that the public response to crime found in the Sparks *et al.* study had been important for radical criminology. In fact it is hardly too fanciful to suggest that radical criminology has been split and reformed into separate camps over this and related issues. The self-styled 'new left realist' school (Lea and Young, 1984; Young, 1986) first accepted the US data on victimisation and its links with race and poverty (Lea and Young, 1984), arguing that crime was not a Robin Hood activity of robbing the rich to help the poor, but a matter of internecine strife *within* sections of the urban poor who preyed upon their own most vulnerable members (p. 45). They also acknowledged that crime was a perceived and present fear for poor and vulnerable people (p. 35). A series of local surveys have been produced within this perspective, contradicting many of the assertions of the national surveys, especially about levels of risk among particular groups (Kinsey, 1984 and 1985; Jones *et al.*, 1986) although they do broadly confirm the BCS findings on the public's views of the seriousness of crime and what one can only describe as the social distribution of fear of crime.

Crime surveys further provide important new sources of data for the study of crime. This material can be used to support and develop various theories and concepts, and it is important for it to be used as widely and as critically as possible (Sparks, 1981). There is some danger of a positivistic renaissance if such surveys are merely used for limited number-crunching purposes; they also need to be paralleled by detailed local studies and by good qualitative studies. Only the latter can really convey the anguish and the lasting harm caused by crime (Maguire, 1980). When the two approaches are linked (Maguire, 1980; Maguire and Corbett, 1987), insights into the complex effects of crime victimisation can be achieved. Crime surveys have been an important factor in recording and making heard the voices of victims of crime. It is clear that, as in many fields of social policy, policies *for* victims were largely developed without consulting victims (Shapland *et al.*, 1985; Walklate, 1986). Sociologists know that what constitutes 'social facts' is highly problematic; however, when new sets of social facts on key social problems are being rapidly generated, it is as well to be standing by and readily prepared to use and assess them.

Public responses to crime

At several stages in this chapter we have observed points in what
has come to be called the 'fear of crime' debate. One of the main
features we noted in surveys of crime were questions about popular
perceptions of crime. At least two clear findings emerge consistently
on this topic. First, crime is seen as a serious problem by many
people (Kinsey, 1984; Lea and Young, 1984; Smith, 1986). Even
quite minor disturbances such as rowdiness or petty vandalism are
seen as threats to order to which the police should respond (Shapland
and Vagg, 1987). There is a considerable broad consensus, too, on
what constitutes serious crime and what the priorities should be
for the police and the courts (Walker, 1978; Levi and Jones, 1985).

However, there is considerable variation in reported levels of
personal fear of crime and what are seen as particular discrepancies
between perceived and likely risks. The BCS's 'statistically average'
risks were reported above, together with some details of the 'high
risk' individuals who are most likely to be victimised – young,
urban, working-class males who are out in public or inside public
houses a good deal (Gottfredson, 1984, p. 31). Yet those who fear
crime most are not those who appear from the surveys to be most
at risk. Women, for example, are reported in all studies to be more
afraid of crime than men, and elderly women more than younger.
In the first BCS, 60 percent of women over the age of 61 in inner
cities felt 'very unsafe' when alone after dark, whereas the figure
for elderly men was 27 percent (Hough and Mayhew, 1983, p. 23).
In the second sweep, respondents were asked about their worries
over becoming the victim of certain types of crime. In no group
of males were even 20 per cent 'very worried' about mugging or
burglary, but over 40 per cent of younger women were 'very
worried' about rape (Hough and Mayhew, 1985, p. 35).

Serious debates and discussions have ensued between social
scientists and others on interpreting the 'fear of crime' reports. On
one side are those who question the whole notion of a 'real' crime
problem. This was for a long time the view of radical and critical
criminologists, who argued that a moral panic was manufactured
by right-wing politicians and the media as a weapon to control the
working class or black people (Harmer, 1982; Sivanandan, 1981).
More recently, 'left realists' such a Lea, Kinsey and Young have
insisted that crime is a 'real' problem which has to be tackled

although they do not support the emphasis Wilson and Kelling give to the maintenance of social order (Kinsey *et al.*, 1985, p. 205). Home Office researchers, in reporting survey findings, have also played down the risks of crime, although, as we shall see, they take them seriously enough to plan for crime reduction and control in other papers.

Another aspect of the debate has focused on the 'rationality' of fears of crime. Since risk and fear seem to be inversely related, anxiety over crime is either a surrogate for something else (Sparks *et al.*, 1977) or irrational and ill-founded (Pearson, 1983). However, Lea and Young (1984) and Jones (1986) argue that such fears are not irrational when more specific risk rates are computed. Women in inner-city areas, for example, are at much higher risk of attack. More sophisticated analyses have gone beyond actuarial categories to explore the construction of the fear of crime. It is clearly related to powerlessness and vulnerability – characteristics obviously prevalent among elderly women, who express the highest levels of anxiety and for whom the effects of victimisation can be devastating (Maguire, 1980; Maguire and Corbett, 1987; Jones, 1987). Rape victims very often feel deeply damaged and face additional and unique problems in the criminal justice system. The publicity surrounding such problems may well have added to the fears women in general express about this crime (Adler, 1987).

Hough and Mayhew (1983, p. 22) declare that 'Fear of crime in Britain is becoming as great a problem as crime itself'. This is certainly a topic where more thoughtful sociological exploration can play a part. It is obvious that there is very real public concern about crime, or at least particular sorts of crime (Benton, 1986) and that crime issues have become public and indeed political issues in a new and distinctive manner. As yet this development has not been adequately explained (but see Dahrendorf, 1985, for an interesting thesis). With crime apparently firmly on the political agenda, social scientists are likely to be faced with situations where solutions are required for problems they have no devised themselves. To see crime taken seriously can be a mixed blessing.

Preventing crime

This chapter is essentially about what in computer language is called an interactive situation. Such situations are common, indeed inevitable, in social science. Sociologists have both independent and subordinate roles in understanding and explaining crime. By the middle of the twentieth century a substantial body of work had been assembled on crime and society. The study of crime and deviance was a topic in its own right. Its findings had begun to make an impact on policy, especially in the USA. In Britain, medical and pyshcological models persisted longer, and probably the one area where social research had major impact was on the intermediate treatment programme for (pre)delinquent young people, where Matza-like notions of diversion were embodied and the need to avoid labelling and stigma recognised (Intermediate Treatment Fund, 1986).

Crime has been publicly presented as an increasingly serious problem in the late twentieth century. It is an ironic mark of the success of the social science enterprise that it is seen overwhelmingly as a social problem for which social solutions have to be found. It is ironic because although policitians, policy-makers and the public are otherwise convinced (partly, at least, because of the gradual spread of sociological ideas – Miller, 1986), *solutions* to the pressing problems of crime are not readily available.

What has happened in practice is that the polity has, so to speak, set an agenda to which social science has returned only a very partial response. Rising crime rates in several Western countries, together with right-wing governments elected with commitments to restore law and order, have formed the background to the agenda setting. There have been particular local conditions, too. Economic recession with exceptionally high levels of unemployment has affected many countries, but especially Britain. New waves of illicit drug use have been notable in some European countries (Pearson, 1987), West Germany in particular. Terrorism was less prevalent in Europe in the 1980s than in the 1970s, although Italy and France were exceptions to this. In Britain there were major disorders in inner cities in 1981 and 1985, and there were the particular crises over policing discussed in Chapter 6.

Pressure to 'Solve' the crime problem was therefore very great. In both the USA and Britain old and new sociological approaches were found wanting in the search for 'realistic' and 'practical' solutions. James Q. Wilson (1975) published a best-selling and influential book in the USA in which he castigated criminologists for their failure to offer practical solutions to crime control. In this and other works with George Kelling (Wilson, 1968; Wilson and Kelling, 1982; Kelling, 1986) he advocated particular forms of policing and police response to crime and disorder. The crux of the Wilson–Kelling hypothesis is a sociological one: 'collective neighbourhood efforts can influence crime and fear of crime . . . community crime control works' (Kelling, 1986, p. 91).

It is not, however, how or why but *whether* it works that is paramount, and prompt policing of trivial disorder is seen as a crucial way of maintaining public confidence and hence public control. As Rock put it,

> *Thinking about crime* is the plain man's guide to crime control . . . [it] berates criminology for its neglect of the politically useful, sifts that knowledge which might be practically employed, and prepares what is tantamount to an agenda for the alert administrator. (Rock, 1979, p. 81)

In Britain, Clarke and his colleagues made a parallel if more moderate critique of what were described as 'dispositional' theories of crime which depicted the distinctive attributes of offenders. Such theories were unhelpful and impractical because they did not lead to practical suggestions for reducing and controlling crime. Instead, in a major change of strategy, the Home Office researchers opted for an 'essentially atheoretical' approach (Trasler, 1986, p. 17) of 'situational crime control' (Clarke and Mayhew, 1980). In more recent work, Cornish and Clarke have refined this concept and given it some theoretical resonance from rational choice theory, an approach derived from economic theory of behaviour and increasingly applied to political action (Downs, 1957; Laver, 1986).

Situational crime prevention

Situational crime prevention describes a series of experiments and enterprises that have in common the assumption that criminal acts can be deterred or displaced by a variety of measures

> directed at highly specific forms of crime which involve the management, design or manipulation of the immediate environment in which crimes occur as in systematic and permanent a way as possible. (Hough *et al.*, 1980)

Bennett (1980, p. 42) suggests that the

kinds of methods used can be categorised under three main headings relating to the level at which they are designed to operate: 1) the individual; 2) the community; 3) the physical environment.

Individuals have, for example, been encouraged to mark their property in order to reduce the risk of burglary (Laycock, 1986) or to have better locks fitted in their homes (Allatt, 1984).

Community crime control has been encouraged in the USA and in Britain, especially in the form of Neighbourhood Watch schemes. These can be of various types – organised by the police or on voluntary initiative – but are based essentially on informal local surveillance and the reporting of deviance (Rosenbaum, 1986; Kinsey *et al.*, 1986, ch. 5). We looked in Chapter 2 at design improvements based on the work of Newman, Coleman and Powers. There have also been experiments in Hartford (Fowler and Margione, 1986) designed to control crime and reduce fear of it in Chicago (Rosenbaum *et al.*, 1986).

Much is claimed for the effectiveness of such experiments. Laycock (1986, p. 71) found in her study in South Wales 'that property marking can reduce the incidence of domestic burglary', and, strikingly, in this experiment there was no displacement in burglary from participants to non-participants. Other small-scale experiments have shown positive results from vandal-proofing telephone boxes or improving car security (Hough *et al.*, 1980). But crime prevention has not proved as simple and clear-cut as practical people might have hoped, and now, ironically, has generated its own considerable conceptual literature (Cornish and Clarke, 1986).

Sociological, political and normative considerations keep on intruding. Neighbourhood Watch, for example, is a version of that reassertion of community as control which we have discussed before. It embodies various quasi sociological assumptions about communities and how they function. In certain situations, in Detroit in the 1970s for example, it appears to have worked well (Kinsey *et al.*, 1986, pp. 88–91). Such schemes have been widely introduced into Britain in the 1980s. But even a minimal sociological sophistication leads one to raise certain key questions. What, for instance, constitutes the neighbourhood or the community for crime control purposes? Will everyone be included? Even, for instance, itinerants and vagrants? What if there are conflicts over aims? As Kinsey *et al*. (1986, pp. 96–7) put it, 'A cohesive community has the information and the ability to communicate to the police. But what happens if community is lacking?'

In a more comprehensive review of American experience, Yin (1986, p. 300) concludes: 'successful crime prevention efforts require joint activities by the residents and police, and the presumed improvement of relationships between these groups'. He observes that 'those communities with the highest levels of crime also may be those in which resident–police relations are difficult to improve' (p. 307), and hence 'the incidence of crime is not likely to be reduced significantly as a result of crime prevention efforts' (p. 308).

Kelling, on the other hand, is much more optimistic, declaring that 'the community crime control movement in the United States had demonstrated great potential to reduce or control crime, disorder and tear' (1986, p. 102). He too, though recognises dangers such as vigilanteeism or racism.

Policies for preventing crime can be derived from every theory discussed in this book. Some, naturally, would be utopian. For a serious Marxist, only a truly socialist society would be crime-free. There is of course the Durkheimian principle of the inevitability and indeed appropriateness of crime in society. But Durkheim, too, opposed excessive crime and proposed social regulation as a cure for anomie, which remarkably resembles community policing and crime control (Reiner, 1984).

Some sociologists have responded to the call for solutions to the crime problem. Kinsey *et al*. propose 'minimal policing', responsive and accountable to local needs. In the 1980s the cry for crime proposals was taken up by new voices – the radical inner-city councils of several London boroughs, Liverpool and the late GLC. They sponsored research studies and experiments in crime control, drawing especially on the 'left realist' school of criminologists.

What began as a decisive break with theory in both America and Britain has apparently already come full circle. Many reasons can be adduced for this. Some are epistemological: knowledge is socially generated and used and is therefore grounded. It cannot be conjured from nowhere. Many of the ideas behind situational crime prevention derive from central social theory traditions and share their flaws and virtues. The problems of community policing are paralleled in many other fields of social policy where community, that Pandora's box of a concept, has been opened. Among other reasons for the reclaiming of crime control within the central tradition of social science are particular ones, in Britain at least, to do with the organisation of and recruitment to the discipline (Rock, 1988). Reclaimed crime control may be. It retains immense scope of development, as well as dangers if badly handled. In the future study of crime, which we are about to try and forecast, it will inevitably feature.

8 Understanding Crime in a Changing Society

In Chapter 1, I suggested that this text was intended to be a guide to the principal attractions of the sociology of crime. A further purpose is to help in the understanding of a world and its problems which are changing rapidly in the late twentieth century. In this, the final chapter, I want to show how the book may, I hope, be profitably used to aid a wider understanding of social change in general and of the distinctive aspects of crime. Equipped with a set of insights and travellers' tips, it will then be time for us to try and anticipate the future.

Understanding the issues

Crime and Society has consisted so far of accounts and criticisms of theories and research about crime. It is now time to ask what can be done with all this material. The answers will depend very much on what the knowledge is wanted for.

While writing this book I have had in mind two images of the student of crime. On the one hand there is the *curious*, the seeker after knowledge, who wants to know, grasp theories, gauge findings; on the other there is the *concerned*, the professional, practitioner or member of the public who wants to apply theories or improve or change things. This is both a simplified distinction and an artificial division between types of knowledge and the purposes for which it can be used. 'Knowledge for what?' has been a key question for social scientists for generations. Max Weber began a considerable (and still developing) debate when in his classic essay on 'Science as a vocation' (1948) he insisted on the distinction between the tasks of the academic who can understand and explain what he observes and the politician whose task is to change things (p. 146). How social knowledge can best be obtained and then how (or indeed if) it should be used and to what ends remain key questions. As I have indicated, I am addressing readers divided rather arbitrarily into the curious and the concerned. Their interest in knowing about crime is likely in both cases to be for purposes concerned with authority.

As we have seen throughout, the role of authority in the state, the police, judiciary and other agencies is crucial in determining what is crime, who is criminal and how they are processed through the system. According to their point of view, those who wish to use sociology in relation to authority may, following Shils's typology, do so as *manipulation* from within, as criticism from outside or *alienation*, or through understanding and affinity to achieve *consensus* (Shils, 1961, p. 1435). Curiously, whether one wants to destroy or support existing societal relations, the possible alternative ways of using social knowledge will be very similar. The ingredients in an anarchist's recipe book are not necessarily different from those in a traditionalist's; it is the menus which will vary.

Bulmer (1982) has proposed a typology of relations between social research and social policy which we can usefully apply to the general understanding of crime and of the specific sources in this book. He distinguishes first, *empiricism*, or 'superior fact gathering', in which data are collected and the 'facts' speak for themselves; second, *engineering*, where social science is used as a technical device to solve policy-makers' problems. Both these models he finds limited and he puts forward a third, *enlightenment*, in which social science may have considerable use and impact, although 'Much of this use is not direct, but a result of long-term infiltration of social science concepts, theories and findings with the general intellectual culture of a society' (p. 48). In order to transform interesting social knowledge into usable knowledge about crime, one has, I believe, to work at these three levels, and it should be possible to use this book and its references in all these ways. Let me give some examples.

Empiricism

More 'facts' are gathered about crime than on most social issues, but they have rarely been 'self-evident' material. In reading this text, while quick answers to questions about how much crime, etc. will not be easy to find, it should become clear that there is a multiplicity of competing sources on these matters. Crime surveys and self-report studies, observational and official accounts have all developed because of the inadequacy of the original official records. There are rarely simple answers to the basic 'factual' questions most people ask about crime, but it should be possible at least to hunt for an answer and certainly to be properly sceptical about some of the 'commonsense' answers one is often assertively offered.

To give just two examples: in Chapter 5 on gender I considered the 'female liberation causes crime' argument (and referred to other discussions of it). This issue was one where 'apparent' facts turned out not to be nearly so apparent after all. In looking at fear of crime and victimisation we also found that there was a complex set of interactions occurring which could be read from empirical research (as in Maguire and Corbett's subtle analyses) but which were far from straightforward.

Engineering

This book is not meant to be a technical crime prevention text and certainly not a guide to the best 'scams'. Yet for those with direct policy concerns at whatever level there are numerous messages to be gleaned. Many are the 'honourable defeat' kind. Strategies such as community development, urban renewal and active work with youth have all been tried as remedies for crime, with modest degrees of success. Currently fashionable (see Chapters 6 and 7) are community policing, neighbourhood watch schemes and 'designing out' crime. In exploring these approaches we found that their roots lay deep in heavy intellectual clay: 'community' solutions are all grounded in massive assumptions about human society and social relations, while designing out crime presupposes rational, risk-averse offenders. All good engineers would, of course, automatically test the soundness of the soil they built upon before erecting anything.

Enlightenment

It is perhaps inevitably at this broader level that I think social science has most to offer in making sense of crime in society.

Perhaps it can also help to make less of it, although that is a trickier question. One of sociology's earliest insights, at once profound, puzzling and perturbing, is Durkheim's observation that crime is part of society, its existence inevitable, even in a healthy one. Durheim did not, however, say that rates and levels of criminality were given and immutable; indeed, sociologists have played major parts directly and indirectly in strategies linked to altering levels of criminality. It is, after all, inherent in the nature of the sociological approach, deriving as the discipline does from intellectual reactions to and theories of social change, that its practitioners believe that states can be altered, institutions restructured and communities be redeveloped. In this they differ from other social sciences which use less flexible paradigms.

There are at least four ways, each illustrated in this book, through which 'enlightenment' can be sought (and has often developed upon) its central topic.

1. The 'good' society

Sociologists are often depicted as misanthropes, churlishly deriding the societies and cultures which nourish them, acid Alcestes at life's banquet. Yet much of the writing we have discussed here is about the 'good' society, or successful socialisation, where crime will be less endemic and fewer offenders flourish. It is clear, for example (see, Chapter 2), that lower crime rates are found in more stable communities where levels of consensual social control are higher. Equally, young women (see Chapter 5) who grow up in the same poverty and in the same housing as their brothers, are less likely to be involved in crime since they inhabit a different world as far as socialisation and social control are concerned. The British, but not the American, police did once, according to some accounts, enjoy a relatively happy period of public confidence and order (see Chapter 6) and have been offered copious versions of the route back to that lost manor or domain.

These insights can offer enlightenment and may well ultimately effect some positive developments. An understanding of the need to enable people to have power and choice in their own environments has underpinned several modern housing projects, aimed at reducing crime and vandalism (Chapter 2). Raising boys in ways rather closer to those expected of girls is not yet a serious contender as a crime control slogan, although it could be a potentially powerful one. Gentling the police, replacing macho cop culture with something more socially aware and sensitive has, however, become a goal of some modern police reformers and the explicit target of several campaigns. Nevertheless, it is in the nature of enlightenment concepts that they begin by seeming remote and unacceptable, and later, when successful, become an item of conventional wisdom.

2. Exposing problems

Some kinds of sociology, especially the sort discussed in Chapter 2, are close to the tradition of muck-raking and investigative journalism which exposes social ills or social conditions which lead to social ills. A long line of sociological studies has done that, from *The Gold Cost and the Slum* (Zorbaugh, 1929) and *The Gang* (Thrasher, 1963) to *The Delinquent Solution* (Downes, 1966) and *The Girls in the Gang* (Campbell, 1984), all the way indeed from *Street Corner Society* (Whyte, 1955) to *Street Woman* (Miller, 1986). An immense range of problems and conditions have been depicted and analysed from which critical insights about social disorganisation, criminogenic social structures, cultures and familial patterns can be gathered.

It is surprising how many of these ideas have proved influential. The 'crime and opportunity' model had a major effect in American social policies in the 1960s (Chapter 3), while the labelling perspective influenced a whole range of later interventions and approaches (Chapter 4). Some of these accounts can, of course, produce a despairing 'so what' response in the social engineering realist with a small budget and no liking for revolutions. To this, the only honest reply is to (a) reassert a faith in serendipity, and b) to point out that, when situations grow really bad, there are often appeals from authority for ideas for solutions, and very often there are resources available.

3. Sensitising concepts

One of the things social science can do best is to frame and develop concepts which can then be used either in research or more widely in policy-making or public discourse. 'Relative deprivation', 'status', 'stigma', 'total institution' are a few examples of such powerful concepts which have been widely used in all those ways since the mid-twentieth century. They are the ultimate in guide books: they redraw familiar territory in a new fashion so as to highlight key and less observed points.

Two of the main such paradigm shifts in the study of crime are recorded in Chapters 4 and 5. The impact of the 'deviance-lies-in-the-eye-of-the-beholder' thesis has been profound. It is interesting, for instance, to observe the official efforts made in many countries affected by the AIDS epidemic in the 1980s *not* to stigmatise deviant lifestyles associated with higher risks of infection, in order that campaigns to prevent the spread of the disease could be successful. (This was particularly true of the UK and the USA, but less so in the USSR and West Germany.) As we saw in Chapter 5, gender is a newer and still contentious topic in the study of crime. It is likely to have greater future impact as a sensitising concept as issues such as rape, domestic violence, the sexual abuse of children and prevention policies are re-examined.

4. Scanning the horizon

Although I shall do so later in this chapter, I think it is generally an unwise thing for a social scientist to try and predict the future. What we can more confidently do is to report on trends and observations likely to affect that future. This is particularly crucial with crime, which is in many ways a reflection of society itself, thrown back from a distorting mirror, and is thus likely to change in step with certain social changes. For this reason alone, any would-be crime controller needs some sociological insights in their filing system. This will range from basic demographic data to understanding value changes and some of the conceptual shifts discussed above. In Chapters 6 and 7 we saw two profoundly important changes occurring – the disenchantment with the police and the rise of the victim movement. Studying both these, and as we saw they have been well-researched, can at the very least help us to foresee the next such development.

To conclude this section it may be helpful to look at a few examples which illustrate the points I have been stressing. Pearson's *The New Heroin Users* (1987) is one of many studies which examine the problems of hard drug abuse in modern society. The book is itself based on a commissioned study, undertaken for a health policy body (Pearson *et al.*, 1986). In this more popular account, Pearson uses interviews extensively to illustrate the processes of using heroin, 'chasing the dragon', etc. among young people in the North of England in the 1980s. It becomes clear that the drug is not necessarily as automatically addictive as drug culture legend has it, and that its use has to be learned over a period. 'Epidemic heroin use' affected 'working-class communities which were already battered by . . . widespread unemployment and wretched housing' (p. 190). But Pearson emphasises that bad social conditions do not 'cause' addiction, although it spread among them and has to be eradicated there, not by whisking people away to treatment. This careful ethnographic study offers many insights and much material. It adds to many of the ideas we have already discussed about 'crime areas', 'community' and solving crime problems. It proffers both enlightenment and (tentative) solutions.

The links between drug use and crime have been much discussed in the late twentieth century; so too have those between unemployment and crime. Illicit drug use is in itself a crime and is associated with many other offences as users seek funds to pay for their supplies. The relationship between crime and unemployment is in itself problematic. By no means everyone accepts that there is a positive and causal link. In the recession of the 1930s, crime rates appear to have *fallen* in some of the depression-hit societies.

Some modern studies have explored these questions. Farrington *et al.* (1986) looked at the careers of over 400 young males in London and found that 'crime rates were higher during periods of unemployment than during periods of employment' (p. 335). This was particularly true of offences involving material gain. In a New York study Svridoff and McElroy (1984) also found a strong relationship and that it was particularly marked for black youth. Correlations do not, of course, prove causation, as these authors point out. Box (1987) sought to test out the 'recession-causes-crime-rates-to-rise' theory by examining some fifty American and British studies. He concluded that

1. Income inequality is strongly related to criminal activity – with the exception of homicide.
2. The relationship between overall unemployment and crime is inconsistent (p. 96).

Box concludes that the most appropriate research has yet to be done. He argues that more equitable income distribution would reduce crime rates. Farrington *et al.* also cite experiments in giving financial and other benefits to ex-prisoners, some of which had an impact on recidivism rates (p. 353). Again this work provides both 'engineering' and understanding, if only of the complexities of the issues and the difficulties of finding clear and hard answers.

The future

Having, I hope, offered a small pocket tool-kit to go with the travel guidance offered so far in this volume, it is now perhaps time to move on to a look at the future. I began this section by distinguishing between concern and curiosity in the study of crime. This does provide a useful starting point for examining future prospects in the study of crime. We need to explore two distinct universes in order to find out, first, what is likely to happen to social science, especially sociology, and second, what may occur in the field of crime. How these universes will interact will provide our range of predictions, if not our answers.

The future of sociology

Anthony Giddens has proposed *Nine Theses on the Future of Sociology* (1987). Perhaps the most significant feature of these propositions about the parent discipline of criminology is how remote several of them seem from our concerns within the subject. He insists that the future of sociology is, so to speak, grand, indeed global: 'The dominant object of analysis of sociology will be substantially rethought' (p. 32). He forecasts the future of social science as being very much concerned with 'the study of the world system' (p. 34), with an emphasis, especially in sociology, away from detailed empirical work and towards more armchair-based theorising about long-term social transformations (pp. 41–3). Giddens does suggest four probable developments which are likely to make sense to the 'curious' student of crime and help him or her to make more sense of the topic they are studying. These are:

1. that there will be greater theoretical synthesis in sociology which will make debate in the subject more coherent (p. 29);
2. that there will be much greater involvement of sociology in social policy-making (p. 44);
3. that the significance of social movements such as the peace movement or the women's movement will grow (p. 48);

4. that sociology will be as controversial as ever (p. 50).

Giddens's tone is confident, his predictions relatively optimistic. We can recognise in some of them trends already discerned in the study of crime. Association with social policy, for example, has always in the end proved unavoidable for the student of crime. Theoretical and intellectual syntheses are also already developing. This has at least as much to do with what is *taught* to those who learn about crime as with the researchers' and planners' concerns (Rock, 1988). Two social movements – feminism and the victim–community control movement – have already changed some of the assumptions of academic research on crime. As to the controversy which follows sociology around, this often seems to be a myth. Yesterday's heretical view becomes today's orthodoxy, but as it does so the original prophet may remain unhonoured or even continue to be reviled. Many once-challenging ideas from social science have become incorporated into conventional wisdom. Most people now accept that educational performance is related to family background, and many recognise that prison does not rehabilitate offenders. The dilemma for sociologists may not be of appearing outrageous so much as that of Moses's sister when he was found in his cradle in the bullrushes. Does claiming kinship damage the infant's chances of survival?

The coasts of Britain used to be dotted with tide mills. These mills gained the power to turn their wheels from the water flooded into their mill pools at high tide. Criminology in Britain has functioned rather like a tide mill. The source of its power – the accumulated wisdom and concepts – came from outside, from the mainstream, the tides surging and ebbing through sociology. It has not been, on the whole, a source of generation in itself, but has been renewed from without, renovated by teams from the mainland, as in the 1960s, or suddenly jolted by feminists and popular movements in the 1970s and 1980s. I do not see this position changing dramatically; it is too well-established.

The study of crime would benefit greatly, however, from being less isolated, more integrated in mainstream social science. Resistance, for instance, to the incorporation of gender has been much stronger here than in other areas of social science. It seems to me, too, that it makes for much greater intellectual coherence to study crime within other contexts and alongside other subjects.

Could a sociology of victims of crime, or of public reactions to it, have taken so long to develop if deviance and welfare were not so generally distinct as subject areas in both higher education and central government? From an academic standpoint Giddens sees closer integration and synthesis as likely and desirable prospects; Rock suggests that for organisational and political reasons, too, these will occur. While the study of crime may remain conceptually distinct within the realm of sociology, it will flourish much more if it is less conceptually distinctive. There are one or two restored and working tide mills still in existence. They survive supported by a combination of public and voluntary effort; they may grind a little, symbolic corn on power from the mill pool, but they are always connected to the national grid.

Both sociology and criminology in the United States of America are in a much more vigorous state than in Britain, although some of these points can also be made about the state of the art there. The disjuncture with mainstream sociology is most notable there. Some key differences worth stressing (and predicting) are that the political climate for using academic research in policy had long been more auspicious in the USA, and was particularly so during the 1960s when concepts such as differential opportunity were used as the basis for delinquency-reducing policies in the ghettos (Marris and Rein, 1974). Political dimensions appear to have much greater significance for social science in the USA than in the UK, although sociology is by no means exclusively identified with the liberal establishment in the States (Fox Piven, 1987). On the contrary, as some of the studies cited in Chapter 7 indicate, there was an important criminological conservative renaissance in the 1970s. If one believes in a 'pendulum' theory of self-correcting swings, then there could be a more radical trend in the 1990s in both the American polity and the academy. What remains, and is likely long to remain, most distinctive about the USA is its high levels of recorded crime. In this it differs from most other advanced industrial societies.

Crime in the future

Predicting the future of an academic study area is risky enough, even though the enterprise is relatively small and the area bounded. Scanning the horizon to see what may happen in the field of crime is a still harder task because, as the history of even the quite recent past shows, so many unexpected factors can have an important effect, and even known variables may not link with any consistency. High levels of unemployment, for example, were related to low rates of recorded crime in the 1930s, but to increased official criminality in modern times (Farrington *et al.*, 1986). Perhaps the single most important lesson to be derived from the sociological study of crime is that the concept itself is problematic. What is called crime, how much it is a current social or political issue, what researchers focus upon – and what gets ignored – all vary and have frequently been contested. Nevertheless, it is possible to make at least some tentative proposals as to what may happen, and I shall do so, conscious that this might help to structure and focus the study of crime. This is, I think, particularly important for those many people who come to crime because of their concern about it as professionals, policy-makers and the growing numbers of members of the community who are involved in various projects.

Propositions about crime

1. Continued concern about crime

There is, it seems, now a permanent agenda on which certain key issues are perpetually recurring items. Crime is one of these and seems unlikely to lose its position. Even if crime rates fall – and I make no predictions in any direction there – concern about particular offences and the experiences of victims is likely to continue, while rising crime rates in themselves would constitute a problem. Along with this concern will go a whole subset of issues on control, treatment of offenders, and social disorder. Demands and pressures on all those involved in the criminal justice system are bound to increase.

2. Crime will continue to be an inconstant social constant

By this I mean that while 'crime' will still make headlines and make (or break) political careers, there are likely to be considerable changes from various sources in what we call crime. New forms of criminal activity may appear, for example. Computers and their capacities for storing and linking data already offer scope for fraud on a literally global scale, and this is bound to be exploited still further. The history of crime is not, however, so much replete with technological innovation as with examples of shifts in public concerns and policies. In the 1960s criminal laws relating to off-course betting, attempted suicide, abortion and adult male homosexual relationships were all changed. In the 1970s and 1980s there has been growing concern about first rape and then the sexual abuse of young children, especially within the family. It would be unwise to try and predict precisely where boundaries might be changed; it is more important to be prepared for change and be equipped to live with permanent instability.

3. There may be a new politics of crime

In Chapters 6 and 7 we saw how a 'new agenda' of topics developed in the study of crime, determined in most cases by outside influences. Policing, victimology and prevention have all become key items, raised and sustained by various groups who all have some stake in them. Crime has, in a sense, become a consumer issue. Not all voices, however, are represented in this new participant politics of crime. Offenders themselves, and communities and groups from whom they are drawn, have been fairly silent, although there are some exceptions. Prostitutes' organisations, for example, have organised protests over police practices and community reactions in Britain, France and the USA. Ethnic communities and miners and their families have also sought to protest about their members' treatment by the police. If, as seems likely, the new politics of crime continues to flourish, it is bound to politicise a wider range of individuals and groups who have some stake to preserve in the enterprise.

4. Changing social conditions will affect crime

Crime is a product of society, an outcome of social definitions of individuals' situated behaviour. As aspects of the society change, so will its outcomes, although one cannot be confident about predicting in what ways. It is nevertheless sensible to note likely social developments and their probable impact on crime. I have already mentioned *unemployment*, which will almost certainly remain at high levels in most Western countries for many years and is now associated not only with increased criminality but also with urban riots. *Race relations* and their links with crime are already highly charged issues and are not likely to diminish in seriousness. In the USA, the issues are at least clear, if considerable; in Britain they were masked for a long time by lack of recording (Walker,

1987a and 1987b; Home Office, 1986). 'Looking to the future, there is only one prediction that can be made with little fear of contradiction: there will be no racial peace without racial justice' (Stone, 1985, p. 158).

Other areas of society where changes may affect crime could include *family life* and *gender roles*. An increasing number of children in modern societies spend part of their childhood in a one-parent family, where the single parent is almost invariably the mother. These families are among the poorest and worst housed and live in disproportionate numbers on the least sought-after housing estates. At the same time, there are growing numbers of very elderly people, again mainly women living on their own. Much of this pattern of indepedent living for women is an acceptance of reality, not a chosen preference, and there is little evidence that all its implications for informal social control, vulnerability to victimisation, etc. have been fully worked through (Rock, 1987b; Jones, 1987).

5. 'Crime' will create crime

I am not predicting new techniques of bioengineering in which criminals might be cloned for fell purpose by a science fiction villain. Rather, I am focusing on the issue of feedback (Wilkins, 1964). That is, because crime is 'news', it is reported and repeated, perhaps imitated, almost certainly responded to. It is both the major fodder of the mass media in capitalist societies and, in a sense, their creation. Victim surveys show how fearful old people remain at home, leaving empty streets to the unseen mugger and the unwary victim. All the other predictions I have suggested are likely to mean more crime stories and media interest, and hence a further growth in the cycle. Social research plays and will play its role in this theatre too: the collection of scholarly papers on policing cited in Chapter 6 became the subject of the front-page news story in the *Daily Mirror*.

Towards a synthesis

Given the likely futures of crime and of social science, will it be possible to continue the somewhat uncertain history I have described in this book into the twenty-first century? Paradoxically, *as a field of study*, if in no other way, prospects look more promising than they have done for a long time. All the elements for making a full landscape with figures, in which crime is a feature, have been assembled, even though some of them are temporarily stored in remote warehouses. Giddens suggests that sociologists should in future favour at least armchair-based theorising, especially conceptual innovation. The empirical material, he argues, is either often already available or unnecessary (Giddens, 1987, p. 43). While this is not entirely true for the study of crime, there is an important message here – that concepts and the ordering of existing material in new ways can be most fruitful. This must be, I think, a co-operative endeavour among social scientists themselves and also with others, all of whom have knowledge and understanding, albeit of different kinds. Researchers on crime have, at some periods, favoured bar-stool sociology; I am arguing for what might be called a sofa or seminar sociology.

For those who, whatever the future brings, will be studying and perhaps dealing with crime, I should like to conclude with three modest proposals which may be of use. First, there are immense resources at your disposal to be used: use them. I have tried to indicate some of them in this book; following them up should lead you to vast treasures. Much work, for example, has already been done on delinquency, policing, and victims. Read it and analyse it, see whether it aids the explanation and understanding of the issues – and go beyond it. Second, the existing heritage contains quantities of heirlooms in the form of paradigms and models which still have analytical or explanatory power, as I have tried to show. Some have been underused, lost like mini skirts or flared trousers to intellectual fashion changes, yet are still worth using and exploiting. Finally, there is a general point to stress whether one is heading for a session of sofa sociology or the more traditional, for crime students, mean streets kind. Crime is a peculiar conflation of human endeavours; studying it a strange if fascinating occupation. By definition it is an inherently unstable and uncertain enterprise. Be prepared: expect the unexpected.

Bibliography

Adler, F. (1975) *Sisters in Crime* (New York: McGraw-Hill).

Adler, Z. (1982) 'Rape – The Intention of Parliament and the Practice of the Courts', *Modern Law Review*, vol. 45.

Adler, Z. (1987) *Rape on Trial* (London: Routledge).

Advisory Commission on Civil Disorders (1968) Report (New York: Bantam).

Alderson, J. (1979) *Policing Freedom* (Plymouth: MacDonald & Evans).

Alderson, J. (1983) 'Police', in D. Walsh and A. Poole (eds), *A Dictionary of Criminology* (London: Routledge & Kegan Paul).

Allatt, P. (1984) 'Fear of Crime: The Effect of Improved Residential Security on a Difficult to Let Estate', *Howard Journal*, vol. 24.

Allen, H. (1987) 'Rendering them harmless: The Professional Portrayal of Women Charged with Serious Violent Crime' in Carlen and Worrall (eds).

Amir, M. (1971) *Patterns in Forcible Rape* (Chicago: University of Chicago Press).

Anderson, N. (1961) *The Hobo* (Chicago: University of Chicago Press).

Archer, D. and Gartner, R. (1984) *Violence and Crime in Cross-National Perspective* (New Haven: Yale University Press).

Atkinson, J. M. (1971) 'Societal Reactions to Suicide: The Role of Coroners' Definitions', in S. Cohen (ed.).

Auld, J., Dorn, N. and South, N. (1986) 'Irregular Work, Irregular Pleasures: Heroin in the 1980s', in Matthews and Young (eds).

Austin, R. L. (1981) 'Liberation and Female Criminality in England and Wales', *British Journal of Criminology*, vol. 21, no. 4.

Baldwin, J. (1979) 'Ecological & areal studies', in Morris and Toury (eds) vol. I.

Baldwin, J. and Bottoms, A. (1976) *The Urban Criminal: A Study in Sheffield* (London: Tavistock).

Banks, O. (1981) *Faces of Feminism* (Oxford: Martin Robertson).

Barnes, H. E. and Teeters, N. K. (1951) *New Horizons in Criminology* (New York: Prentice Hall).

Barrett, M. and Macintosh, M. (1982) *The Anti Social Family* (London: Verso).

192

Beccaria, C. (1754) *Essay on Crimes and Punishments*, Milan.
Becker, H. S. (1963) *Outsiders: Studies in the Sociology of Deviance* (London: Macmillan).
Becker, H. S. (ed.) (1964) *The Other Side* (New York: Free Press).
Becker, H. S. (1966) Introduction to Shaw (1966).
Becker, H. S. (1967) 'Whose Side are We On?' *Social Problems*, vol. 14, no. 3.
Becker, J. (1977) *Hitler's Children* (London: Michael Joseph).
Bennett, J. (1981) *Oral History and Delinquency* (Chicago: University of Chicago Press).
Benton, S. (1986) 'What Can Law-makers and Police Do About Rising Crime?', *New Statesman*, 14 November. 'Left Shifts on Law and Order', *New Statesman*, 21 November.
Berger, P. and Luckmann, T. (1967) *The Social Construction of Reality* (New York: Double Day/Anchor).
Biderman, A. D. and Reiss, A. J. (1967) 'On Explaining the "Dark Figure" of Crime', *Annals of the American Academy of Politics* and *Social Science*, November.
Blair, I. (1985) *Investigating Rape* (London: Croom Helm).
Blumer, H. (1939) *Critiques of Research in the Social Sciences: An Appraisal of Thomas and Znamicki's 'The Polish Peasant in Europe and America'* (New York: Social Science Research Council).
Boltomore, T. and Nisbet, R. (eds) (1978) *A History of Sociological Analysis* (London: Heinemann).
Bottomley, K. and Pease, K. (1986) *Crime and Punishment* (Milton Keynes: Open University Press).
Bottoms, A. (1974) 'On the Decriminalization of English Juvenile Courts', in R. Hood (ed.) *Crime Criminology and Public Policy* (London: Heinemann).
Bottoms, A. (1983) 'Neglected Features of Contemporary Penal Systems', in D. Garland and P. Young (eds) *The Power to Punish* (London: Heinemann).
Bottoms, A. (1986) 'Intermediate Treatment', address to the British Society of Criminology.
Bottoms, A. E., Mawby, R. I. and Walker, M. (1987) 'A Localized Crime Survey in Contrasting Areas of a City', *British Journal of Criminology* vol. 27, no. 2.
Bottoms, A. and Sheffield, C. (1983) 'Feasibility Report for Research into Immediate Treatment', mimeo (Cambridge: Institute of Criminology).
Bowker, L. H. (1985) 'The Effects of National Development on the Position of Married Women in the Third World: The Case of Wife Beating', *International Journal of Comparative and Applied Criminal Justice*, vol. 9.
Bowlby, J. (1946) *Forty-four Juvenile Thieves: Their Characters and Home Life* (London: Baillière, Tindall and Cox).
Bowlby, J. (1953) *Child Care and the Growth of Love* (Harmondsworth: Penguin).
Box, S. and Hale, C. (1983) 'Liberation and Female Criminality in England

and Wales', *British Journal of Criminology*, vol. 23, no. 1.

Box, S. (1983) *Power, Crime and Mystification* (London: Tavistock).

Box, S. (1987) *Recession, Crime and Punishment* (London: Macmillan).

Braithwaite, J. (1984) *Corporate Crime in the Pharmaceutical Industry* (London: Routledge and Kegan Paul).

Brake, M. (1985) *Comparative Youth Culture* (London: Routledge and Kegan Paul).

Brogden, M. (1982) *The Police: Autonomy and Consent* (London: Academic Press).

Brogden, M., Fielding, N. and Waddington, P. A. J. (1986) 'Review Symposium', in *British Journal of Criminology*, vol. 26, no. 1.

Brodgen, M. (1987) 'The Emergence of the Police: The Colonial Dimension', in Reiner and Shapland (eds).

Brophy, J. and Smart, C. (eds) (1985) *Women-in-Law* (London: Routledge and Kegan Paul).

Brown, D. and Iles, S. (1985) *Community Constables: A Study of Policing Initiative*, Research and Planning Unit Paper 30 (London: HMSO).

Brown, J. and Howes, G. (eds) (1975) *The Police and the Community* (Farnborough: Saxon House).

Brownmiller, S. (1973) *Against Our Will (Men, Women and Rape)* (Harmondsworth: Penguin).

Bulmer, M. (1982) *The Uses of Social Research* (London: Allen and Unwin).

Bulmer, M. (1984) *The Chicago School of Sociology* (Chicago: University of Chicago Press).

Bulmer, M. (1986), *Neighbours: The Work of Philip Abrams* (Cambridge: Cambridge University Press).

Bunyan, T. (1977) *The Political Police in Britain* (London: Quartet).

Burgess, E. W. (1966) 'Discussion' in Shaw C. *The Jack Roller*.

Cain, M. (1973) *Society and the Policeman's Role* (London: Routledge and Kegan Paul).

Cameron, M. O. (1964) *The Booster and the Snitch* (London: Free Press of Glencoe).

Campbell, A. (1981) *Girl Delinquents* (Oxford: Blackwell).

Campbell, A. (1984) *The Girls in the Gang* (Oxford: Basil Blackwell).

Carlen, P. (1976) *Magistrates' Justice* (Oxford: Martin Robertson).

Carlen, P. (1983) *Women's Imprisonment* (London: Routledge and Kegan Paul).

Carlen, P. (ed.) (1985) *Criminal Women* (Cambridge: Polity Press).

Carlen, P. and Worrall, A. (eds) (1987) *Gender, Crime and Justice* (Milton Keynes: Open University Press).

Carson, W. G. (1970) 'White Collar Crime and the Enforcement of Factory Legislation', *British Journal of Criminology*, vol. 10.

Castells, M. (1978) *City, Class and Power* (London: Macmillan).

Chambers, G. and Millar, A. (1987) 'Proving Sexual Assault: Prosecuting the Offender or Persecuting the Victim?', in Carlen and Worrall (eds).

Chambliss, W. (1978) *On the Take: From Petty Crooks to Presidents* (Indiana: Indiana University Press).

Chatterton, M. (1976) 'Police in Social Control', in J. F. S. King (ed.)

Control Without Custody (Cambridge: Institute of Criminology).

Chesney-Lind, M. (1980) 'Rediscovering Lilith: Misogyny and the "New Female Criminality"', in C. Taylor Griffiths and M. Nance (eds) *The Female Offender* (Vancouver: Simon Fraser University).

Chibnall, S. (1979) *Law and Order News* (London: Tavistock).

Cicourel, A. (1968) *The Social Organization of Juvenile Justice* (New York: Wiley).

Clarke, A. H. and Lewis, M. J. (1982) 'Fear of Crime Among the Elderly', *British Journal of Criminology*, vol. 22, no. 1.

Clarke, R. V. and Mayhew, P. (1980) *Designing Out Crime* (London: HMSO).

Clarke, R. V. and Hough, M. (1984) *Crime and Police Effectiveness*, Home Office Research Study No. 79 (London: HMSO).

Clarke, R. V. (1983) 'Situational Crime Prevention: its theoretical basis and practical scope', in Tonry and Morris (eds).

Clarke, R. V. (1984) 'Opportunity-Based Crime Rates', *British Journal of Criminology* vol. 24, no. 1.

Clinard, M. (1968) *The Sociology of Deviant Behaviour*, 3rd edition (London: Holt, Rinehart and Winston).

Clinard, M. (1978) *Cities with Little Crime* (Cambridge: CUP).

Clinard, M. B. (1983) *Corporate Ethics and Crime: The Role of Middle Management* (Beverly Hills: Sage).

Clinard, M. and Yeager, P. (1980) *Corporate Crime* (New York: Free Press).

Cloward, R. and Ohlin, L. (1960) *Delinquency and Opportunity* (London: Collier-Macmillan).

Cockburn, A. and Blackburn, R. (1969) *Student Power* (Harmondsworth: Penguin).

Cohen, A. K. (1955) *Delinquent Boys* (London: Free Press).

Cohen, A. K., *et al.* (eds) (1956) *The Sutherland Papers* (Bloomington: Indiana University Press).

Cohen, A. K. and Short, J. F. (1958) 'Research in Delinquent Subcultures', *Journal of Social Issues*, vol. 14, no. 3.

Cohen, A. K. (1965) 'The Sociology of the Deviant Act: Anomie Theory and Beyond', *American Sociological Review*, vol. 30.

Cohen, A. K. (1966) *Deviance and Control* (Englewood Cliffs: Prentice Hall).

Cohen, L. and Telson, M. (1979) 'Social Change and Crime Rate Trends'. *American Sociological Review*, vol. 44.

Cohen, P. (1981) 'Policing the Working-Class City', in Fitzgerald *et al.* (eds).

Cohen, P. S. (1968) *Modern Social Theory* (London: Heinemann).

Cohen, S. (ed.) (1971) *Images of Deviance* (Harmondsworth: Penguin).

Cohen, S. (1972 and 1980) *Folk Devils and Moral Panics*, (Oxford: Martin Robertson).

Cohen, S. (1981) 'Footprints on the Sand: A Further Report on Criminology and the Sociology of Deviance in Britain', in Fitzgerald *et al.* (eds).

Cohen, S. and Scull, A. (eds) (1983) *Social Control and the State* (Oxford: Blackwell).
Cohen, S. (1985) *Visions of Social Control* (Cambridge: Polity Press).
Coleman, A. (1985) *Utopia on Trial* (London: Hilary Shipman).
Coote, A. and Campbell, B. (1982) *Sweet Freedom* (London: Picador).
Cornish, D. B. and Clarke, R. V. (1986) 'Situational Prevention, Displacement of Crime and Rational Choice Theory', in Heal and Laycock (eds).
Corrigan, P. and Frith, S. (1976) 'The Politics of Youth Culture', in S. Hall and T. Jefferson (eds).
Corrigan, P. (1979) *Schooling the Smash Street Kids* (London: Macmillan).
Coser, L. A. (1978) 'American Trends', in T. Bottomore and R. Nisbet (eds) *A History of Sociological Analysis* (London: Heinemann).
Cousins, M. and Hussain A. (1984) *Michel Foucault* (London: Macmillan).
Cowie, J., Cowie, V. and Slater, E. (1968) *Delinquency in Girls* (London: Heinemann).
Cressey, D. R. and Sutherland, E. H. (1978) *Criminology*, 10th edition (Philadelphia: Lippincott).
Critchley, T. (1978) *A History of Police in England and Wales* (London: Constable).
Dahrendorf, R. (1985) *Law and Order* (London: Stevens).
Davidson, R. N. (1981) *Crime and Environment* (London: Croom Helm).
Davis, N. J. (1972) 'Labelling Theory in Deviance Research' *Sociological Quarterly*, vol. 13, no. 4.
Deem, R. (1978) *Women and Schooling* (London: Routledge and Kegan Paul).
Dell, S. (1971) *Silent in Court* (London: Bell).
DHSS (1980) *The Black Report* (London: HMSO).
Dingwall, R. (1982) Review of Bulmer (ed.) *Social Research Ethics*, in *Sociology*, vol. 16, no. 4.
Ditton, J. (1977) *Part-time Crime* (London: Macmillan).
Dobash, R. Emerson and Dobash, R. P. (1979) *Violence Against Wives* (London: Open Books).
Dobash, R. P. and Dobash, R. Emerson and Gutteridge, S. (1986) *The Imprisonment of Women* (Oxford: Blackwell).
Douglas, J. B. (1967) *The Social Meanings of Suicide* (Princeton University Press).
Douglas, M. (1970) *Purity and Danger: An Analysis of Pollution and Taboo* (Harmondsworth: Penguin).
Downs, A. (1957) *An Economic Theory of Democracy* (New York: Harper Row).
Downes, D. M. (1966) *The Delinquent Solution* (London: Routledge and Kegan Paul).
Downes, D. (1979) 'Praxis Makes Perfect: A Critique of Critical Criminology', in Downes and Rock (eds).
Downes, D. and Rock, P. (eds) (1979) *Deviant Interpretations* (Oxford: Martin Robertson).
Downes, D. and Rock, P. (1982) *Understanding Deviance* (Oxford: Clarendon).

Durkheim, E. (1949) *The Division of Labour in Society* (New York: Free Press).

Durkheim, E. (1952) *Suicide* (London: Routledge and Kegan Paul).

Durkheim, E. (1964 & 1973) *The Rules of Sociological Method* (New York: Free Press).

Eaton, M. (1985) 'Documenting the Defendant: Placing Women in Social Inquiry Reports', in J. Brophy and C. Smart (eds) *Women in Law* (London: Routledge and Kegan Paul).

Eaton, M. (1986) *Justice for Women?* (Milton Keynes: Open University Press).

Edwards, S. (1981) *Female Sexuality and the Law* (Oxford: Martin Robertson).

Edwards, S. (1984) *Women on Trial* (Manchester: Manchester University Press).

Ely, P. (1985) 'Delinquency and Disillusion', in Manning (ed.).

Ennis, P. (1967) *Criminal Victimisation in the United States: A Report of a National Survey* (Washington: US Government Office).

Erikson, K. T. (1966) *Wayward Puritans: A Study in the Sociology of Deviance* (New York: John Wiley).

Evans, D. (1980) *Geographical Perspectives on Juvenile Delinquency* (Farnborough: Gower).

Eysenck, H. J. (1977) *Crime and Personality* (London: Paladin).

Faris, D. (1970) *Chicago Sociology: 1920–1932* (Chicago: University of Chicago Press).

Farrington, D. and Dowds, E. A. (1985) 'Disentangling Criminal Behaviour and Police Reaction', in D. Farrington and J. Gunn (eds) *Reactions to Crime: The Police, Courts and Prisons* (Chichester: Wiley).

Farrington, D., Gallagher, B., Morley, L., St. Ledger R. J. and West, D. J. (1986) 'Unemployment, School Leaving and Crime', in *British Journal of Criminology*, vol. 26, no. 4.

Fine, B. and Millar, R. (eds) (1986) *Policing the Miners' Strike* (London: Lawrence and Wishart).

Fisher, B. M. and Strauss, A. L. (1978) *Interactionism*, in Bottomore and Nisbet (eds).

Fitzgerald, M., McLennan, G. and Pawson, J. (eds) (1981) *Crime and Society: Readings in History and Theory* (London: Routledge and Kegan Paul).

Foucault, M. (1967) *Madness and Civilisation* (London: Tavistock).

Foucault, M. (1977) *Discipline and Punish* (London: Allen Lane).

Fowler, F. J. and Mangione, T. W. (1986) 'A Three-Pronged Effort to Reduce Crime and Fear of Crime: The Hartford Experiment', in Rosenbaum (ed.).

Fox Piven, F. (1987) plenary address to the Social Administration Association, Edinburgh.

Fyvel, T. R. (1963) *The Insecure Offenders* (Harmondsworth: Penguin).

Garland, D. (1985) *Punishment and Welfare* (Aldershot: Gower).

Garfinkel, H. (1967) *Studies in Ethnomethodology* (Englewood Cliffs: Prentice Hall).

Geis, G. (1962) 'Towards the Delineation of White-collar Offences', *Sociological Inquiry*, vol. 32, no. 2.

Geis, G. (1967) 'White Collar Crime: The Heavy Electrical Equipment Antitrust Cases of 1961', in M. B. Clinard and R. Quinney (eds) *Criminal Behaviour Systems* (New York: Holt, Rinehart and Winston).

Genders, E. and Player, E. (1986) 'Women's Imprisonment. The Effects of Youth Custody', *British Journal of Criminology*, vol. 26, no. 4.

Gershuny, J. (1979) 'The informal economy: its role in industrial society' *Futures*, Feb.

Giallombardo, R. (1966) *Society of Women: A Study of a Woman's Prison* (New York/London: Wiley).

Giallombardo, R. (ed.) (1972) *Juvenile Delinquency: A Book of Readings*, 2nd edition (New York: John Wiley).

Gibbens, T. and Prince, J. (1963) *Child Victims of Sex Offences* (London: Institute for the Study and Treatment of Delinquency).

Gibbons, D. (1968) *Society, Crime and Criminal Careers* (New Jersey: Prentice Hall).

Gibbs, J. (1966) 'Conceptions of Deviant Behaviour: The Old and the New', *Pacific Sociological Review*, vol. 8, no. 1.

Giddens, A. (1971), 'Durkheim's Political Sociology', *Sociological Review*, vol. 19, no. 4.

Giddens, A. (1987) *Social Theory and Modern Sociology* (Cambridge: Polity Press).

Gifford, Lord (1986) *The Broadwater Farm Inquiry* (London: Karia).

Glaser, D. (1956) 'Criminality Theories and Behavioural Images', *American Journal of Sociology*, vol. 61, no. 5.

Goffman, E. (1968) *Stigma* (Harmondsworth: Penguin).

Gold, M. (1963) *Status Forces in Delinquent Boys* (Ann Arbor: University of Michigan).

Gold, M. (1970) *Delinquent Behaviour in an American City* (Belmont: Brooks Cole).

Gottfredson, M. (1984) *Victims of Crime: The Dimensions of Risk*, Home Office Research Study No. 81 (London: HMSO).

Gouldner, A. (1970) *The Coming Crisis of Western Sociology* (New York: Basic Books).

Gove, W. (ed.) (1975) *The Labelling of Deviance* (London: Wiley).

Gregory, J. (1986) 'Sex, Class and Crime: Towards a Non-Sexist Criminology', in Matthews and Young (eds).

Gurr, T. R. (1976) *Rogues, Rebels & Reformers* (Beverly Hills: Sage).

Gurr, T. R. (1979) 'On the History of Violent Crime in Europe and America', in H. Graham and T. Gurr (eds) *Violence in America* (Beverly Hills: Sage).

Hagan, J. (1977) *The Disreputable Pleasures* (Toronto: McGraw-Hill).

Hain, P. (ed.) (1980) *Policing the Police* (London: Calder).

Hall, P. (1985) 'The Social Crisis', *New Society*, vol. 74, no. 1195.

Hall, S. and Jefferson, T. (eds) (1976) *Resistance Through Rituals* (London: Hutchinson).

Hall, S., Cutcher, C., Jefferson, T. and Roberts, B. (1978) *Policing the Crisis* (London: Macmillan).

Hanmer, J. (1977) 'Violence and the Social Control of Women', in G. Littlejohn *et al.* (eds) *Power and the State* (London: Croom Helm).

Hanmer, J. and Saunders, S. (1984) *Well-Founded Fear* (London: Hutchinson).

Hanmer, J. and Maynard, M. (eds) (1987) *Women, Violence and Social Control* (London: Macmillan).

Hargreaves, D. (1967) *Social Relations in a Secondary School* (London: Routledge and Kegan Paul).

Harman, C. (1982) 'The Law and Order Show', in *Socialist Review*, vol. 1.

Harris, R. and Webb, D. (1987) *Welfare, Power and Juvenile Justice* (London: Tavistock).

Harrison, P. (1983) *Inside the Inner City* (Harmondsworth: Penguin).

Hay, D., Linebaugh, P. and Thompson, E. P. (1975) *Albion's Fatal Tree* (London: Allen Lane).

Heal, K., Tarling, R. and Burrows, J. (eds) (1985) *Policing Today* (London: HMSO).

Heal, K. and Laycock, G. (eds) (1986) *Situational Crime Prevention: From Theory Into Practice* (London: HMSO).

Heathcote, F. (1981) 'Social Disorganisation Theories', in Fitzgerald *et al.*

Hebdige, D. (1976) 'Reggae, Rastas and Rudies, in Hall and Jefferson (eds).

Heidensohn, F. M. (1968) 'The Deviance of Women: A Critique and an Enquiry', in *British Journal of Sociology*, vol. xix, no. 2.

Heidensohn, F. (1969) 'Prison for Women' *Howard Journal*.

Heidensohn, F. (1975) 'The Imprisonment of Females' in McConville, S. (ed.), *The Use of Imprisonment* (London: Routledge & Kegan Paul).

Heidensohn, F. (1981) 'Women & the Penal System' in Morris, M. & Gelsthorpe, G. (eds) *Women and Crime* (Cambridge: Institute of Criminology).

Heidensohn, F. (1985) *Women and Crime* (London: Macmillan, and New York University Press).

Heidensohn, F. (1986) 'Models of Justice: Portia or Persephone? Some Thoughts on Equality, Fairness and Gender in the Field of Criminal Justice', *International Journal of the Sociology of Law*, vol. 14.

Heidensohn, F. M. (1987) 'Women and Crime: Questions for Criminology', in Carlen and Worral (eds).

Henry, S. (1978) *The Hidden Economy* (Oxford: Martin Robertson).

Henry, S. (1985) Review of Clinard (1983), *British Journal of Criminology*, vol. 25, no. 1.

Henry, S. and Mars, G. (1978) 'Crime at Work', *Sociology* vol. 12, no. 2.

Hepburn, J. (1984) 'Occasional Property Crime', in Meier (ed.).

Heyl, B. (1979) *The Madam as Entrepreneur* (New Brunswick).

Hillyard, P. (1986) Review of Reiner (1985), in *Journal of Social Policy*, vol. 15, Pt 4.

Hirschi, T. (1969) *Causes of Delinquency* (Berkeley: University of California Press).

Hirst, P. (1972) 'Marx and Engels on Law, Crime and Morality', *Economy and Society*, vol. 1, no. 1.

Holdaway, S. (ed.) (1979) *The British Police* (London: Edward Arnold).

Holdaway, S. (1983) *Inside the British Police* (Oxford: Blackwell).

Home Office (1985) *Report of the Commissioner of Police of the Metropolis for the year 1984*, Cmnd 9541 (London: HMSO).

Home Office (1986) *Home Office Statistical Bulletin*, 17/86.

Hope, T. (1985) *Implementing Crime Prevention Measures*, Home Office Research Study, No. 86 (London: HMSO).

Hough, J. M., Clarke, R. V. and Mayhew, P. (1980) 'Introduction', in Clarke and Mayhew (eds).

Hough, M. and Mayhew, P. (1983) *The British Crime Survey*, Home Office Research Study No. 76 (London: HMSO).

Hough, M. and Mayhew, P. (1985) *Taking Account of Crime: Key Findings from the Second British Crime Survey*, Home Office Reseach Study No. 85 (London: HMSO).

Hough, M. (1985) 'Organisation and Resource Management of The Uniformed Police' and 'Managing with Less Technology', in Heal *et al.* (eds).

Hough, M. (1987) 'Thinking About Effectiveness', in Reiner and Shapland (eds).

Humphreys, L. (1970) *Tearoom Trade: Impersonal Sex in Public Places* (Chicago: Aldine).

Hutter, B. and Williams, G. (eds) 1981 *Controlling Women* (London: Croom Helm).

Hutter, B. (1986) 'An Inspector Calls', *British Journal of Criminology*, vol. 26, no. 2.

Iles, S. (1985) 'Women Terrorists and the Press: The Role of Medicalization and Sexualization as Depoliticizers by the State', in *Quarterly Journal of Ideology*, vol. ix, no. 3.

Iles, S. C. (1986) 'Patriarchal Therapeutism', unpublished PhD thesis, University of Kent.

Intermediate Treatment Fund (1986) *Youngsters in Trouble – The Way Ahead* (London: ITF).

Jackson, B. and Marsden, D. (1966) *Education and the Working Class* (Harmondsworth: Penguin).

Jenkins, P. (1984) 'Varieties of Enlightenment Criminology', *British Journal of Criminology*, vol. 24, no. 2.

Johnson, T., Misner, G. and Brown, L. (1981) *The Police and Society*. Englewood Cliffs: Prentice Hall.

Jones, G. (1987) 'Elderly People and Domestic Crime', *British Journal of Criminology*, vol. 27, no. 2.

Jones, K. and Fowles, A. J. (1984) *Ideas on Institutions* (London: Routledge and Kegan Paul).

Jones, S. (1986) *Policewomen and Equality* (London: Macmillan).

Jones, T., Maclean, B. and Young, J. (1986) *The Islington Crime Survey*,

Crime Victimisation and Policing in Inner City London (Aldershot: Gower).
Kelling, G. (1986) 'Neighbourhood Crime Control and the Police: A View of the American Experience, in Heal and Laycock (eds).
Kinsey, R. (1984) *Merseyside Crime Survey: First Report, Nov. 1984* (Liverpool: Merseyside Metropolitan Council).
Kinsey, R. (1985) *Crime and Policing on Merseyside*, Final Report (Liverpool: Merseyside Metropolitan Council).
Kinsey, R., Lea, J. and Young, J. (1986) *Losing the Fight Against Crime* (Oxford: Blackwell).
Kitsuse, J. and Dietrick, D. (1959) 'Delinquent Boys: A Critique', *American Sociological Review*, vol. 24.
Klein, D. (1976) 'The Aetiology of Female Crime: A Review of the Literature', in L. Crites (ed.), *The Female Offender* (Lexington: D. C. Heath).
Kolankiewiecz, G. (1985) 'Review' of Kwasniewski (1984), *British Journal of Criminology*, vol. 25, no. 4.
Kornhauser, R. R. (1978) *Social Sources of Delinquency: An Appraisal of Analytic Models* (Chicago: University of Chicago Press).
Knudten, R. D. (1970) *Crime in a Complex Society* (Illinois: Dorsey Press).
Kwasniewski, J. (1984) *Society and Deviance in Communist Poland: Attitudes Towards Social Control* (Leamington Spa: Berg).
Lasch, C. (1977) *Haven in a Heartless World* (New York: Basic Books).
Laver, M. (1986) *Social Choice and Public Policy* (Oxford: Blackwell).
Laycock, G. (1986) 'Property Marking as a Deterrent to Domestic Burglary', in Heal and Laycock (eds).
Lea, J. and Young, J. (1984) *What Is To Be Done About Law and Order?* (Harmondsworth: Penguin).
Lees, S. (1986) *Losing Out: Sexuality and Adolescent Girls* (London: Hutchinson).
Lemert, E. M. (1951) *Social Pathology* (New York: McGraw-Hill).
Lemert, E. M. (1964) 'Social Structure, Social Control and Deviation', in M. B. Clinard (ed.), *Anomie and Deviant Behaviour* (New York: Free Press).
Lemert, E. M. (1967) 'Role Enactment, Self, and Identity in the Systematic Check Forger', in *Human Deviance, Social Problems and Social Control* (Englewood Hills: Prentice Hall).
Leonard, D. (1978) *Sex and Generation* (London: Tavistock).
Leonard, E. B. (1982) *Women Crime and Society. A Critique of Criminology Theory* (New York and London: Longman).
Levi, M. and Jones, S. (1985) 'Public and Police Perceptions of Crime Seriousness in England and Wales', in *British Journal of Criminology*, vol. 25, no. 3.
Líazos, A. (1972) 'The Poverty of the Sociology of Deviance: Nuts, Sluts and Perverts', *Social Problems*, vol. 20, no. 1.
Lombroso, C. and Ferrero, W. (1895) *The Female Offender*, with an introduction by W. D. Morrison (London: T. Fisher Unwin).
Lombroso, C. (1913), *Crime: its Causes and Remedies*. Boston.
Loney, M. (1983) *Community Against Government* (London: Heinemann).

Luckenbill, D. (1984) 'Murder and Assault', in Meier (ed.).

Lustgarten, L. (1987) 'The Police and the Substantive Criminal Law', in Reiner and Shapland (eds).

Lyman, S. M. and Scott, M. B. (1970) *A Sociology of the Absurd* (New York: Apleton Century Crofts).

McBarnet, D. (1979) 'Arrest: The Legal Context of Policing', in Holdaway (ed.).

McConville, S. (1981) 'Editorial Note', *British Journal of Criminology*, vol. 21, no. 3.

McLeod, E. (1982) *Woman Working: Prostitution Now* (London: Croom Helm).

Maguire, M. (1980) *Burglary in a Dwelling: The Offence, The Offender and The Victim* (London: Heinemann).

Maquire, M. and Corbett, C. (1987) *The Effects of Crime and the Work of Victims Support Schemes* (Aldershot: Gower).

Malinowski, B. (1926) *Crime and Custom in Savage Society* (London: Routledge & Kegan Paul).

Mandaraka-Sheppard, A. (1986) *The Dynamics of Aggression in Women's Prisons in England* (Aldershot: Gower).

Mann, M. (1985) *Defending White Collar Crime* (New Haven: Yale University Press).

Mannheim, H. (1940) *Social Aspects of Crime in England Between the Wars* (London: Allen and Unwin).

Mannheim, H. (1965) *Comparative Criminology*, vols I and II (London: Routledge and Kegan Paul).

Manning, N. (ed.) (1985) *Social Problems and Welfare Ideology* (Aldershot: Gower).

Manning, P. (1977) *Police Work* (Cambridge, Mass: MIT Press).

Manning, P. (1979) 'The Social Control of Police Work', in Holdaway (ed.).

Marcuse, H. (1964) *One Dimensional Man* (London: Sphere).

Mark, R. (1978) *In the Office of Constable* (London: Collins).

Maris, P. and Rein, M. (1967) *Dilemmas of Social Reform* (London: Routledge & Kegan Paul).

Mars, G. (1982) *Cheats at Work* (London: Allen & Unwin).

Marsh, I. (1986) *Crime* (London: Longman).

Marshall, T. (1985) *Alternatives to Criminal Courts* (Aldershot: Gower).

Matthews, R. (1986) 'Beyond Wolfenden? Prostitution, Politics and the Law', in Matthews and Young (eds).

Matthews, R. and Young, J., (eds) (1986), *Confronting Crime*. London: Sage.

Matza, D. and Sykes, G. (1961) 'Delinquency and Subterranean Values', *American Sociological Review*, vol. 26.

Matza, D. (1964) *Delinquency and Drift* (London: Wiley).

Matza, D. (1969) *Becoming Deviant* (New Jersey: Prentice Hall).

Maxfield, M. (1984) *Fear of Crime in England and Wales*, Home Office Research Studies No. 78 (London: HMSO).

Mayhew, H. (1862) *London Labour and the London Poor*, vols I–IV (London: Griffin).

Meier, R. F. (ed.) (1984) *Major Forms of Crime*, Criminal Justice Systems Annual, vol. 21 (Beverly Hills: Sage).

Mendelsohn, B. (1956) 'The Victimology', in *Etudes Internationales de Psycho-Sociologie Criminelle*, no. 1.

Merton, R. K. (1949) *Social Theory and Social Structure* (New York: Free Press).

Miller, E. (1986) *Street Woman* (Philadelphia: Temple).

Miller, R. (1986) – see under St John–Brooks.

Miller, W. B. (1958) 'Lower Class Culture as a Generating Milieu of Gang Delinquency', *Journal of Social Issues*, vol. 14, no. 3; reprinted in Giallombardo (ed.) (1972).

Miller, W. R. (1979) 'London's Police Tradition in a Changing Society', in Holdaway (ed.).

Millman, M. (1982) 'Images of Deviant Men and Women', in M. Evans (ed.) *The Women Question* (London: Fontana).

Mishra, R. (1981) *Society and Social Policy*, (2nd edn) (London: Macmillan).

Mitchell, J. (1971) *Women's Estate* (Harmondsworth: Penguin).

Mitchell J. and Oakley, A. (eds) (1986) *What is Feminism?* (Oxford: Blackwell).

Moore, C. and Brown, J. (1981) *Community Versus Crime* (London: Bedford Square Press).

Morash, M. (1984) 'Organized Crime', in Meier (ed.).

Morgan, P. (1985) 'Constructing Images of Deviance: A Look at State Intervention into the Problem of Wife-battering', in N. Johnson (ed.) *Marital Violence* (London: Routledge and Kegan Paul).

Morris, A., Giller, H., Szwed, E. and Geach, H. (1980) *Justice for Children* (London: Macmillan).

Morris, N. and Tonry, M. (and V. V.) (1979, 1980, 1981, etc.) *Crime and Justice. An Annual Review of Research*, vols. 1, 2, 3, etc. (Chicago: University of Chicago Press).

Morris, P. and Heal, K. (1981) *Crime Control and the Police*, Home Office Research Study No. 67 (London: HMSO).

Morris, T. P. (1957) *The Criminal Area* (London: Routledge and Kegan Paul).

Moulds, E. (1980) 'Chivalry and Paternalism: Disparities of Treatment in the Criminal Justice System', in Datesman, S. and Scarpitti, F. (eds) *Women, Crime and Justice* (New York: Oxford University Press).

Musto, D. (1973) *The American Disease: Origins of Narcotics Control* (Yale University Press).

Nagel, I. *et al.* (1980) 'Sex Differences in the Processing of Criminal Defendants', in D. Kelly Weisberg (ed.) *Women and the Law: The Social Historical Perspective* (New York: Schenkman).

Newman, O. (1972) *Defensible Space: People and Design in the Violent City* (London: Architectural Press).

Nisbet, R. A. (1966) *The Sociological Tradition* (London: Heinemann).
Nye, I. and Short, J. (1957) 'Scaling Delinquent Behaviour', *American Sociological Review*, vol. 22.
Oakley, A. (1982) *Subject Women* (Oxford: Martin Robertson).
Pahl, R. E. (1984) *Divisions of Labour* (Oxford: Blackwell).
Park, R. (1929) 'The City as a Social Laboratory', in Turner (ed.) (1967).
Park, R. (1967), in Turner (ed.).
Park, R., Burgess, W. E. and McKenzie, R. D. (eds) (1925) *The City* (Chicago: University of Chicago Press).
Park, R. and Burgess, W. E. (1927) *The Urban Community* (Chicago: University of Chicago Press).
Parker, H., Casburn, M. and Turnbull, D. (1981) *Receiving Juvenile Justice* (Oxford: Basil Blackwell).
Parker, H. and Giller, H. (1981) 'More and Less the Same: British Delinquency Research Since the Sixties', *British Journal of Criminology*, vol. 21, no. 3.
Parker, T. (1962) *The Courage of his Convictions* (London: Hutchinson).
Parker, T. (1963) *The Unknown Citizen* (London: Hutchinson).
Parker, T. (1965) *Five Women* (London: Hutchinson).
Parker, T. (1965) *The Plough Boy* (London: Hutchinson).
Parsons, T. (1937) *The Structure of Social Action* (New York: McGraw-Hall).
Patrick, J. (1973) *A Glasgow Gang Observed* (London: Eyre Methuen).
Pearson, G. (1975) *The Deviant Imagination* (London: Macmillan).
Pearson, G. (1983) *Hooligan: A History of Respectable Fears* (London: Macmillan).
Pearson, G. (1987) *The New Heroin Users* (Oxford: Blackwell).
Petrie, G. (1971) *A Singular Iniquity: The Campaigns of Josephine Butler* (London: Macmillan).
Philips, D. (1977) *Crime and Authority in Victorian England: The Black Country 1835–60* (London: Croom Helm).
Philips, D. (1983) 'A Just Measure of Crime: Authority, Hunters and Blue Locusts', in Cohen and Scull (eds).
Phipps, A. (1986) 'Radical Criminology and Criminal Victimization: Proposals for the Development of Theory and Intervention', in Matthews and Young (eds).
Pizzey, E. (1973) *Scream Quietly or the Neighbours Will Hear* (Harmondsworth: Penguin).
Platt, A. (1975) 'Prospects for a Radical Criminology in the US', in Taylor *et al.* (eds).
Plummer, K. (1979) 'Misunderstanding Labelling Perspectives', in D. Downes and P. Rock (eds) *Deviant Interpretations* (Oxford: Martin Robertson).
Plummer, K. (1983) *Documents of Life* (London: Allen and Unwin).
Pollak, O. (1950) *The Criminality of Women* (New York: A. S. Barnes/Perpetuo).
Polsky, N. (1969) *Hustlers, Beats and Others* (Chicago: University of Chicago Press).

Power, A. (1981) 'How to rescue council housing', *New Society*, 4 June.

Power, A. (1988) *Property before People* (London: Allen & Unwin).

Punch, M. and Naylor, T. (1973) 'The Police: A Social Service', *New Society*, vol. 24.

Punch, M. (1979) *Policing the Inner City* (London: Macmillan).

Punch, M. (ed.) (1983) *Control in the Police Organization* (Cambridge, Mass.: MIT Press).

Quattrocchi, A. and Nairn, T. (1968) *The Beginning of the End* (London: Panther).

Quinney, R. (1970) *The Social Reality of Crime* (Boston: Little, Brown).

Quinney, R. (1973) 'Crime Control in Capitalist Society: A Critical Philosophy of Legal Order', *Issues in Criminology*, vol. 8.

Quinney, R. (1975) *Criminology: Analysis & Critique of Crime in America* (Boston: Little, Brown).

Randall, S. and Rose, V. M. (1984) 'Forcible Rape' in R. Meier (ed.).

Randall, V. (1982) *Women and Politics* (London: Macmillan).

Raynor, P. (1985) *Social Work, Justice and Control* (Oxford: Blackwell).

Reckless, W. (1961) *The Crime Problem*, 3rd edition (New York: Appleton Century Crofts).

Reiner, R. (1978) *The Blue-Coated Worker* (Cambridge University Press).

Reiner, R. (1984) 'Crime, Law and Deviance: The Durkheim Legacy', in S. Fenton, *Durkheim and Modern Sociology* (Cambridge: Cambridge University Press).

Reiner, R. (1985) *The Politics of the Police* (Brighton: Wheatsheaf).

Reiner, R. and Shapland, J. (eds) (1987) 'Why Police? Special Issue on Policing in Britain', *British Journal of Criminology*, vol. 27, no. 1.

Reiner, R. and Shapland, J. (1987) 'Why Police?' in Reiner and Shapland (eds).

Reiss, A. J. (1964) 'The Social Integration of Queers and Peers', in Becker (ed.).

Reiss, A. J. (1971) *The Police and the Public* (New Haven: Yale University Press).

Reith, C. (1956) *A New Study of Police History* (London: Oliver and Boyd).

Renvoize, J. (1982) *Incest: A Family Pattern* (London: Routledge and Kegan Paul).

Rex, J. and Moore, R. (1967) *Race, Community and Conflict* (Oxford: Oxford University Press).

Richardson, H. J. (1969) *Adolescent Girls in Approved Schools* (London: Routledge and Kegan Paul).

Riley, D. and Shaw, M. (1985) *Parental Supervision and Juvenile Delinquency*, Home Office Research Study no. 83 (London: HMSO).

Roberts Chapman, J. (1980) *Economic Realities and the Female Offender* (Lexington: Lexington Books).

Robin, G. (1977) 'Forcible Rape: Institutionalized Sexism and the Criminal Justice System', *Crime and Delinquency*, vol. 23, no. 2.

Rock, P. (1979a) 'The Sociology of Crime: Symbolic Interactionism and Some Problematic Qualities of Radical Criminology', in Downes and Rock (eds).

Rock, P. (1979b), Review of Wilson (1975), in *British Journal of Criminology*, Vol. 19, no. 1.

Rock, P. (1986) *A View from the Shadows* (Oxford: Clarendon).

Rock, P. (1987) 'Crime Reduction Initiatives on Problem Estates' in Hope, T. and Shaw, M. (eds) *Communities and Crime Reduction* (London: HMSO).

Rock, P. (1988a) 'Governments: Victims and Policies in Two Countries', *British Journal of Criminology*, vol. 28, no. 1.

Rock, P. (1988b) 'The Present State of Criminology in Britain', *British Journal of Criminology*, vol. 28, no. 2.

Rock, P. and Cohen, S. (1970) 'The Teddy Boy', in V. Bogdanor and R. Skidelsky, *The Age of Affluence: 1951–1964* (London: Macmillan).

Rock, P. and Heidensohn, F. (1969) 'New Reflections on Violence' in D. A. Martin (ed.) *Anarchy and Culture* (London: Routledge and Kegan Paul).

Rosenbaum, D. P. (ed.) (1986) *Community Crime Prevention: Does it Work?* (Beverly Hills: Sage).

Rossi, P. H. *et al.* (1974) 'The Seriousness of Crimes: Normative Structures and Individual Differences', *American Sociological Review*, vol. 39.

Rubington, E. and Weinberg, M. (1968, 1973) *Deviance: The Interactionist Perspective* (1st and 2nd editions) (New York: Macmillan).

Russell, D. (1975) *Rape: the Victim's Perspective* (New York: Stein & Day).

Russell, D. (1984) *Sexual Exploitation* (Beverly Hills: Sage).

Rutter, M. and Giller, H. (1983) *Juvenile Delinquency* (Harmondsworth: Penguin).

Sampson, R. and Castellano, T. (1982) 'Economic Inequality and Personal Victimisation,' *British Journal of Criminology* vol. 22, no. 4.

Samuel, R. (1981) *East End Underworld: Chapters in the life of Arthur Harding* (London: Routledge and Kegan Paul).

Scarman, Lord (1981) *The Brixton Disorders, 10–12 April 1981* (Scarman Report), Cmnd 8427 (London: HMSO).

Scheff, T. (1966) *Being Mentally Ill* (London: Weidenfeld and Nicholson).

Schofield, M. (1965) *The Sexual Behaviour of Young People* (Harmondsworth: Penguin).

Schur, E. M. (1965) *Crimes Without Victims* (Englewood Cliffs, N.J.: Prentice-Hall).

Schur, E. M. (1971) *Labelling Deviant Behaviour: Its Sociological Implications* (London: Harper and Row).

Schwendinger, J. and Schwendinger, H. (1978) 'Studying Rape: Integrating Research and Social Change', in Smart and Smart (eds).

Scraton, P. (1985) *The State of the Police* (London: Pluto).

Scraton, P. and Gordon, P. (eds) (1984) *Causes for Concern* (Harmondsworth: Penguin).

Scull, A. (1977) *Decarceration* (Englewood Cliffs, N.J.: Prentice-Hall).

Sellin, T. and Wolfgang, M. (1964) *The Measurement of Delinquency* (New York: Wiley).

Shapland, J., Willmore, J. and Duff, P. (1985) *Victims in the Criminal Justice System* (Aldershot: Gower).

Shapland, J. and Vagg, J. (1987) 'Using the Police', in Reiner and Shapland (eds).

Shaw, C. (1930, 1936) *The Jack Roller: A Delinquent Boy's Own Story* (Chicago: University of Chicago, reprinted 1966).

Shaw, C. R. and Mckay, H. D. (1942) *Juvenile Delinquency and Urban Areas* (Chicago: Chicago University Press).

Sheldon, W. H. (1949) *Varieties of Delinquent Youth: An Introduction to Constitutional Psychiatry* (New York: Harper).

Shils, E. (1961) 'The Calling of Sociology', in T. Parsons, E. Shils, K. D. Naegele and J. R. Pitts (eds) *Theories of Society* (New York: Free Press).

Short, J. F. (1958) 'Differential Association with Delinquent Friends and Delinquent Behaviour', *Pacific Sociological Review*, vol. 1, no. 1.

Short, J. F. and Strodtbeck, F. (1965) *Group Process and Delinquency* (Chicago: University of Chicago Press).

Sieh, E. (1987) 'Garment Workers: Perceptions of Inequity and Employee Theft', in *British Journal of Criminology*, vol. 27, no. 2.

Simon, R. J. (1975) *Women and Crime* (Toronto/London: Lexington).

Sivanandan, A. (1981) 'From Resistance to Rebellion', *Race and Class*, vol. II.

Skinner, A. (1985) *A Bibliography of Intermediate Treatment 1968–84* (Leicester: National Youth Bureau).

Skolnick, J. (1966) *Justice Without Trial* (New York: Wiley).

Skolnick, J. (1969) *The Politics of Protest* (New York: Bantam).

Smart, B. (1985) *Michel Foucault* (London: Ellis Horwood and Tavistock).

Smart, C. (1977) *Women, Crime and Criminology, A Feminist Critique* (London: Routledge and Kegan Paul).

Smart, C. (1979) 'The New Female Criminal: Reality or Myth', *British Journal of Criminology*, vol. 19, no. 1.

Smart, C. (1981) 'Law and the Control of Women's Sexuality', in Hutter and Williams (eds), 1981.

Smart, C. (1984) *The Ties that Bind* (London: Routledge and Kegan Paul).

Smart, C. and Smart, B. (eds) (1978) *Women, Sexuality and Social Control* (London: Routledge and Kegan Paul).

Smith, A. D. (1962) *Women in Prison* (Library of Criminology) (London: Stevens).

Smith, D. A. and Visher, A. C. (1980) 'Sex and Involvement in Deviance/Crime': A Quantitative Review of the Empirical Literature', *American Sociological Review*, no. 45, pp. 691–707.

Smith, D. J. and Gray, J. (1983) *Police and People in London: The Police in Action*, vols I–IV (London: PSI).

Smith, D. J. and Gray, J. (1985) *Police and People in London. The PSI Report* (Aldershot: Gower).

Smith, D. (1986), Foreword to S. Jones, *Policewomen and Equality*.

Smith, S. (1982) 'Victimisation in the Inner City', *British Journal of Criminology*, vol. 22, no. 4.

Smith, S. (1986) *Crime, Space and Society* (Cambridge: Cambridge University Press).

Smith, S. J. (1984) 'Crime in the News', *British Journal of Criminology*, vol. 24.

Southgate, P. (1986) *Police–Public Encounters*, Home Office Research Study, No. 90 (London: HMSO).

Sparks, R., Genn, H. G. and Dodd, D. J. (1977) *Surveying Victims* (Chichester: Wiley).

Sparks, R. (1981) 'Surveys of Victimisation: An Optimistic Assessment', in M. N. Tonry and R. Morris (eds) *Crime and Justice*, vol. 3.

Stanko, E. (1984) *Intimate Intrusions* (London: Routledge and Kegan Paul).

Stanko, E. (1988) 'Fear of crime and the myth of the safe home', in M. Borad and K. Yuo (eds) *Feminist Perspectives on Wife Abuse* (London: Sage).

Stanko, E. (1987) 'Typical Violence, Normal Precaution: Men, Women and Interpersonal Violence in England, Wales, Scotland and the USA', in Hanmer and Maynard (eds).

St. John-Brooks, C. (1986) 'Selling the Sciences', interview with Roberta Miller, *New Society*, vol. 78, no. 1247.

Steffensmeier, D. I. (1978) 'Crime and the Contemporary Woman: An Analysis of Changing Levels of Female Property Crime, 1960–75', *Social Forces*, vol. 57.

Stone, J. (1985) *Racial Conflict in Contemporary Society* (London: Fontana).

Styles, J. (1987) 'The Emergence of the Police: Explaining Police Reform in 18th and 19th Century England', in Reiner and Shapland (eds).

Sudnow, D. (1965) 'Normal Crimes: Sociological Features of the Penal Code in a Public Defender Office', *Social Problems*, Winter, vol. 12.

Sutherland, E. H. (1940) 'White Collar Criminality', *American Sociological Review*, vol. 5, no. 1.

Sutherland, E. H. (1945) 'Is "White-Collar Crime" Crime?' *American Sociological Review*, vol. 10, no. 2.

Sutherland, E. H. (1961) *White Collar Crime* (New York: Holt Rinehart and Winstone).

Sutherland, E. and Cressey, D. (1960) *Principles of Criminology* (Philadelphia: Lippincott) and *Criminology* 10th edn 1978.

Suttles, G. (1968) *The Social Order of the Slum* (Chicago: Chicago University Press).

Suttles, G. (1972) *The Social Construction of Communities* (Chicago: Chicago University Press).

Sykes, G. and Matza, D. (1957) 'Techniques of Neutralization: A Theory of Delinquency', *American Sociological Review*, vol. 22; reprinted in Giallombardo (ed.) (1972).

Svindoff, M. and McElroy, J. (1984) *Employment and Crime* (New York: Vera Inst of Justice).

Tannenbaum, F. (1938) *Crime and the Community* (New York: Columbia University Press).

Tappan, P. W. (1947) 'Who is the Criminal?', *American Sociological Review*, vol. 12, no. 1.

Taylor, L. (1971) *Deviance and Society* (London: Michael Joseph).

Taylor, I., Walton, P. and Young, J. (1973) *The New Criminology* (London: Routledge and Kegan Paul).

Taylor, I., Walton, P. and Young, J. (1975) *Critical Criminology* (London: Routledge and Kegan Paul).

Thomas, W. I. (1923) *The Unadjusted Girl* (Boston: Little, Brown).

Thompson, K. (1982) *Emile Durkheim* (London: Tavistock).

Thorpe, D. H., Smith, D., Green, C. J. and Paley, J. H. (1980) *Out of Care: The Community Support of Juvenile Offenders* (London: Allen and Unwin).

Thrasher, F. M. (1927, 1963) *The Gang* (Chicago: Phoenix Press, reprinted 1963).

Toby, J. (1974) 'The Socialization and Control of Deviant Motivation', in D. Glaser (ed.), *Handbook of Criminology* (Chicago: Rand-McNally).

Toner, B. (1982) *The Facts of Rape* (London: Arrow Books).

Tonry, M. and Morris, N. (1980 *et seq.*) *Crime and Justice: An Annual Review of Research*, vols. 1, 2, 3, etc. (Chicago: University of Chicago Press).

Topliss, E. (1978) 'The Disabled', in P. Brearley *et al.* (eds) *The Social Context of Health Care* (Oxford: Martin Robertson).

Townsend, P. (1979) *Poverty in the UK* (Harmondsworth: Penguin).

Townsend, P. and Davidson, N. (eds) (1982) *Inequalities in Health: The Black Report* (Harmondsworth: Penguin).

Trasler, G. (1986) 'Situational Crime Control and Rational Choice: A Critique', in Heal and Laycock (eds).

Tuck, M. (1985) Foreword in Hope (1985).

Turner, R. (ed.) (1967) Introduction to *Robert E. Park on Social Control and Collective Behaviour* (Chicago: University of Chicago Press).

US Dept of Justice (1983) *Criminal Victimisation in the United States 1981*, Statistics Bulletin (Washington, DC: US Government Printing Office).

Ungerson, C. (ed.) (1985) *Women and Social Policy* (London: Macmillan).

Vaughan, D. (1983) *Controlling Unlawful Organizational Behaviour* (Chicago: University of Chicago Press).

Von Hentig, H. (1949) *The Criminal and His Victim* (New Haven: Yale University Press).

Walby, S. (1986) *Patriarchy at Work* (Cambridge: Polity).

Walker, L. E. A. (1987) 'The Social Control of Women by Labelling them "Bad" or "Mad"', in *Contemporary Psychology*, vol. 32, no. 7.

Walker, Martin (1987) *Guardian* 12 Jan.

Walker, M. (1978) 'Measuring the Seriousness of Crime', *British Journal of Criminology*, vol. 24, no. 1.

Walker, M. A. (1987a) 'Interpreting Race and Crime Statistics', *Journal of Royal Statistical Society*, A 150.

Walker, M. A. (1987b) 'The Ethnic Origin of Prisoners', in *British Journal of Criminology* vol. 27, no. 2.

Walker, N. D. (1987), *Crime and Criminology*. Oxford: Oxford University Press.

Walklate, S. (1986) 'Reparation: A Merseyside View', in *British Journal of Criminology*, vol. 26, no. 3.

Walkowitz, J. (1980) *Prostitution and Victorian Society* (Cambridge: Cambridge University Press).

Ward, D. A. and Kassebaum, G. G. (1966) *Women's Prison* (London: Weidenfeld).

Webb, D. (1984) 'More on Gender and Justice: Girl Offenders on Supervision', *Sociology*, vol. 18, no. 3.

Weber, M. (1948) 'Science as a Vocation', in H. Gerth and C. Wright Mills (eds) *From Max Weber* (London: Routledge and Kegan Paul).

Weis, J. G. (1971) 'Dialogue with David Matza', *Issues in Criminology*, vol. 6, no. 1.

West, D. and Farrington, D. (1971) *Present Conduct and Future Delinquency* (London: Heinemann).

West, D. and Farrington, D. (1973) *Who Becomes Delinquent?* (London: Heinemann).

West, D. and Farrington, D. (1977) *The Delinquent Way of Life* (London: Heinemann).

West, D. J., Roy, C. and Nichols, F. L. (1978) *Understanding Sexual Attacks* (London: Heinemann).

White, J. (1986) *The Worst Street in North London* (London: Routledge and Kegan Paul).

Whyte, W. F. (1955) *Street Corner Society* (2nd edition) (Chicago: University of Chicago Press).

Wilkins, L. T. (1964) *Social Deviance* (London: Tavistock).

Willis, P. (1977) *Learning to Labour* (London: Saxon House).

Willis, P. (1978) *Profane Culture* (London: Saxon House).

Wilson, E. (1983) *What is to be Done About Violence Against Women?* (Harmondsworth: Penguin).

Wilson, H. (1980) 'Parental Supervision: A Neglected Aspect of Delinquency', *British Journal of Criminology*, vol. 20.

Wilson, H. (1982) 'Parental Responsibility and Delinquency: Reflections on a White Paper Proposal', *Howard Journal*, vol. 21.

Wilson, H. (1987) 'Parental Supervision Re-examined', in *British Journal of Criminology*, vol. 27, no. 3.

Wilson, J. (1975) *Thinking About Crime* (New York: Basic Books).

Wilson, J. and Kelling, G. (1982) 'Broken Windows: The Police and Neighbourhood Safety', in *Atlantic Monthly*, March.

Wilson, J. Q. (1968) *Varieties of Police Behaviour* (Cambridge: Harvard University Press).

Winslow, R. (1968) *Crime in a Free Society*, selections from the President's Commission on Law Enforcement and Administration of Justice (California: Dickenson).

Wolff, K. (1978) 'Phenomenology and Sociology' in Bottomore and Nisbet (eds).

Wolfgang, M. (1959) *Patterns in Criminal Homicide* (Philadelphia: University of Pennsylvania Press).

Wood, J. (1984) 'Groping Towards Sexism: Boys' Sex Talk', in A. McRobbie and M. Nava (eds) *Gender and Generation* (London: Macmillan).

Wootton, B. (1959) *Social Science and Social Pathology* (London: Allen and Unwin).

Yin, R. K. (1986) 'Community Crime Prevention', in Rosenbaum (ed.).

Young, J. (1970) *The Drugtakers* (London: McGibbon and Kee).

Young, J. (1986) 'The Failure of Criminology: The Need for a Radical Realism' in R. Matthews and J. Young (eds) *Confronting Crime* (London: Sage).

Young, J. (1985) 'Broadwater Farm', Middlesex Polytechnic Centre for Criminology (mimeo).

Young, M. and Willmott, P. (1973) *The Symmetrical Family* (London: Routledge and Kegan Paul).

Zeldes, I. (1981) *The Problems of Crime in the USSR* (Illinois: Thomas).

Zorbaugh, H. (1929) *The Goldcoast and the Shun* (Chicago: Chicago University Press).

Index